NARCISSUS
and
OEDIPUS

The Children of Psychoanalysis

Victoria Hamilton

with a new Foreword by
Eric Rayner

and a new Preface by
Murray M. Schwartz

MARESFIELD LIBRARY

London
KARNAC BOOKS

First published in 1982 by
Routledge & Kegan Paul Limited

This edition reprinted by
H. Karnac (Books) Ltd.
58 Gloucester Road
London SW7 4QY
1993
by arrangement with the author.

British Library Cataloging in Publication Data

Hamilton, Victoria
Narcissus and Oedipus: The Children of
Psychoanalysis. – New ed. – (Maresfield
Library)
I. Title II. Series
150.19

ISBN 1–85575–062–7

Printed in Great Britain by BPCC Wheatons Ltd, Exeter

Acknowledgements

I began working on many of the ideas contained in this book during the summer of 1967. This summer was a transitional period between the completion of my philosophy degree at University College, London, and the beginning of my psychoanalytic studies at the Tavistock Clinic, including my practical work with children in schools and clinics. During the vacation, I was inspired by the work of Gregory Bateson, whom I was lucky to hear and meet at the Dialectics of Liberation Congress held in London. This book owes much to my love of philosophy and to my teachers in the philosophy department at University College, London. I am particularly indebted to Professor Richard Wollheim and to Mr G. A. Cohen for their teaching and their personal interest in me as a student.

During my psychotherapy training at the Tavistock Clinic, I was introduced to the two main frameworks which have guided the development of my psychoanalytic thinking: Attachment Theory and Object-Relations Theory. I am immensely indebted to Dr John Bowlby for his intellectual inspiration and personal contact. His work on the early infant–mother attachment provided me with the most fascinating and coherent account of child development. The films of James and Joyce Robertson, which were shown at the Tavistock Clinic, have further convinced me of the overwhelming importance of separation in the life of a child. My understanding of Object-Relations theory has been gathered from two sources. The first of these is the work of Melanie Klein, which was transmitted to me in seminars and supervisions during my training at the Tavistock. I am particularly indebted to Frances Tustin for the imaginative understanding and rigour with which she invested my weekly supervision hours. Her originality provided an important bridge to my second source – namely, the work of those non-aligned members of the Object-Relations School referred to, in England, as the 'Middle Group'. The clinical seminars given by Dr D. W. Winnicott during the last two years of his life (1969–70) remain an unforgettable experience.

The members of Staff at Uxbridge Child Guidance Clinic, particularly Dr Ronald Urquhart, provided me with a supportive and enthusiastic setting to pursue my clinical experience with young children. I would like to thank the staff and the children who attended the clinic between the years 1969 and 1972.

My thoughts return to an artist, Mr Robert Stewart, Head of the Department of Design at the Glasgow School of Art, for his interest in my art work and his friendship during the embryonic stages of my writing career.

Many friends have read parts of the ms. My thanks go, first, to my husband, Nicholas Tufnell, who has read numerous versions of the manuscript; he has listened to me, discussed and teased out many of the fundamental ideas in this book. He has provided clarification at all levels from the theoretical to the grammatical. I wish to thank Mr Jeffrey Steingarten and Ms Caron Smith for their reading and editing of early versions of the manuscript. For the completion of the final ms., I am indebted to Mr Peter Mezan, who came out to California for ten days to help me organise the manuscript into its final form. His insistence on coherence and precision revived both the book and the author. I wish to thank Professor Herbert Morris and Professor Louis Breger for their careful appraisal of the final edition.

David Godwin of Routledge has been untiring in his support of this project. Without his continuing interest across 6,000 miles and timely requests for progress reports, completion might have been postponed. He could not have been more generous with his attention and editorship of the manuscript. I thank Harry Karnac and Cesare Sacerdoti for believing in the book and keeping the first edition available and for reprinting this new edition. I wish to thank Mrs Evelyn Siegen for her patience and endurance in the typing and correction of several versions of this ms.

I am grateful to all the children, young people and adults who have taught me.

Acknowledgements

For permission to quote from published works, thanks are due to the publishers listed below. Bibliographical details of all the works cited are given in the list of references at the end of the volume. Faber and Faber Ltd., London, in respect of 7 lines from 'Little Gidding'. Reprinted by permission of Faber and Faber Ltd. from *Four Quartets* by T. S. Eliot; also in respect of extracts reprinted by permission of Faber and Faber Ltd. from *Oedipus Rex* by Sophocles, translated by Dudley Fitts and Robert Fitzgerald; Harcourt Brace Jovanovich, Inc., New York, for 7 lines from 'Little Gidding' in *Four Quartets* by T. S. Eliot, copyright 1943 by T. S. Eliot; renewed 1971 by Esme Valerie Eliot, reprinted by permission of Harcourt Brace Jovanovich, Inc.; also for extracts from *Oedipus Rex* translated by Dudley Fitts and Robert Fitzgerald, copyright 1949 by Harcourt Brace Jovanovich, Inc., renewed 1977 by Cornelia Fitts and Robert Fitzgerald, reprinted by permission of the publisher; James Greene and Granada Publishing Ltd. in respect of 'I look into the frost's face, alone' from *Osip Mandelstam* – poems chosen and translated by James Greene; Sigmund Freud Copyrights Ltd., The Institute of Psycho-Analysis, and The Hogarth Press Ltd., for permission to quote from *The Standard Edition of the Complete Psychological Works of Sigmund Freud,* translated and edited by James Strachey in respect of extracts from Freud's Standard Edition, Volumes, 9, 10, 12, 13 16, 17, 19, 21, 23; W. W. Norton & Company Inc., New York, in respect of *Civilization and its Discontents* and *An Outline of Psycho-Analysis* by Sigmund Freud; Penguin Books Ltd., Harmondsworth, in respect of an extract from *Metamorphoses,* translated by Mary M. Innes (Penguin Classics, 1955) pp. 83–87, Copyright Mary M. Innes, 1955, reprinted by permission of Penguin Books Ltd.; Tavistock Publications Ltd., in respect of *Playing and Reality* by D. W. Winnicott; Robert Graves in respect of *The Greek Myths: Vol.* 1 Narcissus and Vol. 2 Oedipus, published by Penguin Books Ltd.

Contents

Foreword

Eric Rayner

This book was originally published over ten years ago. It is undoubtedly important and its writing has beautiful clarity, yet it is little known. In searching for the reason, I only had to look at my own case. Years ago, I glanced at *Narcissus and Oedipus* and quickly saw that quite a lot of it was, as expected, an examination of the two Greek myths. I thought how erudite Vicki Hamilton was, felt a bit humble and unscholarly, and got on with more practical matters. This could not have been more wrong; I would have been practically and theoretically much wiser if I had used this book years ago. The same must apply to other analysts and therapists.

Why is this an important book? Starting very generally, it questions a long-standing bit of psychoanalytic theory. Any body of knowledge has to be capable of changing; to be alive, it has to develop. Some elements must be added, others have to be discarded. How does one decide that a bit of theory is no longer of much use – and how, then, does an intellectual community, like the psychoanalytic one, discard it with dignity and without acrimony? In the sciences this is, in principle, easy: if observations lead to contradictions of it, a theory is dropped or altered. In the humanities, theoretical points of view tend to fall away through disuse, while in religions people may kill each other about such matters. Psychoanalysis often seems to be both scientific and religious, and thus doubt about a bit of theory enshrined by age, especially if from Freud himself, can bring condemnation from pious disciples. Yet a theory that is incapable of change easily becomes anachronistic, and this is no service to Freud or to psychoanalysis.

Hamilton sets about demonstrating that Freud's theory of primary narcissism as a normal developmental stage is largely wrong, so we must think about discarding it. From this it begins to become plain that Freud's notion of psychic energy with its hydraulic qualities is antiquated. Perhaps psychoanalysis needs to think about itself in the light of the systems and structuralist theories now extensively used in both the biological and social sciences. The urgent practical point here is that old mistaken theories, especially when classically honoured, can distort good therapy. Primary narcissism has, of course, been questioned for decades but never so gracefully and cogently as by Hamilton. It should be required reading, at least for teachers of psychoanalysis.

Dr Hamilton is a child and adult psychoanalytic practitioner and teacher of long experience. Her literary facility makes the Greek myths seem easy. However, she is also philosophically and logically trained, and this gives her the conceptual precision needed to set about reforming old psychoanalytic habits.

Freud envisaged the infant mind as being like an egg hatching: at first, it has virtually no interest in or energy for emotional interaction with other objects or people. This is primary narcissism. Only slowly, and born of painful frustrations from external objects, do self-absorbed desires give way to relating with objects and the reality sense.

This model of early development was, of course, derived from the clinical observation of older patients; it was extrapolation backwards. Hamilton, like John Bowlby before her, uses the evidence of a host of infant researchers to see how a bit of psychoanalytic developmental theory stands up to findings from direct observation. Early on she gives due warning of where she is going by convincingly showing that the mythical Narcissus himself grew in an object-relational way. Unnoticed by Freud, Narcissus' mother fell madly in love with him at his birth and continued that way. But this is a side-show – the main arena is the psychoanalytic model of development. Hamilton sees Freud's primary narcissism, of psychic egg-hatching, as at one extreme of a continuum of ideas about infantile interactiveness with the environment. She shows that Anna Freud actually made many observations of active interchanges between mothers and infants, but still followed her father theoretically. So did Spitz, Mahler and even Kohut in assuming primary narcissism as the origin of emotional development. Klein is rightly given pride of place for originating the idea of object relations; but she is seen as showing little interest in the infant's actual inter-relating with people. Balint made no bones about his view: narcissism, as in the myth, arises out of the mother's adoration for her baby; it thus rests upon a passive object-relatedness from the beginning. Then comes Bowlby with attachment theory. He systematically gathered a mass of direct evidence concerning the infant's early object-related attachment to his mother – and was slated by many psychoanalysts for his labours. Further away still from Freud's narcissism model, Hamilton sees Winnicott's position, which emphasizes the importance of moment-to-moment mutuality between mother and infant from the beginning.

However, the linchpin of her argument comes not from psychoanalysts, but from infant researchers like Bower, Brazelton, Lewis, Rosenblum and Bell. She amasses the evidence – particularly that using electronic recording – showing that a baby that is awake can be remarkably synchronous and interactive with his environment. For instance, we now know that he tunes in to environmental stimuli minutes after birth, let alone hours or days afterwards. The conclusion is inevitable – social behaviour with synchrony and developing rapport is a primary function. It arises concurrently with states of self-absorption such as sleep; it does not follow after amorphous early narcissism. Thus, frustration cannot be the unique cause of the step to object relating, so Freud's ideas about many things like sublimation must be rethought.

Incidentally, not far from primary narcissism is the notion of primary autism. The originator of this concept, Frances Tustin, has recently clearly stated that in the light of recent infant research she now thinks the idea was erroneous. Would all psychoanalytic writers correct themselves likewise? Freud, I think, would – what about others?

Since 1986, when Daniel Stern summarised infant research findings in his classic, *The Interpersonal World of the Infant*, the general psychoanalytic theory of development ought never to have been the same again. Hamilton's book came before Stern's but has been overshadowed by it. His is much the fuller collection of the evidence. However, she quotes many of the same sources as he does, and the basic thrust of their arguments is identical. She then tackles issues that Stern does not address. She explicitly confronts several psychoanalytic theories directly and shows that their mistakes have serious clinical implications; she also continues to look at development after infancy. Thus Stern and Hamilton complement each other, and Hamilton is all the more worth reading and taking action upon now that Stern is present to add his weight of evidence.

Going on to Oedipus and later childhood, Hamilton shows that the original drama is not simply about a boy's sexual desire for his mother and wish to kill his father. It is also about knowledge and ignorance of reality, the lengths to which people will go to hide uncomfortable truths, and how tragedy is born of such deceits. Here Oedipus is not just an unconscious murderer; he is a man of great stature, because he profoundly desires to bear full responsibility for his actions. He is a hero of the depressive position.

Hamilton sees the myth as emphasising the importance of knowledge, with its growth from the earliest hours of life, through zestful 'holy curiosity', as Einstein called it, towards truly healthy development. She sees how important is the obliteration and distortion of knowledge in psychopathology. She is here close to Bion, but she thinks that he, like many others, is too bound to Freud's vision, which is overbalanced towards pessimism. This can affect the analyst's initial stance in therapeutic technique. Without an interest in early natural curiosity, the analyst may see only the patient's desire to regress, to be narcissistic, to obliterate the truth, and to distort. The analyst can then slip into portraying himself as the only possessor of knowledge in the therapeutic duet – he is, then, only an authoritarian informant, not also a cooperator in a venture into truthfulness. But cooperation alone carries grave dangers too, and I am not sure that Hamilton emphasises these enough. She rightly points out that truths that have optimism in them can be undervalued, but optimism can also breed ignorant complicity between analyst and patient.

What is more, an analytic focus upon knowledge can at worst breed intellectualism at the expense of comprehending childhood emotionality, let alone sexuality. But this hardly does justice to Hamilton's sensitivity. Most of all, her astringent rigour in argument, emphasising the central importance of knowledge structures, makes it plain to us therapy people that it is not only the believers in cooperation who are sloppy. The seemingly tough-minded psychoanalytic pessimists are themselves lazy and self-indulgently pious when they hang on to simple old pessimisms in the cause of classical conservatism.

Whatever useful road we follow in psychoanalysis, it is most unlikely to be easy. For instance, even playfulness in therapy is not just fun: it can be frightening and very difficult. Hamilton's book is certainly not a lazy read – it is definitely hard going. But it grasps both wide vistas of theory and the intimacy of clinical experience. This gives it a beauty that is a joy to read; but the conclusion we must come to is rather awesome. Psychoanalysis must think honestly about changing some of its theory. Without this, it is likely to become anachronistic; yet if we do think of change, we still risk sectarian strife.

Reference

Stern, D. (1986). *The Interpersonal World of the Infant*. New York: Basic Books.

Preface

Murray M. Schwartz

As a theory of the early effects and meanings of early childhood experience, psychoanalysis stands or falls on its conception and reconstruction of infancy and the emergence of self-reflective individual identity. How do we imagine our origins? And to what ends? The answers to these questions have marked the differences between schools of psychoanalytic thought and practice since Freud's discovery of infantile sexuality. As Freud knew, the answers would not be found in the psychoanalytic setting alone, nor in observation alone, but in the multifarious representation of human experience, including literature, mythology, ethology, and the surprising meaningfulness of each person's history. Psychoanalytic knowledge depends on unknowing. Its greatest enemies are its own orthodoxies, as the history of its theoretical conflict reveals all too well.

Victoria Hamilton's *Narcissus and Oedipus: The Children of Psychoanalysis* is a powerful critique of Freud's conception of the infant. Yet her aim is not destructive. Like a good teacher, she makes use of the past of psychoanalysis to liberate it (and us) from its constraints. She guides the reader through an intellectually lucid presentation of the psychoanalytic child as he has evolved through the work of many sensibilities over the decades. Freud's model of 'primary narcissism' depicts the infant as a self-contained, self-enclosed unit forced to accept the reality of frustration and the tragic limitations of Oedipal knowledge. As this infant is progressively re-conceived in the work of Anna Freud, Melanie Klein, Mahler, Kohut, Kernberg, Rosenfeld, and others, the self-contained Freudian infant struggles towards active relatedness, until a new infant is born through the work of

Balint, Bowlby, Spitz, Winnicott, Green, Tustin, Bower, Bateson, and Brazelton. Hamilton traces the progression from a closed system in which the infant is a passive recipient of experience to an open system in which the infant is an agent in relationships – an active participant in the interplay of self, other, and external world from the beginning.

With a literary and philosophic sensitivity that is rare in psychoanalytic writing, Hamilton *reads* the infants of theory through the images and metaphors of these writers, as a good analyst would read the nuances and transformations of expression in the analytic setting. Her aim is to show how psychoanalytic theory and practice can overcome a certain narcissistic self-containment of its own, in which theories tend to mirror the pathologies they are about and, therefore, lead to a tragic view of human knowledge and potential. 'I propose an alternative view of knowing which is not tragic but expansive', she writes.

Hamilton's expansive view is unfolded in her interpretation and use of two master narratives: the myth of Narcissus and the drama of *Oedipus Rex*. Each story is a parable of limitation. Narcissus cannot grasp the image of himself and hears only the echoes of his own lamentations. Oedipus seeks self-knowledge against the deceptions and violations of the parental past. Hamilton's rich reading of these stories is carefully played out in relation to the evidence of child observations, clinical experiences, and the discourses of analytic theories. The result is an enlargement of psychoanalytic sensibility. Scientific thought and poetic representation are held together in the open space of her imagination. The tragic view thus gives way to the potential space of creative living, in both theory and practice.

Since it was first published in 1982, *Narcissus and Oedipus* has become part of a growing psychoanalytic literature that includes and reaches beyond the tragic vision. It remains today an exemplary work – a bridge that links past and future, origins and unbounded possibilities. Like the therapeutic work of the analytic relationship, it enlarges the scope of our vision and enables us to see continuities where there were unmediated gaps and absences. In this new edition, *Narcissus and Oedipus* will provide a secure base for continuing explorations of an open psychoanalytic domain that overlaps the borders of many disciplines and receives vital news from regions yet unknown.

NARCISSUS
and
OEDIPUS

Those incidental charms which first attached
My heart to rural objects, day by day
Grew weaker, and I hasten on to tell
How Nature, intervenient till this time
And secondary, now at length was sought
For her own sake. But who shall parcel out
His intellect by geometric rules,
Split like a province into round and square?
Who knows the individual hour in which
His habits were first sown, even as a seed?
Who that shall point as with a wand and say
'This portion of the river of my mind
Came from yon fountain?' Thou, my Friend! art one
More deeply read in thy own thoughts; to thee
Science appears but what in truth she is,
Not as our glory and our absolute boast,
But as a succedaneum, and a prop
To our infirmity. No officious slave
Art thou of that false secondary power
By which we multiply distinctions, then
Deem that our puny boundaries are things
That we perceive, and not that we have made.
To thee, unblinded by these formal arts,
The unity of all hath been revealed,
And thou wilt doubt, with me less aptly skilled
Than many are to range the faculties
In scale and order, class the cabinet
Of their sensations, and in voluble phrase
Run through the history and birth of each
As of a single independent thing.
Hard task, vain hope, to analyse the mind,
If each most obvious and particular thought,
Not in a mystical and idle sense,
But in the words of Reason deeply weighed,
Hath no beginning.

William Wordsworth, *The Prelude*, Book II

Introduction

Narcissus and Oedipus – the Children of Psychoanalysis – is a book about child development which I have organised around the two well-known Greek myths, Narcissus and Oedipus. It is in two parts with a transitional section, in which I discuss some of the transformations which take place between the narcissistic and oedipal stages of development. I return to the Greek myths because they have played an important role in the articulation of psychoanalytic theory. They name two stages in early development conceptualised by Freud as 'primary narcissism' and the 'Oedipus complex'. The myths recount two dramas, turned tragedies, in the spectrum of human relationships: one dyadic and confluent and ultimately sterile, the other triadic and dissonant and ultimately destructive. Against this literary backcloth, I draw on the theory and practice of ethology and communication theory so as to expand the discipline of psychoanalysis which Freud created almost one hundred years ago.

The following outline of my use of myth and of the two theoretical models which inform my thinking is intended to direct the reader through the three parts of the book. In each part, I include specific illustrations drawn from both clinical practice and ethological research. Parts I and II begin with an exposition of the relevant myth. My aim in investigating the myths is not to claim or seek archetypal 'evidence' for my views but to invite the reader to look at them, and thereby the theory of psychoanalysis, in a different light. Since they are works of literature, the myths provide a space for the play of imagination in a way that good research may not. For example, it did not occur to me, at first, that narcissism was a term which could be used to describe a relationship until my imagination was fired by Robert Graves's poetic rendering of the love affair between Narcissus and Echo. Similarly, it was the reading of Sophocles' *Oedipus Rex* which brought into sharp relief the many elements of deception surrounding Oedipus' adoption, which marred his youthful curiosity and heroic search for self-knowledge. The play portrays the tremendous complexity involved in our urges to explore the world about us and to gain knowledge about ourselves. It intensified my interest in the origins of exploration, play and knowing and contributed greatly to my understanding of an adopted boy and his adoptive parents who were in psychotherapy with me.

Part I: The myth of Narcissus

A common view of the narcissist is of someone who cannot love another and who loves and admires only himself. We may also imagine a person who is – or thinks he is – beautiful and attractive in appearance and whose self-absorption takes the form of a fascination with his own image.

Freud took this popular view and constructed a theory of 'primary narcissism' which was pivotal to his theories of child development and adult pathology. Since 1914, when Freud published his paper 'On Narcissism', many elaborations of, and disagreements with, his views have appeared in psychiatric and psychoanalytical journals, particularly in the last decade. In these recent works, an interesting connection, observed by Freud, has been drawn between narcissistic self-love and an impoverished sense of self. For many of us, the wish to love, and to be loved by, another remains unfulfilled. At the same time, our efforts towards self-sufficiency seem equally vain. Both endeavours lead to isolation. How can I love, be loved and yet be self-possessed?

The answer to this dilemma lies somewhere in the way we think about a person and about ourselves. Many of the disputes between conflicting psychoanalytic schools are related to varying concepts of a person. For instance, we cannot decide whether narcissism is a normal stage of human development or whether it is a secondary, 'defensive' aberration until we decide what it is that develops out of what. How do we describe the primary state of being?

Let us go back to the image in the mind of the man who started it all. Let us see how Freud thought it all began.

Two images: 'a bird's egg';
'an amoeba'.

Freud used the image of 'a bird's egg' to describe the closed 'psychical system' of the new-born infant.

> A neat example of a psychical system shut off from the stimuli of the external world, and able to satisfy even its nutritional requirements autistically . . . is afforded by a bird's egg with its food supply enclosed in its shell; for it, the care provided by its mother is limited to the provision of warmth. (Freud, 1911, p. 220)

The new-born infant is like one asleep in a primal state of absolute narcissism. From this comfortable enclosure, which is sustained by the brooding mother's warmth, the baby extends feelers into the outside world 'much as the body of an amoeba is related to the pseudopodia which it puts out' (Freud, 1914, p. 75). Amoebae, 'those simplest of living organisms . . . put out protrusions, known as pseudopodia, into which they cause the substance of their body to flow over' (Freud, 1916–17, p. 416). These 'elongations into which the substance of the body extends . . . can be retracted at any time so that the form of the protoplasmic mass is restored' (Freud, 1917, p. 139). Just as the bird's egg image depicts the child's primary state of non-relatedness, 'blissful self-contentment and inaccessibility' (Freud, 1914, p. 89), so the analogy of the amoeba serves to illustrate the child's first relationship to other people. Unlike the egg, the amoeba is minimally, and most reluctantly, related. However, if the individual starts life in an a-social, autistic state, a question arises as to the conditions under which he will extend himself: how does the infant become a social being? Much of Freud's work on the development of the child is addressed to this problem.

According to Freud, the child develops relationships with others when the demands and frustrations imposed by the external world and the limitations of his inner resources force him to seek satisfaction and comfort from without. Only then does the child become social and at all concerned with the well- or ill-being of others. In one of his last works, Freud reiterates his early view that the state of primary narcissism is never given up. The amoeba analogy of relationships is recapitulated: 'Throughout the whole of life the ego remains the great reservoir from which libidinal cathexes are sent out to objects and into which they are also once more withdrawn, just as an amoeba behaves with its pseudopodia' (Freud, 1940, p. 150).

Freud's clinical observations, together with the psychoanalytic model of development he proposed, have affected the ways in which we think about ourselves. In this book, it is Freud's view of relationship as a *secondary* development which is challenged. I do not attempt, as Freud so valuably did, to characterise early relationships by reference to the infant's accompanying unconscious phantasies. This area and the related issue of infant cognitive development remain rich areas for investigation. In Part I, I put forward the view that the development of the child is not a function of the gradual and painstaking socialisation of an original isolate. Development occurs through an interpersonal process of mutual differentiation and individuation out of a primary attachment bond. The child is intensely related from the moment of birth, and, of course, for nine months before that. The problem of development is reformulated. It is no longer a question of how the other, the 'object' as it is called in psychoanalytic literature, is to be added on to an original unit (illustrated by the bird's egg), but of how difference interposes itself in the original, synchronous, mother-child relationship. In my view, primary narcissism theories lead to a misidentification of the central problem of human development. In an original, divided world, a problem arises about linking and object-relating.

To illustrate my position, I use material from three sources. First, I stress the relational nature of the Greek myth of Narcissus and Echo. We are told about the relationship between a sixteen-year-old youth, Narcissus, and his lover-admirer, Echo. This adolescent relationship is grounded in the early relationship between the infant Narcissus 'in his cradle' and his mother, Leiriope. In Graves's words, 'everyone was in love with Narcissus even in his cradle'. The term narcissism would then describe a love-*relationship*. In the light of this interpretation, the later relationship between Narcissus and Echo might serve to illustrate some of the pathologies which result when an early, unconditionally admiring, relationship is perpetuated. Echo is a young woman 'who always answers back' and Narcissus a young man who spurns the admirers who pursue him. Echo is trapped in a primitive relationship of mirroring and echoing in which she cannot initiate dialogue and, it would seem, it is this type of fused relationship from which Narcissus seeks unsuccessfully to free himself and, thereby, 'come to know himself'.

As my second source, I draw upon that body of work which is referred to in the literature as 'Attachment Theory'. Attachment theory concerns itself with the origins of the child's *tie* to the mother. For many people, especially parents, the idea that a *bond* might pose a tricky, theoretical problem and, moreover, have revolutionary significance in the study of infancy, could seem absurd. Of course, the mother and her baby are intensely attached during the first months of life. However, unlike the public at large and the small company of ethologists, psychotherapists are more often faced with isolated individuals whose lives are crippled with pathological attachments and the pathologies of detachment. As is often observed, Freud's views on infant development were derived from his work with adult patients. By contrast, some child psychoanalysts, who developed his ideas, and most child ethologists, for whom fieldwork is a principal source, have based their theories on the direct observation of infants and young children.

When, in 1958, the British psychiatrist and psychoanalyst, Dr John Bowlby, proposed a new approach to the origins of the child's tie to the mother, he introduced the term attachment in order to avoid some of the connotations of the term dependency (Bowlby, 1958, pp. 350–73). In order to clarify the central importance of attachment theory in my work, let me contrast the concepts of attachment, dependency and object-relations.

Unlike dependency relations, both attachments and object-relations refer to affectional ties between one person and another *specific* individual. Whereas dependency implies non-specificity, transience, immaturity and helplessness, object-relations and attachments are enduring, extremely discriminating and bridge gaps in space and time. They are not incompatible with independence and maturity. Attachment theory stresses the long-term nature of attachments, their strong positive affect and their pervasive effect on other behaviours. Although, in all three of these relationships, the importance of the earliest exchanges between mother and infant is stressed, nevertheless dependency relations are conceived of as secondary to the mother's gratification of the infant's basic *drives,* such as hunger and warmth.

The distinction between attachment theory and object-relations theory is more subtle. It could be said that, in the study of infancy, object-relations theory provides a bridge between Freudian drive theory and contemporary attachment theory. Although, in his later works, Freud stressed the enduring importance of the infant-mother tie, his emphasis on orality, the drive theory and the libido theory tended to obscure the primacy which he also accorded to the attachment bond. Some Freudians, particularly of the ego psychology school, view early development as proceeding from an undifferentiated, objectless and narcissistic stage, through a transitional stage, to the establishment of true object-relations some time after eight months of age. Psychoanalysts of the object-relations school, sometimes called the British school because of the works of Balint, Fairbairn, Klein, Winnicott and others, have developed the relational aspect of Freud's ideas. They regard the infant's tie to the mother as primary, but usually emphasise that the first attachment is to a 'part-object', particularly the mother's breast. Part-object relations are usually held to exist between those parts of the body of the subject and object, which serve vital functions such as feeding and elimination. For instance, the baby may experience himself as all mouth and his object as all breast. The development of object relations is marked by the summation of part-objects into wholes. The concept of part-objects implies that the newborn is not capable of whole object relations and has no idea of person constancy. In contrast to the Freudian theories of an early narcissistic, passive, objectless stage, many of the object-relations theorists stress the infant's intentionality and his contribution to the quality of the first relationship.

Attachment theory, while agreeing, on the one hand, that the neonate does not have a concept of person constancy and, on the other, that he is an active being capable of initiating responses in other people, differs over the importance of the breast relationship and stresses the nature of the *interaction* between the mother and the infant. The attachment theorist studies both the contribution of the infant's actions and their effects upon his caretaker, *and* the care-giver's sensitivity, acceptance, co-operation and accessibility towards the infant. Interpersonal interaction is stressed from the beginning of life.

Two distinguishing characteristics of the attachment view are the use of the paradigm of systems theory in order to conceptualise the *interactional* nature of the infant–mother tie and the placing of early social behaviour in an *evolutionary* context. Many attachment behaviours only make sense when they are viewed as having survival advantages in the environment of evolutionary adaptedness. In Bowlby's view, for instance, the primary function of attachment and the reciprocal maternal behaviour is the protection of the infant from predators. Other attachment theorists place less emphasis on this function.

Attachment theory also draws an important distinction between attachment and attachment behaviours. Attachment *behaviours* are diverse and may even be mutually exclusive of one another. Attachment theorists are not in complete agreement over the criteria of these behaviours. For example, there is great interest in the nature of the interplay between attachment and exploratory behaviours. Although seemingly mutually exclusive, in that a child who seeks close contact with his mother cannot simultaneously turn away from her to explore his environment, they are nevertheless interdependent. Without a secure attachment, exploration tends to have a detached, restless and hyperactive quality.

The concept of *attachment* is more abstract than its behaviours and can be thought of as an inner construct or governor, organising the various, and often conflicting, patterns of attachment behaviour. Inherent in attachment theory is the notion that the first infant-mother relationship creates that structure which governs later attachments. Since an attachment is like an inner construct, it is stable and exists across space and time. A characteristic of many attachment *behaviours*, on the other hand, is that they are 'proximity-seeking' and, consequently, disappear if and when they achieve their aim.

Attachment theory emphasises different patterns of behaviour to those conceptualised in psychoanalysis by reference to the oral, anal, phallic and genital stages and their respective contributions to the development of object-relations. A primary attachment behaviour of special interest to me is grasping,[1] the development of which in the early, synchronous stage of relationships may mark an important step in the individuation process. Freud tended to emphasise the 'narcissistic' gratifications in the child's achievement of motor skills. But the achievement afforded by the successful grasp is, in another sense, a differentiation *away* from the narcissistic type of relationship. The grasp frees the child from synchronous and mirroring interactions. For it is the baby's successful grasp of an object which inserts the outside world into the intense, largely exclusive, play between himself and his mother. The fully co-ordinated grasp, where eyes, arm, fingers and object of desire meet, is achieved around five months. To the observer, the successful grasp signifies that the child is now able to reach out for objects and to get what he wants for himself. It marks the child's ability to experience himself as an effective agent. In this respect, the grasp is a precursor of crawling and walking; its success or failure may set the stage for the child's experience of autonomous action. Whereas, previously, the child was simply in a relationship, the grasp affords him the new opportunity to forge direct links between himself and the outside world. He learns not only about the external objects he fondles, but also about the mobility and strength of his own body. Through the achievement of the grasp, the child has it in his own hands to push away or to pull towards. He can make or break a connection.

In the Greek myth, the death of Narcissus coincides with the failed grasp. He does not die because he falls in love with himself, but because he falls in love with a phantasm – his mirror-image – which is ungraspable. Narcissus cries:

> I am in love and see my loved one, but that form which I see and love, I cannot reach. . . . My distress is all the greater because it is not a mighty ocean that separates us, nor yet highways or mountains, or city walls with close-barred gates. Only a little water keeps us apart. My love himself desires to be embraced: for whenever I lean forward to kiss the clear waters he lifts up his face to mine and strives to reach me . . . What I desire, I have. My very plenty makes me poor. How I wish I could separate myself from my body. A new prayer this, for a lover, to wish the things he loves away! (Ovid, 1955, p. 86)

A common complaint is, 'Oh, but it doesn't make any difference.' Whatever we do, we seem unable to make a mark. Whatever we touch seems to slip through our hands. Over and over again, we reach out but we seem to miss it, we never quite get there. The life we long to embrace passes by. The grasp, or its failure, becomes a metaphor for life. I am not claiming that such complaints rest exclusively upon the individual history of the grasp, but I am saying that the grasp helps to create the infant's conception of externality. His feeling of competence affects both the eagerness with which he explores his environment once he can crawl and the crawling behaviour itself. An infant who is apathetic about his surroundings may remain in the synchronous realm of the visual and echolalic, in which he is mainly attuned to reflected images and answering voices. Some pathologies of narcissism are characterised by this kind of passivity. Even a successful performer, who seems so full of confidence, can experience himself as a product, or organ, of others.

Together with the Greek myths and attachment theory, a third influence on my thinking has been the work of Gregory Bateson. Much of Bateson's research is based on the application of the cybernetic paradigm to the study of social systems. There is an obvious link between Bateson's work, child ethology and attachment theory in that they share a commitment to the cybernetic model. Gregory Bateson is a British anthropologist who grew up in, and was educated at, Cambridge, England. His father, William Bateson, was a well-known geneticist. Bateson, the younger, left the academic atmosphere of Cambridge in the 1930s when he went to Bali; since then, he has spent the majority of his time in the United States. Over the last forty-five years, his attention has ranged over the fields of aesthetics, animal communication, anthropology, evolution, genetics, linguistics, philosophy, psychiatry and religion. From his study of Balinese culture (Bateson, 1936), to more recent research into schizophrenia (Bateson, 1960, pp. 477–91), to contemporary work on the theory of evolution (Bateson, 1979), Bateson has applied the systemic or cybernetic method. A primary rule of this approach is that any phenomenon, whether it is the clinging behaviour of a Balinese infant, the 'word salad' of a schizophrenic or the addictive behaviour of an alcoholic, is only intelligible in its context. An event forms part of an ongoing system. There are no schizophrenics without families and no infants without mothers.

Let us look at some of the features of the cybernetic model

which have particular relevance to the model of infancy and child development presented in this book.

1 Cybernetic explanation, unlike causal explanation, is always *negative*. In cybernetic explanation, we do not look for a specific cause of an event, but we consider all the possible alternatives which could have occurred and then ask ourselves why most of these alternatives were not followed so that a particular event was one of the few which did occur.

The negative nature of cybernetic explanation is conceptualised by the term *'restraints'*. What were the restraints upon a particular system such that a number of alternatives were knocked out? Bateson illustrates the differences between restraints which are negative and clues which are positive by the following example.

> For example, the selection of a piece for a given position in a jigsaw puzzle is 'restrained' by many factors. Its shape must conform to that of its several neighbours and possibly that of the boundary of the puzzle; its colour must conform to the colour pattern of its region; the orientation of its edges must obey the topological regularities set by the cutting machine in which the puzzle was made; and so on. From the point of view of the man who is trying to solve the puzzle, these are all clues, *i.e.*, sources of information which will guide him in his selection. From the point of view of the cybernetic observer, they are *restraints*. (Bateson, 1967, pp. 29–32)

Bateson regards the theory of evolution under natural selection as 'a classical example' of the cybernetic type of explanation (1967, p. 29). The emphasis is less that the fittest survive than that the fittest are those life-forms which are not eliminated by environmental pressures. Animals survive, reproduce and evolve within the restraints of many opposing variables. Niko Tinbergen, the ethologist and zoologist, has described the life of animals observed in their natural habitat as 'a multi-dimensional tightrope act' (Tinbergen, 1973, p. 200). Success depends upon coping with a bewildering variety of obstacles. However, it may never occur to the healthy and happy man that there are infinitely more ways in which he could have failed than the narrow road to his success. Like the puzzle-solver, the successful man looks at the positive steps to his goal and does not think that his achievement is the end-product of numerous adaptations to restraints. Bowlby has suggested that we call the successful outcome of an activated behavioural system 'goal-corrected' rather than 'goal-directed' (Bowlby, 1969, p.69). The concept of goal-corrected behaviour is similar to the cybernetic concept of 'feedback' in that the goal-corrected system is constantly checked by reference to the discrepancy between performance and goals.

A further implication of this approach is that no single adaptation is viewed as ideal; it is always the compromise result of many different, and often conflicting, demands. When we analyse human behaviour, we usually study one behavioural characteristic and one environmental pressure at a time. The broader context is thereby lost to view. We do not see that many activities compete, and, moreover, that different environmental pressures may dictate incompatible ways of being met. Freud's concept of 'over-determination' – namely, that a piece of behaviour or a thought has many determinants – can be seen as a positive counterpart to the concept of negative restraints. In place of the assumption that an event has multiple *causes*, we view the event as the end-product of a process of *elimination* of many factors, none of which may be causally related to the final outcome. Conflict behaviour – such as that between approach and withdrawal – and the emotional state of ambivalence have been of particular interest to psychoanalysts. When two behavioural systems are activated, a person may exhibit 'compromise' behaviour (Bowlby, 1969, p. 99) in which he plays out fragments of two different systems. Some tics or stereotyped inappropriate gestures can be seen in this way. Or a person might 'redirect' (Bowlby, 1969, p. 100) a particular behavioural system on to another goal in the way that has been traditionally described in the psychoanalytic literature as displacement. Actions or feelings are 'displaced' (Bowlby, 1969, p. 100) from one person on to another person or object. In a novel environment, even a curious, securely attached, child may exhibit both clinging and exploratory behaviour. Tinbergen discusses the compromises involved in the camouflage of birds. Camouflage is protective as long as the animal is motionless; however, the bird also has to eat, which requires motion. 'While they could feed more efficiently if they never had to freeze, and would be better protected against predators if they never had to move, they can do neither, and selection, rewarding overall success rather than any isolated characteristic, has produced compromises' (Tinbergen, 1973, pp. 154–5).

2 The subject matter of cybernetics is not events and objects but the *information* carried by events and objects. This feature is of particular relevance to the communicational nature of attachment behaviours and to the whole domain of meaning in human action, which is the subject matter of psychoanalysis. Bateson points out that there is no information or communication without context. A word acquires meaning in the larger context of the utterance, which again has meaning only in a relationship.

Studies of the noise-making aspects of an infant's babbling in isolation from his communicational partner ignore the context in which sounds gain their meaning (Bower, 1977). Bateson and others have applied this principle to their study of apparently meaningless 'schizophrenese' (Bateson, 1955, pp. 39–51; 1956, pp. 251–64). The schizophrenic's 'word salad' acquires meaning through the study of the communicational patterns and family relationships in which this aberrant speech form has developed. In his study of autistic children, Tinbergen observes that the speech defects and stereo-typies of autistic children are usually secondary developments due to unsolved motivational conflicts. Speech therapy or the teaching of social skills are unlikely to be effective if the treatment relationship excludes the understanding of the context in which the motivational ambivalence is maintained at an irresoluble level (Tinbergen, 1973, p. 195). In the analytic setting, communication between doctor and patient may acquire meaning in the highly specific context of the transference relationship. A rule of the analytic setting is that the analyst and the analysand attempt to understand various idiosyncratic and ineffective ways of relating to others through the transference of these patterns from past figures on to the analyst.

3 The communicational subject matter of cybernetics relates to two other central concepts, 'feedback' and 'redundancy'. Bateson believes that 'patterning' or 'predictability' are 'the very essence of communication' (Bateson, 1968, pp. 614–26). The predictability of particular events is technically called 'redundancy'. Information depends upon predictability. And predictability is dependent upon restraints. Bateson gives the following exam-

ple: If, for instance, 'I see the top part of a tree standing up, I can predict – with better than random success – that the tree has roots in the ground. The percept of the tree top is redundant with (i.e., contains "information" about) parts of the system which I cannot perceive owing to the slash provided by the opacity of the ground' (Bateson, 1967, pp. 29–32). The world of the schizophrenic or autistic child would seem to lack redundancy. The autistic child, who has a particular difficulty with *verbal* communication, would seem unable to make predictions across the slashes. A world which lacks patterning or redundancy is characterised by 'noise'; that is, a clamouring multitude of perceptions and sensations through which there is no clear passage.

4 Since the subject matter of cybernetics is information, concepts which imply localisation are inappropriate. We cannot look for pieces of information in a person's neurophysiology. In this respect, information is like contrast, symmetry, correspondence, difference, etc. As Bateson says, the

> contrast between this white paper and that black coffee is not somewhere between the paper and the coffee and, even if we bring the paper and coffee into close juxtaposition, the contrast between them is not thereby located or pinched between them. Nor is that contrast located between the two objects and my eye. (Bateson, 1967, p.32)

A further consequence of the cybernetic view, in contrast to the nineteenth-century model of the hard sciences, is that nothing – that which is not – can be a cause. Information theory refers to this type of cause by the term 'zero message'. In the world of information and ideas, we do not investigate forces, drives, impacts or energy exchanges. In psychoanalysis, we look at the meaning conferred upon concrete events. Zero information is important to the discipline of psychoanalysis and to the study of attachment. Zero messages, such as absence or unresponsiveness, may cause extremely strong emotions. Bateson illustrates a zero cause by the 'letter which you do not write'. This non-letter 'can get an angry reply' (Bateson, 1970, p. 452). Take, for example, the case of two neighbours who met frequently. A couple of weeks go by without meeting. Each person begins to wonder what has happened and to attribute various motives to the other. Perhaps he said the wrong thing, perhaps the neighbour does not like him any more, perhaps the neighbour has found another friend. Both talk to a third neighbour, exclaiming 'I can't understand it, nothing happened.' It does not occur to either of the first two neighbours that the answer does not lie in anything positive, such as an offence, but in an absence of response. Nothing happened. But because nothing happened, each believes that something must have happened. They begin to search for positive clues.

The features of cybernetic theory, which I have attempted to elucidate above, affect the conception of development and change which we bring to our study of infancy and childhood. For instance, within the cybernetic paradigm, we do not ask, is this piece of behaviour caused by a constitutional or an environmental factor? The problem of development is formulated negatively in terms of 'feedback' and 'restraints'.

Transition: The transformations of narcissism and the transition to the Oedipal phase

This section of the book centres on the problem of differentiation and the transitional structures which mediate the intense relatedness of the mother–infant dyad and the child's sense of personal identity and agency in the world about him.

At about eight months, when he begins to crawl, the child frees himself from his mother's arms and begins to make unsupported approaches towards, departures from, and reunions with, the people to whom he is attached or who evoke his curiosity. The child marks out a boundary where previously there was an overlap. Both child and mother are engaged in differentiating themselves out of the primary affectional bond. At this point, it begins to make sense to talk of an emerging sense of personal identity. The mother now provides the child with 'a secure base for exploration' (Bowlby, 1969), or background of safety. Some pathologies of narcissism, auto-erotism and, perhaps, some types of autism may have their roots in this phase of development. Frances Tustin, who has studied autistic children from an object–relations point of view, has observed that the mothers of autistic children are not unable to form relationships, neither are they simply cold or distant as was sometimes thought. But they are in a muddle about difference and separateness. In this regard, they tend to be inconsistent, oscillating between intense and sensitive contact and emotional withdrawal.

Bowlby's emphasis on the parameter familiar–strange is also pertinent to this transitional stage of development (Bowlby, 1973). 'Eight months anxiety', a term in currency amongst some researchers, often accompanies the child's ability to crawl and is sometimes referred to as 'stranger anxiety'. The stranger throws the child a wager. The stranger is the representative of the unknown. He challenges the child's preference for familiarity. Within the ethological model, 'eight months anxiety' is a function of the 'ambivalent motivation' (Tinbergen, 1973, p. 185), which the child feels as he works out a balance between his desires for the familiar and the strange. If his explorations were to proceed completely untrammelled by fear, the child would soon die. The child's sense of danger and caution arises precisely through these interactions with the unknown. If, on the other hand, anxiety overwhelms curiosity, the child may attempt to retreat back into the safe, warm cocoon of early narcissistic relationships. The stranger brings into sharp relief the security the child feels in relation both to his mother's presence and to her predictable absences, out of both of which the background of safety is formed.

The view of exploration presented in this book differs from the Freudian view. In psychoanalysis, there is an assumption that knowledge develops in a context of separation, pain and frustration. For Freud, exploration and mature scientific curiosity were transformations of illicit, sexual interests. If a child was to be educated into his cultural heritage, the repression or sublimation of his essentially anti-social sexuality was deemed to be obligatory. As a result, there has been a tendency in psychoanalysis to characterise curiosity in a negative way and to regard creativity as an attempt to make reparations. In my view, though sexuality is certainly of intense interest to a child, there is something odd about attributing his eagerness for knowledge to a redirection of sexual excitation. It seems to me that a child's explorations flourish not in conditions of privation and frustration, but within a secure attachment. The secure child approaches the external world with an intense and, in Einstein's words, 'holy curiosity'.

Part II: The myth of Oedipus

In Part II, I follow a similar procedure to Part I. I begin with the Greek myth of Oedipus the King and reinterpret the oedipal stage of development in the light of the myth and the contemporary models of ethology and systems theory.

Freud brought the myth of Oedipus to the notice of the general public and the psychoanalytic world through his formulation of the 'Oedipus complex'. The Oedipus complex maps out the vicissitudes of triangular relationships which have their origins in the relationship between the child and his two parents. The child of three to five years of age is engaged in a three-person relationship in which the father plays an increasingly focal role. The child wants to get in between his parents. This wish entails the idea that he gets rid of one parent so as to enjoy an exclusive love-relationship with the other. The resolution of this dilemma has far-reaching implications for the child's view of reality. In order to come to terms with the 'reality principle', he must abandon his early attempts to organise the world about him in accordance with the 'pleasure principle' (Freud, 1911), through which his selfish or 'narcissistic' wishes and needs are fulfilled. The Oedipus complex is resolved or 'dissolved' by a renunciation of childish, sexual wishes, which are inherently anti-social, and by an 'identification' with the parent of the same sex. The little boy no longer wishes to eliminate his father but to be just like him.

Freud introduced the novel, sometimes unwelcome, idea that sexuality and anxiety form a major part of the life of little children. His views have been expanded by later writers on child psychoanalysis so as to include even the life of the young infant. My own views, though sometimes at variance with existing analytic views, are nevertheless a continuation of this project. Freud emphasised that aspect of the oedipal drama which deals with illicit sexuality and incestuous wishes. The social system in which Freud lived and worked was 'sick' with repressed sexuality. Freud had the courage to bring to light the unimagined effects which sexuality has upon men's lives. In his interpretation of the Oedipus legend, he was, perhaps influenced by this social factor. In this book, however, I focus instead on that aspect of the myth and of Freud's interpretation of it which concerns the search for knowledge about one's origins. The *Oedipus Rex* tells us about a young man's departure from his familiar home of Corinth and his eventful journey to the strange city of Thebes in quest for knowledge of his true origins. To me, it is more a tale about an individual's search for personal identity than a parable about the acting-out of hidden, incestuous wishes. The tragedy of the play is more a function of the deceptions and evasions which mar the lives of all the characters. The play tells us what happens when knowledge is withheld, denied and obscured. In this sense, it bears on what I regard as psychoanalysis's essentially 'tragic' view of knowledge and knowing. To me, it is a view which characterises more the roots of a particular pathology than the normal growth of knowledge.

Oedipus is an adopted child whose search for his origins proves to be disastrous because of the web of ignorance and deceit in which he and his family are entangled. For Freud, the 'real' meaning of the myth is that every little boy of a normal family wishes to kill his father and sleep with his mother. But, the topic of Sophocles' play is not just deeds done in dreams or wishes. Oedipus is not at all consoled by Jocasta's observation that 'many men, in dreams, have lain with their mothers! No reasonable man is troubled by such things.' Sophocles' play is about 'blind deeds', leading to social destruction, for which personal guilt or intentionality have little bearing. The 'pollution' of Thebes escalates out of the blind actions of the deceived, and deceiving, members of the house of Kadmos. Oedipus is aware that no *individual* action, including suicide, can rectify the social system of Thebes. The context of responsibility is larger than the wishes or actions of any individual and beyond restitution by the reparations of any individual.

In summary, the central theme of the book is that development proceeds from the intensely social to the personal. Problems of differentiation are emphasised more than those of object- or person-relating. In normal circumstances, attachment and object-relating may be taken for granted, being the secure base out of which differentiation occurs. The developing 'ego' may be thought of as an internal governor which functions, like the mother, as a secure base and as the regulator of the child's rapidly shifting, emotional, field. The eager search for knowledge about the external world and one's self is seen more as the natural fruit and accompaniment of differentiation than the product of predominantly negative experiences such as pain, absence or the frustration of sexual wishes.

Part I of this book is considerably longer than Part II. This imbalance may strike the reader as odd. However, since, in my view, our initial picture of infancy affects all later views of development, it becomes important to paint this picture as clearly, and fully, as possible. The earlier chapters of Part I, in which I discuss existing, psychoanalytic views of infancy, are intended to set the scene for the thesis I develop throughout the book. Thus, the major portion of Part I (chapters 1–4) is theoretical and, therefore, may be of more interest to psychoanalysts than to other readers. If the reader so chooses, he may read the Introduction, the Preface to Part I (including the diagram on p. 28, which is alluded to throughout the book) and then skip to chapter 3. Chapters 1 and 2 are more accessible to psychoanalysts not only because, as with any specialised discipline, the language of the tradition is a technical language of its own, but also because the antecedent beliefs and assumptions upon which the traditional theory is based are less immediately available. Furthermore, this obscurity in language sometimes represents an obscurity in thinking.

By contrast, the reader who is not psychoanalytically trained may find chapters 3–6 more comprehensible. The view presented in chapter 3 is, I think, more representative of the layman's view of infancy. Chapter 4 presents some of the recent findings about the newborn, upon which a new conception of infancy can be built. In addition, chapters 3 and 4 are closer to my views and are, therefore, important to the understanding of my thesis. In chapters 5 and 6, I use the myth of Narcissus, and some illustrations drawn from clinical practice, to develop my own interpretation of narcissism and early infancy.

Part I

NARCISSUS

I look into the frost's face, alone:
It's going nowhere,
Which is where I come from.
Miraculous! The breathing plain all ironed,
Without a crease.
The sun screws up its eyes in laundered destitution,
Finds calm and consolation . . .
Innocent as bread, snow crunches in one's eyes.

Osip Mandelstam

The myth of Narcissus[1]

Narcissus was a Thespian, the son of the blue nymph Leiriope, whom the River-God Cephisus had once encircled with the windings of his streams, and ravished. She gave birth to a child with whom one could have fallen in love even in his cradle, and she called him Narcissus.

She is the first to test the reliability of the blind seer Teiresias. Teiresias has been condemned to eternal blindness by Hera, the wife of Zeus, in revenge for Teiresias' verdict in Zeus' favour on an argument between herself and her husband as to whether women get far more pleasure out of love than men. They consult the wise Teiresias because he has experienced love both as a man and as a woman. Zeus, in recompense for Teiresias' loss of sight, gives him the power to know the future.

Leiriope asks Teiresias if Narcissus will live to a ripe old age? 'Yes, if he does not come to know himself' (Ovid), or '. . . provided that he never knows himself' (Graves). This pronouncement seemed to be nothing but empty words. However, it was justified by the outcome of events: the strange madness which afflicted the boy and the nature of his death proved its truth.

Even as a child anyone might excusably have fallen in love with Narcissus, and when he reached the age of sixteen, his path was strewn with heartlessly rejected lovers of both sexes; for he had a stubborn pride in his own beauty.

Among these lovers was the nymph, Echo, who could no longer use her voice, except in foolish repetition of another's voice. She still had a body then, she was not just a voice; but although she was always chattering, her power of speech was no different from what it is now. This loss was a punishment for having entertained Hera with an endless flow of talk while Zeus' concubines, the mountain nymphs, evaded her jealous eye and made good their escape. When Hera realised this, she said, 'I shall curtail the powers of that tongue which has tricked me: you will have only the briefest possible use of your voice.' And in fact she carried out her threats. Echo still repeats the last words spoken, and gives back the sounds she has heard.

One day Narcissus went into the woods to net stags and was seen by the talkative nymph, Echo, who always answers back. She stealthily followed him through the pathless forest, longing to address him, to make flattering overtures to him, to approach him with tender pleas, but unable to speak first. She was ready to do what her voice would allow, to wait for sounds which she might re-echo with her own voice.

At last Narcissus, finding that he had strayed from his companions, shouted:

'Is anyone here?'

'Here!' Echo answered, which surprised Narcissus, since no one was in sight.

'Come!'

'Come!'

'Why do you avoid me?'

'Why do you avoid me?'

'Let us come together here!'

'Let us come together here!' repeated Echo who never again would reply more willingly to any sound and joyfully rushed from her hiding place to embrace Narcissus.

Yet he shook her off roughly, and ran away.

'I will die before you ever lie with [touch] me', he cried.

'Lie with me!' Echo pleaded.

But Narcissus had gone and Echo spent the rest of her life in lonely glens. Yet still her love remained firmly rooted in her heart, and was increased by the pain of having been rejected. Her anxious thoughts kept her awake and made her pitifully thin and she pined away for love and mortification, until only her voice remained and is the only part of her that still lives.

One day, Narcissus sent a sword to Ameinius, his most insistent suitor, after whom the river Ameinius is named; it is a tributary of the river Helisson, which flows into the Alpheius. Ameinius killed himself on Narcissus' threshold, calling on the gods to take revenge on Narcissus for his treatment both of his admirers and of the spirits of the waters and the woods.

'May he himself fall in love with another, as we have done with him! May he too be unable to gain his loved one?'

Artemis heard the plea, and made Narcissus fall in love, though denying him love's consummation. At Donacon in Thespia he came upon a spring, clear as silver, and never yet disturbed by cattle, birds, wild beasts, or even by branches dropping off the trees that shaded it; and as he cast himself down, exhausted, on the grassy verge to slake his thirst, he fell in love with his reflection.

While he sought to quench his thirst, another thirst grew in him, and as he drank, he was enchanted by the beautiful reflection that he saw. He fell in love with an insubstantial hope, mistaking a mere shadow for a real body. As he lay on the bank, he gazed at the twin stars that were his eyes, at his flowing locks, worthy of Bacchus or Apollo, his smooth cheeks, his ivory neck, his lovely face where a rosy flush stained the snowy whiteness of his complexion, admiring all the features for which he was himself admired. Unwittingly, he desired himself, and was himself the object of his own approval, at once seeking and sought, himself kindling the flame with which he burned. At first he tried to embrace and kiss the beautiful boy who confronted him. How often did he vainly kiss the treacherous pool, how often plunge his arms deep in the waters, as he tried to clasp the neck he saw! But he could not lay hold on himself. He did not know what he was looking at, but was fired by the sight, and excited by the illusion that deceived his eyes. Presently he recognised himself, and lay gazing enraptured into the pool, hour after hour.

Stretched on the shady grass, he gazed at the shape that was no true shape with eyes that could never have their fill, and by his own eyes he was undone. How could he endure both to possess and yet not to possess?

'I am in love, and see my loved one, but that form which I see and love, I cannot reach: so far am I deluded by my love. My distress is all the greater because it is not a mighty ocean that separates us, nor yet highways or mountains, or city walls with close-barred gates. Only a little water keeps us apart. My love himself desires to be embraced: for whenever I lean forward to kiss the clear waters he lifts up his face to mine and strives to reach me. You would think he could be reached – it is such a small thing that hinders our love. Certainly it is not my looks or my years which you shun, for I am one of those the nymphs have loved. With friendly looks you proffer me some hope. When I stretch out my arms to you, you stretch yours towards me in return: you laugh when I do, and often I have marked your tears when I was weeping. You answer my signs with nods, and, as far as I can guess from the movement of your lovely lips, reply to me in words that never reach my ears.

'Alas! I am myself the boy I see. I know it: my own reflection does not deceive me, I am on fire with love for my own self. It is I who kindle the flames which I must endure. What should I do! Woo or be wooed? But what then shall I seek by my wooing? What I desire, I have. My very plenty makes me poor. How I wish I could separate myself from my body! A new prayer this, for a lover, to wish the things he loves away!'

Grief was destroying him, yet he rejoiced in his torments; knowing at least that his other self would remain true to him, whatever happened. (Graves)

'I have no quarrel with death, for in death I shall forget my pain; but I could wish that the object of my love might outlive me: as it is, both of us will perish together, when this one life is destroyed.' (Ovid, p. 86)

Echo, although she had not forgiven Narcissus, grieved with him. As often as the unhappy boy sighed 'Alas!', she took up his sigh, and repeated 'Alas!'

His tears disturbed the water, so that the pool rippled and the image grew dim:

'Where are you fleeing? Let me, by looking, feed my ill-starred love.' He beat himself and his white marble skin turn red tinged with purple. When he saw this in the water, he could bear it no longer. As golden wax melts with gentle heat, as morning frosts are thawed by the warmth of the sun, so he was worn and wasted away with love, and slowly consumed by its hidden fire. His fair complexion with its rosy flush faded away, gone was his youthful strength, and all the beauties which lately charmed his eyes. Nothing remained of that body which Echo once had loved.

She sympathetically echoed 'Alas! Alas!' as he plunged a dagger in his breast, and as he gazed into the familiar waters said his last words, 'Ah youth, beloved in vain, farewell!' and expired. (Graves)

He laid down his weary head on the green grass, and death closed the eyes which so admired their owner's beauty. (Ovid)

His blood soaked the earth, and up sprang the white narcissus flower with its red corollary, from which an unguent balm is now distilled at Chaeronea. This is recommended for affections of the ears (though apt to give headache), and is a vulnerary, and for the cure of frostbite. When the pyre was being prepared, his body was nowhere to be found. Instead of his corpse, they discovered a flower with a circle of white petals around a yellow centre.

When this story became known, it brought well-deserved fame to the seer Teiresias. It was told thoughout all the cities of Greece, and his reputation was boundless.

Preface: some theoretical views

The state of sleep is able to re-establish the likeness of mental life as it was before the recognition of reality, because a prerequisite of sleep is a deliberate rejection of reality. . . . It will rightly be objected that an organisation which was a slave to the pleasure principle and neglected the reality of the external world could not maintain itself alive for the shortest time, so that it could not have come into existence at all. The employment of a fiction like this is, however, justified when one considers that the infant – provided one includes with it the care it receives from its mother – does almost realise a psychical system of this kind. . . . – A neat example of a psychical system shut off from the stimuli of the external world, and able to satisfy even its nutritional requirements autistically, is afforded by a bird's egg with its food supply enclosed in its shell; for it, the care provided by its mother is limited to the provision of warmth. (Freud, 1911, pp. 219–20)

Our present ego-feeling is, therefore, only a shrunken residue of a much more inclusive – indeed, an all-embracing – feeling which corresponded to a more intimate bond between the ego and the world about it. If we may assume that there are many people in whose mental life this primary ego-feeling has persisted to a greater or lesser degree, it would exist in them side by side with the narrower and more sharply demarcated ego-feeling of maturity, like a kind of counterpart to it. In that case, the ideational contents appropriate to it would be precisely those of limitlessness and of a bond with the universe.

(Freud, 1930, p. 68)

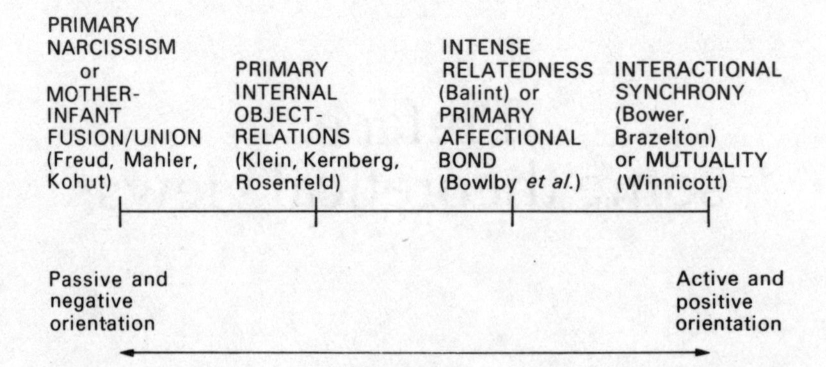

Figure 1

In this preface, I review various conceptualisations of the mental state of the newborn infant. This comparative review forms the backcloth against which I place that view of infancy which I regard as most fertile for research and which best reflects the many new discoveries about the remarkable capacities of the newborn. My aim is to suggest how the research incorporated in the concept of 'interactional synchrony' (Bower, 1977, p. 30) might contribute to a new psychoanalytic theory of child development. Many of the models of infancy – Freudian, object-relations, attachment – agree that in the neonate we see a human being in his least differentiated state. Ontogenic development proceeds from a primary state of amorphous globality or chaos, through a second stage in which discrete parts or circumscribed subsystems emerge, to a third stage in which that which has been differentiated or 'split' is co-ordinated or integrated. However, there is disagreement over the conceptualisation of this primary state of undifferentiation – for example, isolation, autism, psychosis, fusion, chaos, unity, bliss, persecutory anxiety, terror, unintegration, etc. – and over the attribution of passivity or activity, and sometimes intentionality, to the infant.

In the spectrum of viewpoints represented in the nearby diagram, I depict four positions on the infant's primary state, a state which is often accorded a duration of three to six months. I arrange these on a continuum, which goes from states of non-relation and passivity, at one end, to states of relation and activity, at the other. In the first two positions, the newborn's attitude to his world is predominantly negative. The extra-uterine environment is experienced as a source of disturbance or persecution. As one moves along the spectrum, one may envisage the infant as not only more active, but also more connected to, sensorially aware of, and *positively* orientated towards, his primary attachment figure and the world around her.

I have chosen various key figures in psychoanalysis to represent these positions. Nevertheless, since the issues of relatedness and difference are often unclear, some writers occupy more than one position on my spectrum. At the end of this three- to six-month period, the fusion theorists face the problem of duality, individuation, discontinuity and dissonance – how one becomes a person. Those theorists who attribute autonomy and a negative orientation to the infant face problems of linking, harmony and positive affect towards others – how one comes to love another. The interactionalist concept of two 'partners in a dyadic bond' is designed to combine both the attributes of closeness or merger and of duality and autonomy.

I suggest that it is the issue of the onset and extent of the infant's contribution which divides up conflicting schools of thought. The more commonly acknowledged distinction between the Freudian and object-relations schools does not adequately reflect this issue. Not all the relational theories attribute agency or intentionality to the infant, neither do all the primary narcissism theorists deny the infant's sense of relatedness. Like so much of the ambiguity in psychoanalytic thought, this equivocality is a consequence of, even a tribute to, the breadth and originality of Freud's work. His thinking took many different, and richly suggestive, directions at different times, not all of which he fully developed. In the two quotations above, for example, Freud gave two different accounts of the primary state of the infant, one of self-sufficient isolation (the bird's egg), the other of a blissful state of union. These contrary accounts have given rise to two quite different views of early development and to two different traditions or schools within psychoanalysis. The one views the newborn as an undifferentiated isolate, the other as undifferentiated, but within a state of affectionate relation. In either case, little autonomy or awareness of difference is attributed to the infant.

I draw a fundamental distinction between those theories of development which proceed from a primary state of isolation or union, in which autonomy is non-existent (let us name these the 'unity' theorists), and, on the other hand, those which postulate an original diversity or duality.

Amongst the unity theories, I include Freud's theory of primary narcissism, Mahler's concept of normal primary autism, and other Freudian and object-relations theories which postulate a primitive state of fusion or merger between mother and infant. Kohut's work on narcissism and his concept of the 'self-object' fall into this category. When development originates out of a state of oneness, the notions of autism and of fusion meet up, as they did in Freud's theory. In either the autistic or the fused state, there is no awareness of distinction. Nevertheless, there is an important difference in that fusion entails relationship of some kind, whereas the egg symbolises oneness and self-containment. For Freud, the sleeplike state of withdrawal involved 'a deliberate rejection of reality'.

On the diversity side, I place attachment theorists, some object-relations theorists, such as Balint, Klein and (at times) Winnicott, and all interactional theorists. Some attachment and object-relations theorists conceptualise the early relationship in both active and passive modes. Winnicott, for instance, sometimes talks of the mother–infant unit as if the infant was incapable of initiative and, at other times, particularly in his later works, he describes the 'overlap' of two 'play' areas between mother and infant in interactional terms. In some versions of attachment theory, a pre-attachment phase, parallel to Freud's pre-object-related phase, is posited. Questions then arise as to the dating and criteria of 'true' object-relations or attachment proper. This cut-off point in development is related to issues of the infant's autonomy and powers of discrimination. These conceptualisations of the earliest mother–infant relationship acknowledge the intensity of the *bond* but, like Freud, describe the connection in more passive terms, such as 'pre-logical fusion of subject and object' (Milner, 1952), mother–infant 'unit', etc. The dialogue, or dance or play of movement, through which mother–infant synchrony is achieved, is lost in these descriptions.

The interactionalists view the neonate as distinct from the

mother and capable of activating, and contributing to the quality of, the relationship which develops between them. Ainsworth, Bell, Bruner, Bower, Brazelton, Klaus, Rosenblum *et al.* seek to redress the imbalance in the psychological literature in which the infant is viewed as a *passive* organism, which responds to maternal and environmental factors and is subject to internal pressures. In a recent volume, *The Effect of the Infant on Its Caregiver*, Lewis and Rosenblum focus attention 'on the impact of the infant as *a source of the* information, regulation and indeed even the malevolent distortion of the caregiver's behavior' (Lewis and Rosenblum, 1974, p. ix). To describe these reciprocities, the interactionalist invokes one of the central tenets of systems or information theory: elements of behaviour only convey information or have meaning in so far as they occur in a context. Without context, there is no communication. The interactionalist divides up behaviours into contexts such as play, feeding, changing, etc., which then confer pattern or predictability on the ongoing sequence. Crying, as every mother knows, has a variety of meanings. The context helps to designate the cry as an initiator or a response in the ongoing exchange between the mother and the infant which, at this stage of infancy, never ceases, even when the mother is absent. Nevertheless, as Brazelton *et al.* observe, there remains a problem for the interactionalist to account for the evolution of the individual and to distinguish the relative contributions of each member of the dyad (Brazelton *et al.*, 1974, p. 75).

In the field of psychoanalysis, the Kleinian school have been instrumental in bringing attention to the infant's contribution to the earliest person-relationship. In terms of the tricky issue of the evolution of the individual, the Kleinians would seem to hold a considerable theoretical advantage. From the Kleinian point of view, the infant is an individual at birth, endowed with complex mental structures. 'Splitting' is the dominant mental operation which follows the intra-uterine state of complete union between mother and foetus. Splitting is the beginning of the long-term process of separation which is precipitated by birth. It seems to me that Melanie Klein, like the interactional psychologists of today, set out to redress an imbalance in the psychoanalytic literature on infant development in which the infant was perceived as a passive, mindless creature, unrelated to the world about him. The Kleinian group cite recent psychological research as confirmatory of their views on the infant's contribution to his relationships and his complex mentation. However, they can be criticised for their belief in primitive mental structures which are not confirmed by the findings of research on infant cognition, for their underestimation of the maternal contribution and for the predominantly negative quality with which the earliest object-relationship is described. To build her picture of the infant as a unique individual capable of thinking and of constructing his relationship with his mother, Klein ignored the child's interactional context and his powers of cognition, perception and problem-solving outside the realm of 'phantasy'.

Thus, the diversity theories of infant development fall into two groups (positions 2 and 4) depending upon the emphasis they place on the positive or negative aspects of mother–infant relations. In the interactional view, not only does the mother seek to synchronise with her infant, the infant also wishes to link harmoniously with his care-giver. In the Kleinian view, the young infant's tie to the mother is suffused with anxiety, pain, envy, greed and destructiveness. Linking is secondary and is associated with reparative wishes towards the mother for damage done to her.

1
Primary narcissism and primary fusion/union

The difficulty for primary unity theories is the formulation of difference. It takes at least two x's – people or messages – to make a difference. Without difference, there is no change and no development. When there is only one thing – as expressed in the primary autism postulate – or two things in a relationship of perfect fusion or unison, nothing happens, because there is no new information. Each person is drawn to the other in a relationship of replication. This is an extreme case. Although the state of oneness or fusion can facilitate human development, as in the post-partum period when the close tie between mother and infant guarantees survival, its persistence can lead to various narcissistic pathologies, an excellent illustration of which is offered in the exchange between Narcissus and Echo.

Freud made an all-important qualification to his use of the bird's egg 'fiction' – namely, 'provided one includes with it the care it receives from its mother' (Freud, 1911, p. 220). Freud's point, taken up by writers such as Mahler and Winnicott, is that, in the first hours and days of infant life, the *mother* seeks to replicate the intra-uterine relationship. For her, this goal is temporary, since she is aware that, in physical reality, she and her infant are distinct. It is proposed that the infant, on the other hand, wishes to maintain the illusory relationship as long as possible. For Freud, the law of conservation of energy appeared to be one of the most powerful organising principles in human psychical development. The wish to maintain the status quo or to return to a previous state of equilibrium is given more weight than the desire for new relationships, accomplishments and knowledge. This gives the psychoanalytic conception of development a curiously backward-turning direction. In much psychoanalytic theory, there is a tendency to assume that the most primitive state not only provides the template for all future experience but is also the preferred state. Freud stated that man is 'incapable of giving up a satisfaction he had once enjoyed' (Freud, 1914, p. 94) and, in his paper on narcissism, he concludes that 'the development of the ego consists in a departure from primary narcissism and gives rise to a vigorous attempt to recover that state' (Freud, 1914, p. 100). On balance, therefore, reality, relationship and change create an excess of unpleasure when compared to the self-contained state of primary narcissism. The satisfactions of achievement are related to the mastery of anxieties attendant upon the loss of the primary state. In the state of primary narcissism or primary autism, the achievement of a state of near-perfect homeostasis is postulated. But the external world must impinge; change is necessarily painful. The eggshell cracks, the infant feels dismembered or split. These are all absolute terms, in which change is conceived of as traumatic.

Anna Freud

It may seem curious that, in this résumé of theories of infancy, I do not present the views of such an important pioneer in the field of child analysis and child care as Anna Freud. Clearly, Anna Freud has been a key-figure in the growth of the psychoanalytic movement, particularly in the U.S., and her original studies of young children separated from their parents, made in the Hampstead Nurseries during the Second World War, set the scene for the expanding area of systematic research now devoted to the separation of children from their parents. The importance of her research has been acknowledged by Attachment theorists such as John Bowlby, Christophe Heinicke (1956) and Heinicke and Westheimer (1966), and James and Joyce Robertson (1967, 1968, 1969, 1971, 1976a, 1976b).

The children, originally observed by Anna Freud and Dorothy Burlingham, ranged from birth to four years. Although deprived of their parents, Freud and Burlingham noted that the potential for attachment in these children was very strong and ever-present. Moreover, even when a mother was continuously cross and sometimes cruel, her child would cling and continue to manifest a strong attachment towards her (Freud and Burlingham, 1974). In such cases, it would appear that the attachment develops, despite the lack of gratification. In another study, Anna Freud and S. Dann (1951) observed the behaviour of six children, aged between three and four years, from a concentration camp. These children centred their attachments exclusively upon one another, caring greatly for each other and not at all for anybody or anything else. Again, the children did not meet any of each other's so-called primary, instinctual needs which, in the theory, are purported to lead to object-love.

Like her father and her younger associate, Margaret Mahler, Anna Freud's work is characterised, in my opinion, by a curious and confused juxtaposition of observation and theory. In my view, many of her observations fit more coherently into the attachment or primary object-love model, whereas her theoretical formulations describe an infant who is an extremely isolated and anti-social creature.[1] Anna Freud's theories of infancy do not differ radically from those of Freud – in particular, his theories of primary narcissism and of primary instinctual drives. Taking off from Freud's primary narcissism hypothesis, Anna Freud believes that the child is 'lured', or seduced, by his mother away from his exclusive, auto-erotic, preoccupation with his own bodily needs. Through seduction, the infant's attention is redirected to those persons in the outside world who satisfy his more primary, self-centred, preoccupations. Thus, the all-important step from primary narcissism to object-love is accomplished. If, however, the mother does not provide the child with a steady source of satisfaction, this transformation of narcissistic libido into object-libido remains inadequate and the child becomes fixated at the primary, auto-erotic, level of development.

For the purposes of the spectrum of viewpoints on *early* infancy which I present in Part I of this book, Anna Freud's views represent a direct development of Freud's primary narcissism hypothesis. My omission of her very important work is not meant to underestimate her contribution. The psychoanalytic viewpoints I have chosen to present, such as those of Balint, Klein and Winnicott, on the other hand, represent considerable departures from the primary narcissism hypothesis. The works of two contemporary psychoanalysts, Margaret Mahler and Heinz Kohut, on infant–mother relationships and narcissism respectively, have aroused considerable interest and debate in recent times and may be seen as direct developments of the views of Anna, and Sigmund, Freud.

Margaret Mahler

Margaret Mahler is a research psychoanalyst, working in New York, who has made a major contribution to the psychoanalytic study of early infancy. Since the fifties, she has made a particular study of the 'autistic'[2] and 'symbiotic'[3] phases of *normal* infant development; fixations at these stages are manifested in autistic and symbiotic *pathologies* – an area in child psychiatry to which she has also contributed. From these starting points – namely, her postulates of a *normal*, pre-relational, autistic phase and a *normal*, rudimentary relational, symbiotic phase of narcissism – she has developed and refined her observations of the 'separation–individuation processes' (Mahler, Pine and Bergman, 1975).[4] Through her emphasis on separation–individuation as a stage of development in its own right, subsuming within it the more traditional emphasis on instinctual drives and conflicts, she has brought a new focus to the psychoanalytic understanding of separation–individuation and independence.

Within the context of the spectrum delineated in this chapter, Mahler's work may be viewed as a direct development of the model of early infancy portrayed by Freud and Anna Freud. Mahler's work, though rich in observations of mother–infant *interaction*, nevertheless presents a somewhat passive picture of infancy – a picture consonant with the primary narcissism hypothesis. Although she stresses the infant's adaptability, she thinks that 'the *dynamic* point of view . . . is far less important in the earliest months of life than . . . later on' (Mahler, Pine and Bergman, 1975, p.5). 'Tension, traumatic anxiety, biological hunger, ego apparatus, and homeostasis are near-biological concepts that are relevant in the earliest months' (1975, p.5). Mahler observes a predominance of sleep-like states in early infancy and 'an inborn unresponsiveness to outside stimuli'. Taking up Freud's concept of a 'stimulus barrier', she states that a stage of absolute primary narcissism prevails during the first few weeks of life which is marked 'by the infant's lack of awareness of a mothering agent' (1975, p. 42). Mahler's stress on the infant's 'inborn unresponsiveness' (1975, p. 41) leads her to expand Freud's fiction of the bird's egg so that it permeates her whole conception of development. Her schema is full of egg-like metaphors such as 'hatching', 'cracking', autistic 'shells', etc.

Mahler distinguishes two phases of the primary narcissism[5] stage: normal autism, which lasts for the first few weeks of life, and normal symbiosis, which lasts until about four or five months. Together, these 'are the two earliest stages of nondifferentiation', the former being 'objectless' and the latter 'preobjectal' (1975, p. 48). Thus, despite her concept of the 'mother–infant dual unit' and her stress on the infant's adaptability – he 'moulds' himself to the mother – all of which descriptions suggest an intensely relational point of view, Mahler, like Freud, correlates undifferentiation with unrelatedness and, moreover, with a negative, defensive attitude towards the outside world. During the normal symbiotic phase, the second phase of normal primary narcissism, Mahler observes that the infant manifests 'a dim awareness that need-satisfaction cannot be provided by oneself, but comes from somewhere outside the self' (1975, p. 42). Only 'by way of mothering . . . the young infant is gradually brought out of an inborn tendency toward vegetative, splanchnic regression and into increased sensory awareness of, and contact with, the environment' (1975, p. 42). According to Mahler, the development of object-relations runs parallel to the separation–individuation phase; at about four months, there is a steady increase in awareness of the separateness of self and other. But a lack of awareness of separateness need not entail an inborn unresponsiveness. Orientation towards another person, and specificity of responsiveness, as evidenced by the neonate's turning towards the sound of his mother's voice and his early discrimination of constellations of stimuli in the shape of the mother, can be observed from birth onwards and may exist without any awareness of person constancy. In my view, separation–individuation may be a criterion of one type of person-relating but it is not the necessary criterion either of relatedness or of responsiveness to the mother-figure.

Mahler's theoretical reconstruction of infancy seems inappropriate when juxtaposed with her detailed and complex studies of the to-and-fro relationship of the mother–infant dual unit. Mahler draws on the work of Bowlby and Winnicott, but does not make the theoretical shift which her observations require. When discussing 'holding behaviour', for instance, she tends to lose the dynamic aspect. Holding behaviours are called by Mahler 'the symbiotic organizers of psychological birth' (1975, p. 49). Psychological birth is described as a 'hatching'[6] process; the infant must 'hatch' out of his autistic shell, a development which takes place 'only by way of mothering' (1975, pp. 53–4). Holding seems to have value only in so far as it provides another enclosure out of which the infant emerges. The bird's egg model fosters an essentially reactive view of infant development. The infant hatches in reaction to the mother's symbiotic brooding. The behavioural manifestation of hatching is a 'certain look of alertness' at about four or five months. Mahler says that, 'loosely speaking', an infant with this look ' "has hatched" ' (1975, p. 54). At this stage, Mahler observes the preferential smiling responses which, as Bowlby noted in 1958, is a crucial sign that a specific bond between infant and mother has been established.

Winnicott's concept of holding, by contrast, is linked to his concepts of 'mother–infant mutuality' (1970) and 'playing' (1971a), which take place in the 'overlap' between two people. The holding relationship includes *playful interactions*. Alertness and smiling, Mahler's criteria of hatching, characterise the baby's interactions long before he is four or five months of age. Winnicott's concepts introduce the dynamic point of view into the study of early infancy; they imply relationship and movement. The infant wriggles, turns to look at things including his mother; the mother may slacken her arms, but the infant is still held. At times, Mahler also describes the holding relationship in dynamic terms, suggestive of a partnership. As she observes, the rate of growth during infancy is faster than at any other time of life. The rate of change places a great deal of stress on the mother's capacity for flexibility and resilience, for a mother has built up predictable patterns of organisation over a long time.[7]

As each decade passes, infant research increasingly poses more and more difficult challenges to the two central tenets of the primary narcissism (or autism) hypothesis espoused by Freud and Mahler: first, that the infant's attention is inwardly directed and, second, that he reacts defensively and aversively to all external stimuli. It seems, however, that states of womb-like fusion are temporary and part of a cyclical rhythm. In attempting to adjust to the contemporary view, Mahler makes two qualifications to her theory of primary autism. First, she states that, although the autistic phase is characterised by a relative absence of cathexis of external stimuli, this does not mean that there is *no* responsiveness. Second, the infant brings with him the equipment of 'primary autonomy' (1975, p. 43). But Mahler still does not give this primary autonomy any social context. It is autistically directed. During the autistic phase, the apparatuses of primary autonomy 'obey the rules of the conesthetic organization of the central nervous system' (p. 43). Autonomy is employed in the maintenance of the homeostatic conditions which pertained in foetal life. Thus, though minimally *responsive*, the infant displays a lack both of *orientation towards* the outside world and of *initiation of contact* with *specific* people.

Recent research brings to our notice the other side of the picture: the newborn scans his mother's face, face-to-face looking may evoke a smile and the sound of the mother's voice increases alertness and produces an appearance of readiness. These periods of alertness and sociability alternate with periods of withdrawal, as is observed when a baby averts his gaze or seems to slump into a stupor. He expresses his desire for non-interactional quiet or aloneness. But, from a relational standpoint, these negative-seeming behaviours are nevertheless communications, which may be correctly or incorrectly interpreted. For example, a mother might respond to her baby's withdrawal either by increased activity or by abandonment, both of which are dissonant responses to the baby's communication.

In my experience, the wish for a lasting fusion or total union between two people, which is fulfilled and which succeeds in maintaining a narcissistic relationship against the passage of time – that is, against, disorder, dissonance and novelty – signifies a lack of any sense of continuity in each partner. An individual's sense of continuity develops in the context of *synchronous and reliable interactions*. Winnicott introduced the phrase 'continuity of being' (1960) when describing the 'holding' relationship between a mother and her infant. The sense of continuity over time flourishes in the earliest holding relationship between infant and caretaker. Holding, in distinction to fusion, provides the environment for the experience of 'a continuity of being', the alternative to which is *'reacting'* (1960, p. 47). The point is that the experience of continuity only grows out of a relationship which can tolerate change. Change is inevitable. But the narcissistic relation ultimately denies change and thereby stultifies growth. Change is always experienced as a discontinuity, an interruption of being and, therefore, a reaction. Reacting 'interrupts being and annihilates' (1960, p. 47). Egg-like metaphors suggest disruption, not continuity. Growth is eruptive, even traumatic.

In the myth, Narcissus and Echo are equally caught in a relationship which cannot tolerate change. Echo epitomises the helplessly reactive style of relating; she 'always answers back'. Narcissus is her counterpart; he is prideful. His role in the prideful–admiring relationship signifies a more mature stage of development. Narcissus, at least, has found his own voice. He does not simply echo. When compared to the mirroring posture of Echo, his behaviour exhibits a certain autonomy. Nevertheless, when Narcissus tries to break out of the mirroring relationship, he dies. He dies before he can change – before he may 'come to know himself'. I use the myth to illustrate the point that the search for fusion must be limited. A mother's intense empathy and identification with her baby can go on too long. As Winnicott has observed, a mother may provide excellent initial care in relation to holding (which may be 'the only way in which a mother can show the infant her love' (1960, p. 49) in the early stages) but 'fail to complete the process through an inability to let it come to an end' (1960, p. 53). In later life, the child of such a person may face two alternatives: 'a permanent state of regression' or 'a total rejection' of the other person, even when he or she seems good. In his active rejection of love, Narcissus tries to establish himself outside his partner's orbit. The person whom we pejoratively call narcissistic often displays two contrary tendencies: an overwhelming need both to elicit admiration and to spurn and destroy the attention he excites. Hence, Narcissus' pride. Narcissus both provokes and spurns love. His heartlessness towards others is linked to his wish to cut off their hold on him and to break out of a holding relationship which is inordinately persistent. The narcissistic relationship is static, it abhors change and can end only through its own destruction. When

Narcissus falls in love, he is compelled to react in a way that leads to destruction.

The primary narcissism thesis, like the myth after which it is named, represents a pathological, static relationship. In its Freudian form, it introduces quasi-biological, non-relational, and non-interactional, terms which continue to distort the psychoanalytic study of early attachment. In my view, Mahler's excellent descriptions of the lively to-and-fro of relationships lose coherence when placed in the framework of traditional Freudian metapsychology. Nevertheless, her continued use of Freud's conception of infancy may account for the appreciation, and comparative popularity, of her work amongst analysts. Couched in familiar concepts, her new observations are accessible, whereas the works on mother–infant attachment of Balint, Bowlby, Winnicott and others demand a shift in theoretical perspective.

Heinz Kohut

Heinz Kohut is another psychoanalyst whose theory of narcissism follows from the 'primary fusion' characterisation of early infancy. Kohut is the leading figure of a group of Chicago analysts and the centre of an evolving school of analysts in the U.S.A., who propose a new model of psychoanalysis – namely, 'The Psychology of the Self' or 'Self-Psychology'. Kohut is, perhaps, the most well-known contemporary psychoanalytic writer on narcissism. Where Mahler has elaborated Freud's vision of early infancy through systematic observation and research of infants and children, Kohut has investigated the narcissistic personality as it unfolds in the psychoanalysis of *adults*. Though protogenic of a *theory* of early infant development, Kohut's theory of narcissism is not based on the direct observation of infants or of mother–infant relationships. Thus, Mahler's observations of mother–infant interactions and Kohut's observations of transference relationships during the course of an adult analysis may be seen to complement one another in the way originally envisaged by Freud. In the understanding of human development, analytic reconstruction and direct observation go hand in hand.

It might surprise some 'Kohutians', who regard their work as representative of a *break* with Freud, that I should place Kohut in this position on my spectrum and, moreover, that I view his work as a complement to that of Mahler. Despite Mahler's adherence to traditional Freudian concepts and Kohut's revolutionary claims, both analysts adhere to a similar conception of the primary state of being – that of primary narcissism. In my view, both are trapped in the difficulties and contradictions of Freud's non-relational conception of narcissism. In their reconstructions of the infant's primary state. Kohut and Mahler describe a state of union or fusion between mother and infant, a state originally suggested in the second of the two passages from Freud which I quoted in the preface to this section (Freud, 1930). At the same time, however, their formulations of this primary 'intimate bond', which seem to be consistent with modern attachment theory, are juxtaposed with formulations of a non-related, withdrawn, autistic state, as described in the first quotation from Freud (Freud, 1911) and illustrated by the bird's egg analogy. Thus, their accounts of the intense relationship between mother and infant are distorted through the use of antithetical concepts. Like Mahler, some of Kohut's current popularity in the U.S.A. may stem from the fact that, despite his claims to the contrary, he does not challenge the traditional Freudian premise of human development – namely, pre-object-related narcissism or autism.

Kohut's work on narcissism is nevertheless innovative, if not revolutionary, in that he addresses himself to important matters in psychoanalysis which he feels have been ignored both by traditional Freudians and by analysts in the object-relations group. Self-psychology addresses itself to the vicissitudes which surround the development of a coherent *self*. It is not concerned with the products, or fixations, of drives such as aggression or sexuality; nor is it concerned precisely with the development of object-relations. Kohut attempts to free the conceptualisation of human psychology from quasi-biological concepts, which follow from traditional drive and instinct theory. In this respect, he differs from Mahler and many analysts of the Freudian and Kleinian schools. In pursuit of the search for a coherent self, Kohut outlines a new therapeutic technique – the 'introspective-empathic' stance (Kohut, 1977, p. xiii). He addresses himself to a current, much-discussed, cultural malaise – the loss, and pursuit, of the self.

From the early 1960s there has been a proliferation of psycho analytic papers on the narcissistic personality, on narcissistic love and rage and the genesis, and treatment, of the 'narcissistic disorders'. This development reflects a general trend in psychoanalysis towards the study of early infant experience and a greater commitment among some analysts to analytic psychotherapy with children and adults suffering from psychotic and borderline disorders. Some writers also surmise that the apparent increase in narcissistic disorders results from social factors, such as the mobility and disruption of the family (Goldberg, 1972, p. 7). This interest in early infancy and the various pre-oedipal pathologies arising therefrom has occasioned considerable debate around the continued viability of Freud's model. Kohut's work may be seen as a response to trends which are both general to the culture and peculiar to the discipline of psychoanalysis.

Like many writers on the self, Kohut conceives of the self as a centre of initiative and as an internally cohesive 'unit that tries to follow its own course' (Kohut, 1977, p. 245). With this, many would have little disagreement. In my view, however, Kohut's claims for the revolutionary significance of his self-psychology paradigm are extreme. He seems surprisingly unconversant with many non-Freudian psychoanalytic views which, for some time, have been concerned with what he regards as new. In addition, Kohut seems to over-simplify Freud's own complex, and sometimes inconsistent, views on human psychical development. Kohut attacks two stereotypes which, in part, are of his own making. In his new self-psychology, he seeks to redress the inadequacies of two traditional theories of psychoanalysis: object-relations theory and Freudian drive theory. First, Kohut addresses himself to that theory of development which equates object-relations with *oedipal* object-relations. One result of this equation is that it excludes from the field of study all early states of relative undifferentiation between self and other and, thereby, the pathologies, such as narcissism, which represent developmental arrests at this stage. Second, Kohut criticises the Freudian theory of drives, in which pathology is explained in terms of conflicts between libidinal and aggressive drives. Whereas, in his earlier work, *The Analysis of the Self* (1971), Kohut attempted to present his theory of narcissism from within the traditional Freudian framework of drive psychology, in *The Restoration of the Self* (1977), Kohut repudiates classical drive and defence psychology. I believe, Kohut's theory and practice are an amalgam of

Freudian concepts and object-relations methodology and technique.

According to Kohut, narcissistic disorders stem from an intense vulnerability in the area of the self which was originally weak and uncohesive and whose subsequent attempts at cohesion were thwarted by repeated, unempathic, maternal responses. The 'discovery' of this area of vulnerability through the concept of the 'self-object'[8] has led Kohut to substitute the term 'self-object transferences' for the more common term 'narcissistic transferences' (Kohut, 1977, p. xiv). This type of transference has long since been acknowledged by many analysts, particularly those working with children and psychotics. But, these analysts would see, in this type of transference, the transference of an early *relationship*. Although Kohut declares that the emergence of the self as a firm and healthy structure is dependent upon 'the quality of the interactions between the self and its selfobjects' (Kohut and Wolff, 1978, p. 414) – a statement with which I am in full agreement – he cannot term these interactions relational because of his narrow interpretation of object-relations as oedipal. There is a persisting confusion in Kohut's work between descriptions of relationships, on the one hand, and concepts, on the other, which connote, or refer to, a solipsistic or narcissistic self. Without a relational context, the self-self-object interaction is essentially internal, despite the fact that Kohut declares that the embryonic self is absolutely dependent upon those interactions, pleasurable or painful, smooth or abrasive, which take place between the infant and his caregiver.

In Kohut's view, the major cause of pathology is the disruption of the mother–infant *tie*. When the self-object tie is destroyed precipitately, prior to the development of a cohesive self, the infant experiences the loss of the mother as a break. Kohut describes the self-pathologies which arise from this primary defect in the child's archaic experiences in terms of 'a nameless preverbal depression' and a 'sense of deadness' and 'apathy' (Kohut, 1977, p. 25). Since, in Kohut's experience, analysts have concerned themselves exclusively with libidinal and aggressive ties to objects, he seems unaware of similar accounts of these archaic experiences of rupture of the primary tie: this type of experience has been described as a 'basic fault' (Balint, 1968, 1969), 'nameless dread' and 'psychological catastrophe' (Bion,

1962b), 'nuclear hurt' (Fordham 1966), 'heartbreak' (Laing, 1960), and 'unthinkable anxiety' and 'falling infinitely' (Winnicott, 1958, 1971a). Tustin, writing about autistic processes, quotes Winnicott in order to distinguish her concept of 'psychotic depression' from the kind of 'reactive depression' (a more mature response) which is a conscious reaction to the loss of a loved person.

> For example, the loss might be that of *certain aspects of the mouth* which disappear from the infant's point of view along with the mother and the breast when there is separation at a date earlier than that at which the infant had reached a stage of emotional development which could provide the equipment for dealing with loss. The same loss of the mother a few months later would be a loss of object without this added element of *loss of part of the subject*. (Tustin, 1972, p. 12)

Unlike the above authors, Kohut seems to believe that disorders, which are undeniably connected with the primary defect in the self – the psychotic and borderline conditions and, to some extent, the narcissistic syndromes – are effectively unanalysable. In all these disorders, depression and confusion may be related to a fragmentary, uncohesive, unintegrated and barely differentiated self, resulting in large losses in normal, mental functioning upon which Kohut feels the possibility of analysis depends. Kohut believes that a self which has no defensive structures to cover the primary defect is too fragile to withstand the strains of analytic work. Even when a person has limited protective devices, as in the case of a borderline patient, Kohut considers it inadvisable for the therapist to tamper with defensive structures. However, those analysts who have worked with psychotics and with autistic children seem to agree that the broken heart can mend.

Analysts such as Bion, Laing, Little, Mahler, Meltzer, Rosenfeld and Winnicott have willingly treated these disorders in an analytic setting. In their view, the early relationship can be re-experienced in the safety and reliability of the analytic setting although lengthy periods of silent, non-verbal, bizarre and destructive communications must be tolerated by the therapist, who finds himself very much alone in his consulting room. There is little comfort to be found in the relationships which these persons transfer to the analytic setting. The analyst must find in himself the resources to withstand *not understanding* – as Winnicott (1971a) put it, the analyst must tolerate 'formlessness' and 'nonsense'. He must be flexible, resilient and steady. A further difference between Kohut's understanding of psychosis and the approach of these analysts is his view that psychotics are devoid of defences. Those who have engaged with the bizarre, multi-contradictory, messages of a psychotic, even of three years of age, are presented with a most elaborate set of camouflages; these represent, in part, the interactional dissonance of the primary relationship and, in part, the *aversive* behaviours and *inter-sensory* confusions arising out of the pain of relationship. The bizarre message is certainly, at one level, intended to defend.

In Kohut's psychology, the overriding aetiological factor in the disorders of the self – the psychotic, borderline and narcissistic conditions – is failure in empathy, as this is manifested in the *mirroring* responses of the mother. In analysis, this genetic factor may be offset by the 'introspective-empathic' stance of the analyst. As with the discovery of many new 'paradigms', the redefinition of a field of enquiry by a new school may be linked to the use of a new technique. In the case of self-psychology, this novel technique is the 'introspective-empathic' method. In *The Restoration of the Self*, Kohut declares his 'full acceptance of the consequences of the fact that the psychological field is defined by the observer's commitment to the introspective-empathic approach' (1977, p. xiii).

In my view, the *revolutionary* claims made for this technique stem from Kohut's misleading stereotyping of the classical Freudian method of analysis. Kohut interprets the traditional objective to maintain a rigorous, neutral, observational stance, somewhat akin to that of a physical scientist, as unempathic and aloof. Part of the tremendous difference Kohut sees between the classical analyst and his own current analytic style and persona emanates from the peculiar technique he apparently adopted when he was practising what he regarded as classical analysis.

In 'The two analyses of Mr. Z.' (Kohut, 1979) Kohut describes the differences in treatment and result between two instalments of an analysis undertaken by Kohut of a young man, Mr Z. Each instalment was of about four years duration on a five times a week basis; the instalments were separated by an interval of five and a half years. Kohut attributes much of the success of the second period to the experiences made accessible by his change in theoretical outlook. However, when Kohut describes his interpretative behaviour during the first instalment, one gets the impression not of analytic neutrality, openness and respect but of a somewhat controlling, self-righteous, moralising, analyst who expresses his approval and disapproval. It seems as if Kohut is adhering to some parody of 'the classical analyst', to which Mr Z. responds with the behavioural progress of 'the classical patient'. For surely even the *classical* analyst, whose mind is trained to perceive oedipal material and to point out to the patient his resistances against the acknowledgment of such material, can be attentive and non-directive. When, at the beginning of the second instalment of the analysis, Mr Z. manifested some of the same demanding, self-centred behaviour which had marked the beginning of the first period, Kohut this time listened sympathetically: 'While in the first analysis I had looked upon it in essence as defensive, and had at first *tolerated* it as unavoidable and later increasingly *taken a stand against it*, I now focused on it with the analyst's *respective seriousness vis-à-vis important analytic material*' (my italics).

To me, the second instalment of Mr Z.'s analysis demonstrates the importance of the classical, professional, analytic attitude – namely, respect for the patient's point of view and the capacity to suspend both moral judgment and the pursuit of personal glory through the successful treatment of others. As has often been observed, Freud exhibited both scientific and romantic leanings; indeed, his revolutionary investigation of man's inner world would have been impossible if he had adopted the observational stance of a nineteenth-century behaviourist (Breger, 1980), such as Kohut parodies. The writings of the object-relations authors I listed above exhibit an analytic understanding which is suffused with care, rigour, patience and sensitivity to the pain and complexity of archaic, unordered, non-rational experience.

Kohut's claims for this theory and technique have a strongly inspirational character. The introspective-empathic technique is difficult, if not impossible, to articulate. The elevation of this stance as the definer of the field seems to lead to a neglect of the results of other types of study conducted according to different methods. Kohut's dismissal of those who value the role of observable data to me diminishes the importance he claims for his method. He accuses Freud of pursuing an absolute determinism, in which there is no place for the notions of free will and creation, but his own reductive approach is extremely simplistic and suggestive of an even more extreme determinism than Freud's multi-determined approach. For instance, although Kohut discusses narcissism or the self as it develops within the intimate, undifferentiated relationship between the self and the 'self-object', his thesis that narcissism and object-relationships follow two distinct lines of development is extreme. In this respect, Kohut's self-psychology represents a radical development of the original primary narcissism hypothesis, since, for him, narcissism not only characterises the *primary* state of being, but remains throughout life as a separate organising principle to relationships with other people. Kohut has elevated the status of narcissism to a position of supreme value in contrast to the traditional Freudian view, in which narcissism is seen as a temporary stage of development on the way to object love. No longer is narcissism seen as a substitution for, or primitive form of, object-relatedness. Kohut's goal has been to rescue the narcissistic sector from its position of neglect in psychoanalytic theory as a *transitory* stage on the way to object-love. It now becomes an essential feature of normal adult life. Kohut fears that the labelling of narcissistic structures in adults as defensive, rather than primary, may interfere with the analytic relationship in the following ways: first, with the analyst's *empathy* for the total person of the patient; second, with the emergence of the full narcissistic transferences; third, with the belated undoing of developmental arrests in the here-and-now of the transference through the process of 'transmuting internalisation' (Kohut, 1977).[9] But, it seems to me that Kohut's pursuit of this important goal, valuable in itself, had led him to the peculiar and unnecessary position of positing two separate developmental lines – one egocentric and the other social.

Kohut's arguments are sometimes cavalier and his pronouncement of unanalysability on a wide range of disorders indicates a somewhat comfortable approach to analysis. For instance, creativity, based upon successful 'compensatory' structures, is valued above the understanding of primary defects of which the analysand may even be painfully aware – defects which arise in the context of relationship (see Kohut, 1977, 'The Case of Mr. M.', pp. 15–54). Kohut's view of creativity betrays the essentially solipsistic character of his approach. The 'creative narcissist' (Padel, 1977b) is the final product of a theory which postulates two parallel lines of development – namely, of the self and of object-relations. For instance, a narcissistic treatment may be terminated when one sector within the self has been established 'through which an ininterrupted flow of the narcissistic strivings can proceed toward creative expression' (Kohut, 1977, p. 54). Kohut takes issue with the relational theory of the origins of creativity which has been put forward by the American psychoanalyst, Phyllis Greenacre. Greenacre has suggested that the future artist possesses, in infancy, a greater sensitivity to sensory stimuli from the mother and also to peripheral objects; the artist's creativeness coexists with a love-relationship (Greenacre, 1957, pp. 479–504; 1964, pp. 225–48). According to Kohut, however, creative inspiration comes from an expanded self, that includes the world, rather than from a love affair within an unqualified context of object-love. Kohut views creative artists on a par with fetishists. They are attached to their work 'addictively'; 'during the act of creation . . . they do not relate to their work in the give-and-take mutuality that characterises object love' (Kohut, 1978, vol. I, p. 450). Within the model of primary narcissism or Kohut's psychology of the self, mutuality cannot characterise the primary relationship between the infant and his mother and the world beyond them. The poles of the primary relationship, repeated in the creative endeavour, are infantile grandiosity or assertiveness and maternal empathic mirroring.

Another example of Kohut's absolutism is his use of the concept of mirroring. In his analysis of the narcissistic disorders, Kohut encounters two types of self-object transferences, both indicative of the primary aetiological factor – namely, failure in empathic responsiveness.

> There are two kinds of selfobjects: those who respond to and confirm the child's innate sense of vigour, greatness and perfection; and those to whom the child can look up and with whom he can merge as an image of calmness, infallibility and omnipotence. The first type is referred to as the mirroring selfobject, the second as the idealized parent imago. (Kohut and Wolff, 1978, p. 414)

I would like to discuss my objections to the first type of self-object transference. Kohut has expanded the mirroring concept to include *selective* responsiveness; without acknowledging it, he thereby stretches the mirror model to cover interactions which are not primarily reflective. Some narcissistic pathologies may develop out of a mother's incapacity to reflect back to her baby that which she sees. Winnicott has described the mother's face as the baby's first mirror. He has elucidated the kind of depression which ensues when a baby looks in the mirror and sees an emptiness, a despair, or a mood at variance with that which he expected (Winnicott, 1967). However, there are other narcissistic disturbances, which develop at a later stage of childhood when the baby no longer seeks imitative, reflective responses, but those responses which will facilitate his *differentiation* from his mother. But Kohut still describes these in terms of mirroring. He stresses, for example, the importance of a parent's ability to be the 'joyful mirror' of the child's 'healthy assertiveness' (1977, p. 130). Strictly speaking, assertiveness would be *mirrored* by assertiveness. But two independences do not necessarily create the optimal environment for individuation. At this point, Kohut is really advocating a reciprocal adaptation rather than a mirroring relationship. Indeed, difficulties at this stage may arise just because the mother is unable to readjust the asymmetrical balance of power appropriate to the first months, in which she could control her relatively dependent infant from her own centre of relative independence. Increased assertiveness requires of a parent the capacity to set aside his or her image of what their child should be. At times, the child's parents must be able to suspend aversive reactions to difference and allow the child's differences and similarities to emerge. This calls for an appreciation of difference and contrast, rather than for a mirroring response. A parent who has his own independent centre of initiative and competence, apart from his child, will not experience an overwhelming need for the child's continuing appreciation and responsiveness to his approaches.

Kohut describes two other narcissistic disorders which, again, are not reactions to failures in mirroring, but result from failures in differentiation. These are 'the over-stimulated self' and 'the mirror-hungry personality' (Kohut and Wolff, 1978, pp. 119–22). In the case of the 'over-stimulated self', the child's creative gesture is met by an over-excited response. The child might then feel frightened because of an over-expansion of his excitement so that his whole environment becomes suffused leaving no place for containment. Creativity then becomes equated with grandiosity and 'too-muchness'. Kohut also describes the individual who gives the appearance of a 'mirror-hungry personality' and yet suffers not from a *lack* of mirroring, but from a specific '*fault*' in the mother's responsiveness. The focus of mirroring was selected in accordance with the mother's needs to keep her child dependent upon her.

Kohut's concept of mirroring is useful only if its use is limited. Later, in conclusion to this book, I will suggest that those transferences, which reflect the stage of mother–infant relationship in which *independence* is central, might be named the 'differentiating' transferences. This would restrict the mirroring and merger transferences to the transfer of interactions in which reflection plays a key role. In the differentiating transferences, on the other hand, *selective* responsiveness makes sense. The mirror remains a useful analogy for the representation of the intensely related, reflective, post-natal state. Bower's concept of 'interactional synchrony' (Bower, 1977) would seem to cover more precisely the two very different uses, one imitative, the other more selective, to which Kohut puts his concept of mirroring. A synchronous interaction can be both imitative and yet innovative. Kohut's concept of mirroring is best understood in the context of primary fusion or union in which the infant, at times, seeks out a state of oneness rather than a harmonious interaction. Like other theories, which use the concept of fusion to describe the earliest state of infancy, the conceptualisation of the onset of differentiation is problematic. I believe that this problem may also account for Kohut's insistence on the two separate developmental lines.

I suggest that, in the psychoanalytic theory of development, the notion of primary fusion has led to a radicalisation of the ideas of difference and differentiation. Inevitably, the state of fusion is punctured or fragmented. More relativistic terms which have to do with *processes* of differentiation, selecting and discernment are often described in absolute terms (Pruyser, 1975, pp. 1–47); terms such as 'splitting' and cracking have the connotations of fission, which is the contrasting term to fusion. Mahler's term 'hatching' has similar connotations. Growth is described in all-or-nothing terms in which the young person journeys in and out of a sequence of containers.

In Kohut's theory, differentiation takes place through *two* contrasting processes: mirroring *and* frustration. Mirroring and optimal frustration are the poles through which the self separates itself from its selfobjects and, thereafter, acquires internal cohesion. The parent oscillates between mirroring the child's grandiosity and permitting merger of the child's vulnerable self with the idealised parental imagos, on the one hand, and, on the other, introducing step-by-step delays in the gratification of these needs for union. Frustration is required as the agent of destruction of infantile grandiosity and oneness, which have been reinforced by parental mirroring in the early stage of primary narcissism.

As with Mahler's work, I find many of Kohut's observations valuable, particularly as these relate to his clinical practice; however, these only make sense to me within the context of a primary bond or relationship. At times, Kohut himself espouses the relational view. For instance, Kohut takes issue with the notion of a primary aggressive drive and with the concept of auto-erotism. Both phenomena acquire meaning, according to Kohut, in the context of a relationship. In Kohut's view, both are reactions to failures in the earliest self/self-object *relationship*. The baby is primarily assertive, but not aggressive. Although this assertiveness may seem aggressive, it is in the service of the establishment of a rudimentary self rather than the destruction of the object. In line with this view of aggression, Kohut believes that the infant's confidence is innate. Confidence does not *develop*, but becomes re-established as the child becomes aware of his environment. Drive fixations, such as orality, are defensive against primary depression and fragmentation. Kohut describes destructiveness as a 'disintegration product' (1977, p. 120). Primary depression is not connected to drives such as aggression, but results from the relationship between the self and the empathic self-object, which is life-sustaining. When the relationship fails, absence, emptiness and despair may be transformed into destructiveness. Destructive rage may be manifested in the projection of an impersonal, potential attacker. The infant may experience a potential, hovering, bad presence to fill in the gap of nothingness. Kohut also interprets obsessional activities, such as ordering and voyeurism, in relation to primary depression. The obsessional collects objects or goes over details so as to fill in a gap with familiar details. Bodily obsessions, which have sometimes been seen as fixations at an auto-erotic stage, may be connected to breaks in the sense of continuity between the vulnerable self and the self-object. A preoccupation with part-objects or single symbols, such as faeces, phallus, breast, penis, etc., can be manifestations of a fragmented or depersonalised relationship. Single body parts are extrapolated from their relational contexts and absorbed into obsessive preoccupations; these operations are defensive against failures in parental mirroring of the person's *whole* self. In the case of voyeurism, the person is preoccupied with isolated images which are symbols of the parents' power with which he was not permitted to merge.

Kohut's interpretations of auto-erotism, part-object relations and drive fixations as *secondary* products of unsatisfactory relationships suggest a relational model of infancy. However, Kohut's basic premise of the two separate developmental lines of development fosters instead a non-systemic, additive, building-block, model of the development of the self and the inner world, to which relationships do not contribute.

Just as the state of intense relatedness has not been distinguished from a state of union or fusion, so the processes of differentiation and discrimination have not been adequately distinguished from more extreme and concretised mental acts such as splitting, hatching, fragmenting and chopping. The development of the self is characterised by Kohut in concrete terms in the language commonly used to describe the building of a house. For instance, Kohut asks how the *constituents* of the nuclear self are gathered and integrated, and when they are acquired. The 'nuclear self' of the child 'crystallises' through the following 'structure-building process': (1) when the child's mirroring and idealising needs have been sufficiently responded to; (2) when there have been minor, non-traumatic failures in the responses of the mirroring and the idealised self-objects; (3) when these failures lead to the gradual replacement of the selfobjects and their functions by a self and its functions. In this account, (Kohut, 1977, p. 178) the self is conceived as a solid built up of constituents in which defects, fragments, splits may appear. A major goal of analysis is to fill in the structural defects of the self. When the 'pieces' of 'missing structure' are 'filled in' by the analyst's mirroring, empathic responses, the self is 'restored' (Kohut, 1977; Kohut and Wolff, 1978).

This view of development is based on a part-to-whole model with which Kohut's own observations often seem to disagree – as exemplified in his accounts of auto-erotism and part-object relationships. One of the primary rules of systems or communication theory is the law of non-summativity – the whole is *not* the sum of its parts. The mind or the self is not the sum of its constituents, just as the whole object is not the sum of 'part-objects'. The restored self is not the sum of its missing pieces. This concrete way of describing the development of the self is a description of pathology.

2
Primary internal object-relationships

Melanie Klein

In the early years of psychoanalysis, Anna Freud and Melanie Klein pioneered the field of child psychoanalysis in Europe. Both sought to portray the inner life of the child from infancy to adolescence. Through the medium of play and the tools provided by Freud for adult analysis, they tried to understand the ways in which the child constructed external reality to form a 'psychic reality' or 'phantasy' world. Anna Freud came over to England with her father from Vienna in 1938. Melanie Klein was born in Vienna but had trained and undergone personal analysis in Budapest and Berlin with two eminent psychoanalysts, Sandor Ferenczi and Karl Abraham. In 1926, she arrived in England at the invitation of a Welshman, prominent in the British Society of Psycho-Analysis, Ernest Jones. As Freud had shocked the intellectual world with his revelation of the sexual life of 'innocent' young children of only 3–4 years of age, so Klein exposed this world to the ruthless, innately destructive desires of *infants'* wishes, which, moreover, were directed specifically towards their principal love-object, the mother. Whereas Anna Freud adapted her father's technique to the developmental levels of children of different ages, Klein pursued the rigorous, analytic technique employed in adult analysis. She believed that children could form a transference on to the analyst and that the analysis should be confined to interpretative interventions. Unlike Freud and Anna Freud, she believed that the young infant was a moral creature. (This belief is reflected in the dating of the development of the 'super-ego'.) Maturity was marked by a modulation of this persecutory, archaic morality, a development which usually took place after about four months of age.

Melanie Klein was perhaps the first analyst to focus upon the infant's active contribution to the earliest relationship and to allocate to him a substantial degree of autonomy. In this respect, she presents a contrary picture of the infant to that depicted by Mahler and Kohut. The newborn infant is neither passive nor infinitely malleable and adaptable to the mother's preconceptions. On the other hand, like Freud and Mahler, Klein emphasises the negative attitude of the infant towards the outside world. The negativity she describes does not take the form of a passive withdrawal or even of a homeostatic organisation in order to reproduce the lost intra-uterine state; it takes an active form as the infant projects his pain and anxiety into the mother. The mother acts as a container of the infant's pain and her main function is to modulate the persecutory nature of his existence.

It is important to point out that the Kleinians do not claim to give an objective or descriptive account of what actually happens between mother and infant, but merely to construct the infant's phantasies about his relationship to the mother or breast. Klein made few observations of the maternal and environmental contributions. Although a proponent of infant autonomy, she cannot be called an *inter*actionist. Nevertheless, her construction of 'psychic reality' is supported by a limited number of infant observations and, predominantly, by analytic reconstructions of unconscious object-relations as these are revealed in the transference relationships of children and adults.

In my view, Klein's most valuable contribution to the understanding of human development was to expand Freud's revelations of adult mental life backwards into infancy and to show that the infant brings with him into the world a *complex* mentation. Klein's primary focus on 'psychic reality' did much to destroy the amoeba myth. Klein's picture of the infant is vivid and, in comparison with the amoeba and bird's egg images, extremely detailed. As a theory, Klein's schema is also valuable in that it is detailed and definitive enough to evoke lively, and often heated, debate. The amoeba theory is embryonic and ill-defined. Where Klein helped to win the battle for the individual infant, whose lively existence was blurred by the amoeba myth, the attachment and interactionist theorists have reclaimed the environment as an essential factor in the understanding of early infant-mother relationships. In my view, therefore, Klein occupies a pivotal position in the evolution of the contemporary view of the infant as a complex emotional and psychological human being.

Klein introduced the concept of the 'paranoid-schizoid position' to describe the position occupied by the infant from birth to about six months. The paranoid-schizoid position is characterised by paranoid anxiety and a 'schizoid' splitting of the ego and its objects. The infant is paranoid because of the level of acute persecutory anxiety to which he is victim. He is schizoid in that he views his experiences as divided into all-good or all-bad. He lives in a totalitarian world. These anxieties and splits are stirred up by the innate polarity of the two instincts postulated by Freud – namely, the life instinct and the death instinct. In infancy, the psychic representations of the two instincts are the all-good, ever-present, flowing breast and the all-bad, absent, empty or persecuting breast which threatens the infant with annihilation. In order to cope with such persecution, the primitive ego evolves a series of 'mechanisms of defence'. According to Klein, sufficient ego exists at birth for the infant to experience not only anxiety, but to use defence mechanisms and to form object-relations in phantasy and reality. (Other analysts have ascribed a later date to the structural development of the ego.) To begin with, however, the ego is conceived by Klein as labile and in a constant state of flux; nevertheless, it has an inborn tendency towards integration. Under the impact of the death instinct and intolerable anxiety, this tendency is sometimes swept away and defensive disintegration occurs. The anxiety consequent upon the death instinct is deflected in two directions by the primitive ego: part of it is projected outwards into the original, most important, external object – i.e. the breast – and part of it is converted into aggression which is then directed against persecutors. The first persecutor is, in fact, the life-giving breast. This is because the infant has projected the anxiety consequent upon the death instinct into the breast, thereby converting the breast into a bad and threatening object.

In the face of such pervasive persecution, even from the life-giving source, the mechanisms of defence are experienced as crucial to survival. Indeed, it is these mechanisms which lead to the construction of the child's internal world, including his internal object-relationships. The inner representations of the defences are described by Klein as the child's 'phantasies'. The chief mechanisms are projection, introjection, splitting, denial and projective identification.[1] The extent of the ego's agency in the employment of these defences is a confused issue in Klein's work.

Hanna Segal is an original member of the Kleinian group and her work *Introduction to the Work of Melanie Klein* (Segal, 1973) has become a textbook for students of Kleinian theory. Segal is regarded by many analysts, particularly in England where she works, as the most lucid and creative exponent of Klein's views. In this chapter I lean heavily upon her exposition of Klein's work.

Segal states that, when the mechanisms of defence fail, the ego is 'invaded' by anxiety and the 'disintegration' of the ego may occur as a defensive measure (Segal, 1973, p. 30). 'The ego fragments and splits itself into little bits in order to avoid the experience of anxiety.' The ego uses a defensive mechanism which is 'grossly damaging' to it. In this account, the ego is invaded and overwhelmed and at the same time it retains sufficient autonomy to bring about its own disintegration and fragmentation. Even when all the named mechanisms of defence fail, the ego employs its own undefended state – namely, that of disintegration and fragmentation – as a further defence. Segal states that disintegration 'is the most desperate of all the ego's attempts to ward off anxiety' (p. 30). Segal observes that all the mechanisms of defence (against intolerable anxiety) produce in turn anxieties of their own. For instance, the projection of bad feelings (as a defence against anxiety) leads to external persecution; similarly, the projection of good feelings (as a defence against their destruction by bad feelings) leads to feelings of depletion. It is difficult to imagine how the infant ever gets out of the persecutory world into which he is born, particularly since all his strategies against anxiety contain a propensity for further persecution.

As if she were aware of this vicious circle, Segal comments that her emphasis on the anxieties and defences of the paranoid-schizoid position could give 'a misleading picture' of the infant. A normal infant 'does not spend most of his time in a state of anxiety' (1973, p. 35). Although this is the case in favourable situations, Klein tells us very little about what else is going on and her picture of the infant remains incomplete. Like Freud, Klein believed that no experience in development is ever lost. Thus, any situation can stir up the earliest anxieties and defences and, in a well-integrated personality, all stages are included and none are split off. With this view, most analysts, including many attachment theorists, would agree. However, the latter theorists, with an eye trained towards the observation of normal development outside the clinical situation, describe an attitude, or response, to growth and life which is positive, as much as defensive. I think that Klein was unable to give a more balanced view of development because of two basic assumptions: first, projection (primarily of bad feelings) precedes and predominates over introjection so that the infant cannot receive anything which has not been contaminated by anxiety and aggression; second, the mechanisms of defence, and in particular splitting, serve two functions, one pathological and the other normal. The effect of these assumptions upon the theory of development is that the normal infant seems to lack any positive orientation towards either another person or the outside world. The newborn infant does not seem to want to relate to others except as receptacles of projected pain; neither does he manifest any interest in anything outside his oral pleasures. Even in favourable circumstances, the infant 'spends most of his time sleeping, feeding, experiencing real or hallucinatory pleasures and thus gradually assimilating his ideal object and integrating his ego' (1973, p. 35). The implication here is that even good experiences are shrouded by idealised projections.

Since the mechanisms of defence are allotted the principal role in the construction of the child's inner world – i.e. his mind – they are regarded by Klein as the *achievements* of the paranoid-schizoid position. As Segal states, they are important not only for later development, they even *'lay' its 'foundations'* (1973, p. 35). Splitting, for instance, has a multitude of uses, some of which are active and absolute and others passive and relative. Splitting connotes not only an active cutting off or a passive fragmentation, it also refers to the mental processes of differentiation, discernment and judgment. Indeed, the implication is that all the processes of human cognition develop from the primitive mechanism of splitting. Segal says:

> It is splitting which allows the ego to emerge out of chaos and to order its experiences. This ordering of experience which occurs with the process of splitting into a good and bad object, however excessive and extreme it may be to begin with, nevertheless orders the universe of the child's emotional and sensory impressions and is a precondition of later integration. It is the basis of what is later to become the faculty of discrimination, the origin of which is the early differentiation between good and bad. There are other aspects of splitting which remain and are important in mature life. For instance, the ability to pay attention, or to suspend one's emotion in order to form an intellectual judgment, would not be achieved without the capacity for temporary reversible splitting.

Thus splitting, provided that it is not excessive, 'continues to function in a modified form throughout life' (1973, pp. 35–6).

Persecutory anxiety and idealisation, which are connected to splitting, also have a positive value.

> Some degree of persecutory anxiety is a precondition for being able to recognize, appreciate and react to actual situations of danger in external conditions. Idealization is the basis of the belief in the goodness of objects and of oneself, and is a precursor of good object-relationships. The relationship to a good object usually contains some degree of idealization, and this idealization persists in many situations such as falling in love, appreciating beauty, forming social or political ideals – emotions which, though they may not be strictly rational, add to the richness and variety of our lives. (1973, p. 36)

This picture of the human intellect reiterates Freud's polarisation of emotion and reason into the primary and secondary processes. The passionate infant is not credited with cognitive faculties or with an intellectual capacity to discriminate and co-ordinate. Moreover, the theory lacks any notion of primary mutuality between the infant and other people. For instance, the defensive mechanism of projective identification is characterised by Segal as the

> earliest form of empathy and it is on projective as well as introjective identification that is based the capacity to 'put oneself into another person's shoes.' Projective identification

> also provides the basis of the earliest form of symbol-formation. By projecting parts of itself into the object and identifying parts of the object with parts of the self, the ego forms its first most primitive symbols. (1973, p.36)

In summary, we must, therefore, 'look at the mechanisms of defence used in the paranoid-schizoid position not only as mechanisms of defence which protect the ego from immediate and overwhelming anxieties, but also as gradual steps in development' (1973, p. 36).

How then does the normal individual grow out of the paranoid-schizoid position? According to Segal, the answer is when good experiences, to which both external and internal factors contribute, predominate over bad. Then the ego acquires a belief both in the prevalence of ideal over persecutory objects and in its own life instinct over its death instinct. The infant of four to six months is then able to enter the more mature 'depressive position'. Of course, the introjected ideal objects are continually distorted since the ego projects its own instincts outwards. Nevertheless, through the *repeated* identification with the ideal object, the ego acquires strength without recourse to violent use of the mechanisms of defence. Moreover, the splitting in the ego lessens when the ego feels stronger. In other words, it is the weak ego which contains the propensity to split itself. When, instead of fragmenting itself and its objects, the ego integrates, it thereby lessens its projective mechanisms which in turn enables it to make a clearer discrimination between self and object. The ego is then able to leave temporarily its paranoid-schizoid position *vis-à-vis* the outside world.

The two features of Kleinian theory enumerated above – namely, the primacy of projective (expulsive) over introjective (taking-in) mechanisms and the normal and pathological usage of defence mechanisms – permeate Klein's description of the development of object-relationships. In fact, as with any constructivist theory of reality, there is no 'external reality' which is uncontaminated by mental structures. However, the specific structure or ground-plan according to which reality is delineated and built is the infant's conception of his mother's body. The primary phantasy which influences the child's interpretation of reality is his picture of the parts of his mother's body – termed 'part-objects' – and their connections which he has constructed during the paranoid-schizoid position – that is, prior to his conception of his mother as a whole person. In the paranoid-schizoid position, he is unaware of persons and primarily aware of the mother's breast, his first part-object.

Thus, the most primitive relationship to the mother is oral. Its dominant characteristic is oral sadism. The infant attacks the breast and then incorporates it as both destroyed and destructive. This unhappy part-object relationship is modified by gratifying oral experiences in which the infant relates to a loving breast. Later, the child begins to extend his interest to the whole of the mother's body because of anxieties and frustrations arising in the first breast relationship. The mother's body then becomes the object of phantasies in which it is viewed as the container of all riches, including the father's penis. For a while, the infant enjoys a pleasant relationship to his mother. But this object, in turn, becomes a source of dissatisfaction. Because of his phantasied attacks on the mother's body and its contents, including the incorporated penis, the child *displaces* his interest from her body to the whole world around him. His interest in the larger environment is sustained by its symbolic value as the representation of the mother's body. In Segal's words, 'through symbolisation his interest in his mother's body begins to extend to the whole world around him' (1973, p. 5).

In Kleinian theory, there is little place for interest in novelty or in any external object or person which is not a displacement of something internal which has turned sour. Development takes place because of the pressures of anxiety. As each scenario or relationship becomes diffused with anxiety and destructiveness, the infant is driven outwards to find goodness. Segal describes how the anxieties produced by the internal objects, suffused with badness because of the child's projections, promote the child's search for reassurance in the *real* person of the mother and the parents *as external* objects. In like manner, the child turns towards his father because of anxieties about the internal mother and the breast relationship. He turns to the penis as an object of desire, restitution and reparation in contrast to the internal mother. Although Klein observed playful and loving exchanges both at the breast and in the holding presence of the mother, she did not incorporate these aspects of the relationship into the main body of her work. The primary motivation in the infant's turning *outwards* and *towards* others is counter-phobic as each area of interest becomes contaminated with persecutory phantasies. In relation to Kohut's views on part-object relations and auto-erotic fixations described in the last chapter, many of Klein's descriptions of phantasied object-relations could be conceived as 'disintegration-products'. These destructive and fragmented relationships might signify a break in the primary affectional bond and, moreover, indicate a complete absence of mutuality or of synchronous and playful interactions between mother and child. In Kohut's theory, the overriding aetiological factor in the development of the self is maternal mirroring and empathy; in Klein's theory, anxiety becomes the basis of the development of internal object-relationships and of all individual mental functioning.

In conclusion, I think it is fair to say that, of the theorists who postulate a primitive, divided, autistic and psychotic state (signifying a negative attitude to life), which may be actively directed or passively endured, the Kleinians hold the most extreme position. In my view, the negativity attributed to the young infant is a consequence of non-relational conceptualisations of early infancy. In the case of primary fusion theorists, the infant is conceived of as too *un*differentiated to want to relate; since he is not yet a psychological being, he lacks personal motivation. In Kleinian theory, however, it seems that the newborn infant is *over*-differentiated in that he is subject to such violent, unprotected anxiety that he is driven to relate through the threat of annihilation; his relationships are dominated by destructiveness.

Kleinian/object-relations views on narcissism: Otto Kernberg and Herbert Rosenfeld

Klein's views on infancy have been expanded by a number of contemporary writers on narcissism. Two of these are Otto Kernberg and Herbert Rosenfeld. Otto Kernberg is a well-known writer in the USA; Herbert Rosenfeld is better known in England, where he lives and works. Kernberg is a leading exponent of object-relations theory in the USA; Rosenfeld is a leading figure in the Kleinian group in England. In contrast to the primary narcissism theorists discussed in Chapter 1, Kernberg and Rosenfeld believe that the infant of a few weeks of age has complex object-relations, even though he has little sense of differentiation and is a long way from the achievement of person-permanence and self-constancy. However, in contrast to other object-relations theorists (see chapter 3), such as Balint and Bowlby, the relationship is with an 'internal object'. Interaction with external figures serves only to modify primary phantasy relationships. The term 'internal object' differs from the term 'object representation' to the extent to which the former is often used to refer to phantasy relations exclusively whereas the latter is more a mental map of the object as experienced. Kernberg, differing from Klein on this point, uses the term 'object representation' (Kernberg, 1969, p. 327).

Kernberg and Rosenfeld have studied narcissism as it relates to the first object-relationship in the construction of which the infant takes an active part. Rosenfeld's paper 'On the Psychopathology of Narcissism' (1964, pp. 332–7) begins with a restatement of the confusion between undifferentiation and non-relatedness. The *relatively* undifferentiated infant is nevertheless a *relatively* autonomous and intentional creature. Rosenfeld states his disagreement with theorists who propose that, because narcissism implies an objectless state, we may not talk about narcissistic object-relations. Taking off from Michael Balint's concept of 'primary love' (to be elucidated in chapter 3), Rosenfeld argues that object-relatedness is characteristic of the most primitive state of infancy delineated by the concept of primary narcissism. However, Rosenfeld ignores or misses an important aspect of Balint's concept – namely, that 'primary love' refers to an infant-parent *relationship* based upon a mutual 'interdependence of the two' (Balint, 1937, p. 85). Balint's point is that the infant's early 'mental' life (his 'phantasies') is formed in the context of a relationship. The environment to which the infant relates, which is optimally harmonious and continuous, might be called in Winnicott's terms 'the holding function of the mother' (Winnicott, 1960, pp. 48–9). Phantasies do not represent primarily hostile or cannibalistic impulses towards an internal *part-object*, the breast.

Although Klein's view of infancy differs radically from Mahler's more traditional Freudian concept of primary narcissism, her work may nevertheless be viewed as a direct development of some of Freud's views. A continuum may be drawn from Freud's theory of non-relational, primary narcissism to Klein's theory of internal object-relations via Freud's concept of the 'auto-erotic phase' – an early phase of primary narcissism. Freud viewed primary narcissism as a necessary intermediate stage between auto-erotism and object-love. However, auto-erotism was not strictly speaking objectless since parts of the child's own body, in particular the mouth and lips, are taken as the object of libidinal impulses. The infant takes pleasure in the touching of these zones. This view of the 'erotogenic zones' contains the seeds of the idea of the 'part-object' which was developed by Klein. In Klein's view, the normal infant, who may be deemed 'autistic' or 'psychotic', is intensely related to his 'part-objects', the foremost of which is the mother's breast. These part-object relations are to those parts of the *mother's* body which satisfy the infant's needs. The baby attaches himself to, or withdraws from, or seeks to destroy, these part-objects at whim or, in psychoanalytic terms, from within his illusion of *omnipotence*. In Kleinian theory, therefore, the infant might use self-stimulation of parts of his own body as a defence against disappointments and hostility felt towards parts of his mother's body. His relationship to his part-objects, whether the object is his mother's nipple or his own tongue and lips, is nevertheless narcissistic and self-gratifying.

Rosenfeld claims that primary narcissism may be incorporated into object-relations theory through the concepts of infantile omnipotence and part object-relations. For example, 'The object, usually a part-object, the breast, may be omnipotently incorporated, which implies that it is treated as the infant's possession; or the mother or breast are used as containers into which are omnipotently projected the parts of the self which are felt to be undesirable as they cause pain or anxiety' (Rosenfeld, 1964, pp. 332–3). Like other writers on narcissism, Rosenfeld points out that identification is an important feature in narcissistic object-relations. However, because of his focus on the objects or part-objects to which the infant relates, he discusses identification in terms of identification with an object rather than with the relation to, or between, objects. Thus his concept of identification lacks any notion of mutuality. An example of the latter type of identification is the mirroring relationship which precedes the identification of the child with the mother's face (Lichtenstein, 1964, pp. 52–3; Winnicott, 1967, pp. 111–18). In Rosenfeld's view, the process of identification is explained in terms of the mechanisms of projection and introjection. These two mechanisms illustrate a model of primitive object-relations in which relating is conceived in terms of evacuation or incorporation – putting into others or taking into ourselves; they omit the connotations of imitating, portraying, representing as well as the transitional nature of identification in which the subject identifies in turns with different figures who are themselves related to each other (Padel, 1977a).

In my view, identification presupposes some notion of *linking*. Linking depends upon a sense of continuity, of bridging, which arises in the context of holding. Shirley Hoxter (1975, p. 175), an English child psychotherapist of the Kleinian school, suggests that the baby's experience of the nipple is the first experience of a link. The nipple links the baby's mouth with the breast. Thus, the nipple is the primordial model for connecting and linking. Hoxter makes the point that 'true introjection and integration cannot take place in the absence of the living link' (1975, p. 177). In this sense, linking precedes both introjection and projection – that is, both incorporation and evacuation. Hoxter, like most Kleinians, bases a mental capacity such as connecting on a concrete object which represents that capacity. For Hoxter, the mental or ideational content of linking is created through the nipple experience; for Freud, the ideational content of a bond represents the more amorphous experience of at-oneness with the universe – an 'oceanic feeling' (Freud, 1930, pp. 64–5); for Winnicott, linking represents the earliest holding relationship; for Balint, the mental idea of linking represents the mutual interdependence of mother and infant. The point is that these theorists base their theory of object *relations* upon a primitive experience of linking. Linking or relating do not develop out of evacuation or incorporation. These theorists differ in the ways in which they conceptualise linking. In the Kleinian schema, a theorist is likely to look for a part-object which links, whereas a follower of Winnicott might look for a particular relationship such as holding or mirroring.

Rosenfeld's account of identification is as follows:

> When the object is omnipotently incorporated, the self becomes so identified with the incorporated object that all separ-

> ate identity or any boundary between self and object is denied. In projective identification parts of the self omnipotently enter an object, for example the mother, to take over certain qualities which would be experienced as desirable, and therefore claim to be the object or part-object. Identification by introjection and projection usually occur simultaneously. (1964, p. 333)

The notions of reciprocity and mutuality, based on the primary affectional bond, the composite unit of mother and infant or the living link of the nipple, have no place in this account of the identification process. The infant is dominated by an all-powerful possession of the mother.

From Rosenfeld's perspective, Freud's distinction between primary and secondary narcissism dissolves. All narcissistic object-relations are defensive. Rosenfeld states that object-relations of a narcissistic type are defensive against separateness. Indeed, the mechanisms of introjection and projection already presuppose some self-object differentiation. The acknowledgment of separateness immediately evokes feelings of dependence on the other person which further elicit feelings of anxiety and envy. In Rosenfeld's view, a narcissistic object-relationship obviates both aggression and envy, since feelings of dependence and anxiety are denied through the illusion of omnipotence.

What does omnipotence mean in this context? We are told in the literature that the infant feels all-powerful. Winnicott has made the point that, in the earliest days and weeks of life, the infant is also in a state of near-absolute dependence, since he has little notion of separateness. These contrary attributions may be reconciled in the commonly held hypothesis that infantile omnipotence is sometimes a *defence* against the impotent state of absolute dependence. At other times, omnipotence may characterise assertiveness and an expectation that wishes will be fulfilled. In my view, some of the pejorative connotations attached to the idea of omnipotence follow from the negative characterisation of the more primary state of dependence. On the more general level, the concept of infantile dependence is usually described in terms which lack any notion of *inter*-dependence, mutuality and reciprocity. In relation to the infant's experience of his dependence, it is usually assumed that dependence entails anxiety. However, it seems to me that, in the early days and weeks of life, dependence may sometimes be manifested, or experienced, as anxiety, but, in a reliable holding environment, anxiety would not be the dominant mood. Anxious dependence is a sign of an insecure attachment, or of failure in the holding environment. Winnicott has suggested that the infant only becomes aware of holding when it fails (Winnicott, 1960, p. 52). I suggest that infantile omnipotence might sometimes indicate a similar failure in the infant-mother relationship. In distinction to the infant's confidence and displays of his powers, stemming from reliability which is taken for granted, the tyrannical grandiosity and possessiveness, which characterise defensive omnipotence, might indicate disappointments and ruptures in the infant-mother *relationship*. As Rosenfeld suggests, omnipotence might be one defensive reaction to frightening feelings of dependence. But, in normal circumstances, dependence, which has come to have this pejorative connotation, need not be a painful experience. The infant becomes frighteningly aware of his dependence when holding fails.

Thus, in my view, the feeling of being able to depend upon, or turn to, someone may even be comforting and reassuring. Many analysts, particularly those of a Kleinian orientation, have focused upon the frightening aspect of dependence, which may indeed engender extremely controlling behaviour towards the object of that dependence. However, in my view, the urge to 'omnipotently control' is usually a manifestation of an anxious dependence. Of course, a young infant or child manifests this kind of controlling behaviour many times throughout the day, when a mother must turn her attention elsewhere. Her infant will probably protest over the disruption and may exert pressure upon her to resume their mutual pursuit. Usually, however, he will then turn his attention elsewhere and discover other of his resources (provided that his mother remains close by and available).

Like Kohut and Rosenfeld, Otto Kernberg has made a major contribution to the study of narcissism in relation both to normal development and to pathology (1974, pp. 215–40; 1975, pp. 245–7). In my estimation, Kernberg holds a middle position between the Freudian and Kleinian views on narcissism. His theoretical formulations span the USA school of ego psychology, with its emphasis on structure, dynamics and genetic development, and the British school associated with the work of Klein, with its emphasis on internal objects, primary envy, aggression and the most primitive form of object-relating which is 'projective identification'. Kernberg's work illustrates many of the features which characterise the Kleinian approach, such as the belief in primary negativity towards the object, manifested as envy and aggression, and a consequent emphasis on the negative transference in clinical work. At the same time, Kernberg acknowledges the maternal contribution. He says of the narcissistic patient

> that it is an open question to what extent inborn intensity of aggressive drive participates in this picture, and that the predominance of chronically cold, narcissistic and at the same time overprotective mother figures appears to be the main etiological element in the psychogenesis of this pathology. (1974, p. 221)

Like Goldberg, another contemporary analytic writer on narcissism (1972, pp. 3–7; 1975, pp. 695–99), Kernberg notes that, in the case histories of many narcissistic persons, the mother-figure is not so much cold or withdrawn but, rather, doting and overprotective in a smothering way. In other words, the pathology is connected to problems of differentiation from the mother.

Consistent with their view on infancy, most Kleinian writers on narcissism emphasise the negative attitude of the narcissist. Narcissistic pathology results not from disruptions in the primary affectional bond between mother and infant to which the mother contributes, but from envious and omnipotent attacks made by the infant upon the link between his mother and himself. Since, in Melanie Klein's view, the young infant is in a state of primary, persecutory anxiety, all feelings of dependence upon someone, or something, in the outside environment elicit negative feelings, such as hostility towards, and paranoid fear of, the primary object.

The many different ways in which analysts interpret those breaks in the early mother-infant relationship, which are later manifested in narcissistic pathology, are well illustrated in discussions in the literature of the typical narcissist's self-preoccupation and apparent indifference to others. Again, these interpretations reflect the respective theories held of the infant's primary state of being. Almost all the contemporary psychoanalytic writers on narcissism agree that the narcissistic person suffers from an unusual degree of self-reference in his or her interactions. He seems to lack the skill, or facility, of turning away from his own preoccupations and towards the concerns of others. Although many writers still agree with Freud's thesis that the narcissistic person has not yet reached the stage of object-love, most writers disagree with Freud's view that narcissistic persons are not amenable to psychoanalytic treatment. Freud thought that they manifested a resistance which was like a stone 'wall' which cannot be got over (Freud, 1916–17, part III, p. 423). For Freud, their self-involvement seemed to indicate a complete indifference to others. Freud noted that, in treatment, such patients turn from their physician 'not with hostility but with indifference' (Freud, 1916–17, p. 447). I think that most Kleinian analysts would emphasise instead the active hostility underlying the manifest indifference. In their view, the narcissist has reached the stage of object-love, but he actively rejects his object-relationship.

Thus, in the literature on narcissism, we find a variety of interpretations of the attitude of indifference. Narcissistic indifference may simply represent a primitive state of narcissistic, amoeboid, withdrawal, to which the narcissistic person defensively regresses. Other analysts, such as Balint, Kohut and Goldberg, interpret narcissistic indifference as a defence against a raw and unusual sensitivity to the responses of other people. The narcissist suffers, not so much from a cold indifference, but from a *lack* of differentiation and, indeed, an unusual permeability to the feelings of others. Even Kernberg describes how such patients present a *great need to be loved* and to be admired by others, and present an apparent contradiction between a very inflated concept of themselves and *an inordinate need* for tribute from others. Such persons feel best when the inflated self-concept is matched by the external world. However, when the need to be loved and admired is not met, the person is enraged and may turn away in cold indifference. Kernberg's observation suggests that narcissistic indifference represents a defence against relational issues rather than the repetition of a primary state of withdrawal. From the various accounts I have so far presented, it appears that the attribute 'narcissistic' covers many behavioural characteristics and patterns of relationship. The narcissistic person may be aloof, inflated and self-satisfied, or he may be inordinately dependent upon others and lacking in self-esteem. These narcissistic characteristics are determined by a variety of aetiological factors. The typical narcissist is as contradictory a character as the various theories of early infancy. Some narcissistic characteristics are seen as defensive against a whole spectrum of more basic states or forms of relationship. Others are simple reproductions of 'normal', infantile patterns of behaviour. Some writers attribute a narcissistic personality type to failures in relationship; others attribute it to inborn tendencies. Some narcissists are unusually sensitive to others whilst other appear to be indifferent. It seems to me that the variety of theories on the aetiology of narcissism reflect Freud's original, somewhat inconsistent, views.

Early in part I, I gave two quotations from Freud's work; the first, I took to indicate a non-related, withdrawn state, the second, I suggested could be used to corroborate an attachment view of infancy. Interestingly enough, Freud supported even his most extreme presentation of primary, self-sufficient narcissism with observations from parent-child *relationships*. This aspect of his formulation seems often to be overlooked. In his 1914 paper, Freud says:

> The primary narcissism of children which we have assumed and which forms one of the postulates of our theories of the libido, is less easy to grasp by direct observation than to confirm by inference from elsewhere. If we look at the attitude of affectionate parents towards their children, we have to recognize that it is a revival and reproduction of their own narcissism, which they have long since abandoned. . . . Thus they are under a compulsion to ascribe every perfection to the child – which sober observation would find no occasion to do – and to conceal and forget all his shortcomings. . . . The child shall have a better time than his parents; he shall not be subject to the necessities which they have recognized as paramount in life. Illness, death, renunciation of enjoyment, restrictions on his own will, shall not touch him; the laws of nature and of society shall be abrogated in his favour; he shall once more really be the centre and core of creation – 'His Majesty the Baby', as we once fancied ourselves. The child shall fulfill those

> wishful dreams of the parents which they never carried out – the boy shall become a great man and a hero in his father's place, and the girl shall marry a prince as a tardy compensation for her mother. . . . Parental love, which is so moving and at bottom so childish, is nothing but the parents' narcissism born again, which, transformed into object-love, unmistakably reveals its former nature. (Freud, 1914, S.E. 14, p. 91)

In Freud's description of the fond attitudes of parents towards their offspring, the relationship is suffused with admiration and with omnipotent transferences from the parents to the children. In the Narcissus myth, we are told that everyone was in love with Narcissus even in his cradle. This suggests that the self-referring system of the typical narcissist represents the enclosed, mirroring relationship between the relatively undifferentiated mother and infant. At a later stage of development, the person presenting a fixation at this level of relating seeks out tributes from others, thereby attempting to complete the original circuitry. When the search for completion is successful, the self-referring attitude usually dissolves; temporarily, the person feels complete, he 'forgets himself', as in a state of being in love. He feels linked to others.

In my view, the sense of personal continuity depends upon the experience of holding and upon early synchronous and playful interactions. Continuity is a mental representation of such experiences. The narcissistic person, however, seems to have confused continuity with fusion – that is, with an *unbroken* psycho-physical union. In the earliest weeks of life, a mother may attempt to provide such experiences of total psycho-physical union through her holding. However, when holding is taken for granted, the infant *discovers*, and expresses, wishes to be let down. He also looks around and away from his mother. The narcissistic person replaces continuity with fusion as a defence against discontinuities or abrasiveness in the holding relationship, which might include a lack of responsiveness to the infant's desire to be alone. The infant may not manifest this feeling of dissonance by hostility, but simply avert his eyes or stiffen away from his holder.

The narcissist is also said to suffer from self-reference; this implies that he lacks any notion of the *relativity* of the self. He is unable to see himself in relation to other people and to coordinate the multiplicity of perspectives in which others view him. Some of the disturbances in body image and ensuing hypochondriacal symptoms, to which narcissistic persons are prone, might indicate an inability to deal with the relativity of the self. A person who seems over-preoccupied with how he looks or is seen by others may be engaged primarily in a desperate *search* for the self. The apparent need to refer everything to the self manifests, instead, an absence of a self-construct or sense of self-continuity.

Sheldon Bach is another contemporary psychoanalyst who has contributed to the study of narcissism. In three fascinating papers, Bach (1975, 1977a, 1977b) describes in detail the lack of continuity and the presence of discontinuous self-experiences which characterise the narcissistic state of consciousness. Common narcissistic fantasies, described by Bach, are of 'a wise baby' – that is, someone who is born completely mature – of the double or the androgyne, and of the rope to another world (Bach, 1977b, pp. 281–93). In all these fantasies, temporal and spatial separateness is denied. The narcissistic person, lacking the concept of a continuous self which participates in a *variety* of relationships, clings tenuously and tenaciously to the notion of fusion and non-temporal, i.e. non-terrestrial, joining.

Kernberg and Kohut have engaged in an interesting debate over the aetiology, diagnosis and treatment of the narcissistic person, in which many of the above issues are discussed. The differences in their views relate to their respective conceptions of early infancy. According to Kernberg, Kohut neglects the relationship between narcissistic and object-related conflicts and the crucial role of aggression in the aetiology of narcissism. Kernberg emphasises the predominance of envy, devaluation and splitting over other factors. In Kernberg's schema, 'narcissistic investment (i.e. investment in the self), and object-investment (that is, investment in representation of others and in other human beings), occur simultaneously, and intimately influence each other, so that one cannot study the vicissitudes of narcissism without studying the vicissitudes of object relationships' (Kernberg, 1974, p. 219). 'Narcissism and object relationships always go hand-in-hand' (1974, p. 235). Kernberg considers that narcissistic structures are *defences* against the aggressive and envious factors in object-relationships. Kohut sees the narcissistic disorders as *reflections* of developmental arrest. As Ornstein (1974, p. 246) points out, where Kohut sees an 'inability', Kernberg sees a 'denial' or a 'refusal'. According to Kohut, the patient is simply unable to perceive the analyst as an autonomous person; in Kernberg's opinion, the patient refuses to acknowledge the analyst's independence which has been perceived.

Kernberg makes a clear distinction between normal and pathological narcissism, based upon the narcissistic defences to object-relationships. Kohut places normal and pathological narcissism on a continuum. Both thinkers agree, however, that in normal narcissism, some self-object individuation has taken place. In Kernberg's diagnostic spectrum, narcissistic persons fall on the non-psychotic end of the 'borderline personalities' (1974, pp. 215–16). Their regression is not psychotic because, in their case, ego boundaries are stable and reality-testing is preserved. Narcissistic fusion occurs at a level of development where boundaries have already become stable. Like Rosenfeld, Kernberg considers narcissism to be a defensive reaction to separateness and to an intolerable reality in the interpersonal realm. The narcissistic person's greatest fear is to be dependent on anyone else, because to depend means to hate, envy, and expose himself to being exploited and mistreated and frustrated. Kohut, agreeing that narcissism refers to a stage in which the self has attained some 'cohesiveness', disagrees about the reasons why this process of integration has remained incomplete. For him, it is not the *infant's intolerance* of separateness, but the *object's incapacity* to relate to the infant on the infant's own terms. The evidence for this view is the 'reinstatement' (Kohut, 1971) of the archaic relationship in the transference. Of the three types of narcissistic transference – merger, twinship and mirror – the merger transference is the most primitive and the mirror transference the most developed. Both the merger and the twinship transferences are reinstatements of *regressive* positions taken after the *failure* of the mirror stage. However, even the purest forms of the mirror transference are 'not direct replicas of a normal developmental phase' (1971). The argument stops there since there is no independent variable against which to compare the mirror transference for exact replication. Nevertheless, Kohut declares that the mirror transference is closer to being a therapeutic reinstatement of the normal developmental phase and that, in a correctly conducted analysis, the merger and twinship transferences gradually change into the mirror transference which itself tends 'to become more and more akin to the normal developmental phase' (1971).

Kernberg lists the following differences between normal and pathological narcissism, all of which relate to the degree of aggression: first, the 'grandiose fantasies of normal small children . . . have a far more realistic quality than is the case of narcissistic personalities'; second, the 'small child's over-reaction to criticism, failure, and blame, as well as his need to be the centre of attention, admiration and love, coexist with simultaneous expression of genuine love and gratitude, and interest in his object at times when he is not frustrated, and above all, with the capacity to trust and depend upon significant objects'; third, in 'normal infantile narcissism', the child's 'demandingness' is related to 'real needs', whereas 'the demandingness of pathological narcissism is excessive, cannot ever be fulfilled, and regularly reveals itself to be secondary to a process of internal destruction of the supplies received'; fourth, the 'coldness and aloofness', the 'disregard' of others except when idealised as 'potential sources of narcissistic supply' and the 'contempt' and 'devaluation' of patients with pathological narcissism are 'in striking contrast to the warm quality of the small child's self-centredness'; fifth,

> the normal infantile narcissistic fantasies of power and wealth and beauty . . . do not imply an exclusive possession of all that is valuable and enviable in the world . . . fantasies of narcissistic triumph or grandiosity are mingled with wishes that acquisition of these values will make the child lovable, acceptable by those whom he loves and by whom he wants to be loved. (1974, pp. 219–20)

Kernberg claims that the implication of this set of contrasts is that pathological narcissism is strikingly different from normal narcissism. The chief distinguishing feature is the degree of rejection of relationship in adult narcissists.

Kernberg enumerates the different manifestations of pathological narcissism as these arise in the analytic transference. The denial of the separate existence of the analyst is not matched by a simultaneous fusion as in the case of more regressed patients.

The concept of the grandiose self does not relate to a regressive fusion between the idealised self and the idealised parent images but to the *projection* of the patient's grandiose self on to the analyst. The grandiose self permits the denial of dependence. This denial does not represent an absence of internalised object-relations (as in the case of Kohut's patient who lacks an essential piece of structure because of incomplete internalisations), but is a defence against more primitive, pathological object-relations centred on narcissistic rage and envy. The reactions of resentment, disappointment are less intense in non-narcissistic patients and coexist with the capacity for dependence, separation anxiety and mourning reactions. Moreover, idealisation in non-narcissistic patients does not coexist with an almost complete obliviousness of the analyst. According to Kernberg, the narcissistic grandiose self does not reflect a piece of missing structure or an incomplete cohesion of the self, but manifests 'a condensed, pathological self' (1974, p. 223). The idealisation of the analyst corresponds to a projection of the patient's grandiose self which 'stems from the fusion of some aspects of the real self, the ideal self and the ideal object. This condensation is pathological, and does not simply represent fixation at an early stage of development' (p. 223). In pathological narcissism, there is a total denial of separateness and concern for the object. The piece of missing structure in the relation to the object ensues from the child's destructive attacks on his internal object as a source of supply and goodness and, in particular, from his splitting of the object because of primitive envy and devaluation. Fragmentation of the self and object does not reflect embryonic or incomplete cohesion but an active splitting apart of the already constituted internal self- and object-representations. The salient characteristics of the narcissistic person – fusion, grandiosity and omnipotence – are evidence of this active process of splitting – that is, of a divisive procedure in which a whole is fragmented by envious and destructive attacks upon it by an already differentiated self.

In conclusion, I think that this debate between Kernberg and Kohut reflects the two theoretical views delineated in positions 1 and 2 on my spectrum. Kohut's view of both normal and pathological narcissism emanates from the conception of the infant as a dependent, malleable being in a fused relationship with his mother. Grandiosity and perfection, the search for merger, mirroring and twinship relationships, are normal. Kernberg's view of the distinction between normal and pathological narcissism ensues from a different view of the infant; the baby is aware of his separateness and deals with the dependence which permeates his first object-relations with anger and destructiveness. He seeks to split and divide rather than to merge and simulate.

3
Primary object-love and primary affectional bonds

Michael Balint

Michael Balint, who was born in Budapest in 1896 and was analysed by one of Freud's earliest followers and colleagues, Sandor Ferenczi, was one of the foremost pioneers of the object-relations school. Together with the Scottish psychoanalyst, W. R. D. Fairbairn, he might be regarded as the forerunner of the British 'Middle Group' of analysts – a group which continues to play an important role in the integration and clarification of Freudian and Kleinian theory. In 1939, Balint came to England, where he made important contributions both to the developing theory of psychoanalysis and to general psychiatry and medicine. He is particularly well-known for his innovative groups for general practitioners; through these groups, which were attended by doctors from all over Britain, Balint was able to bring psychiatric and psychoanalytic insights into the lives of the general public (Balint, 1957). Balint's relational concept of 'primary love' brought an entirely new perspective to the theory of infancy and a focus on relationships which was quite different to that of Anna Freud and Melanie Klein. Ferenczi had made a particular study of mother-child relations and his interest in the strength of the mother-infant relationship continued to inspire the Hungarian school of psychoanalysts centred in Budapest. Ferenczi introduced the phrase 'passive object-love' to describe the infant's self-centred, but absolutely dependent, love for the mother. In the 1930s, Michael Balint, his wife, Alice, and colleague, I. Hermann, published a series of papers in which they emphasised the importance of the infant's primary instinct to cling. Hermann observed clinging and grasping movements in the early weeks of the life of infant apes and human babies. He did not postulate that these behaviours were evidence of a primary object-relationship, but Alice and Michael Balint combined his observations with Ferenczi's concept of passive object-love to form their new concept of 'primary object-love'. Primary object-love acknowledges the active role played by the infant, illustrated by his clinging tie to the mother. Primary love is thus descriptive of an active love of the mother. The Balints' view of a primary object-relationship is similar to that of Melanie Klein in that the infant is active and his love is egocentric. However, although unaware of his mother's interests, the infant's relationship is neither destructive nor dominated by orality.

In 1937, at the 'Four Countries Conference' in Budapest, Balint presented his views on 'Early Developmental States of the Ego', proposing the new concept of 'primary object-love' to replace Freud's theory of primary narcissism. In this brilliant exposition of the differences between the Viennese, English and Hungarian schools and their respective uses of the primary narcissism hypothesis, Balint anticipated the theoretical shift which contemporary attachment theory and interactionalist theory have made explicit. (Bowlby's work on the affectional tie between mother and infant (1958) and Winnicott's work on mother-infant mutuality and holding (1970) would seem to be offshoots of Balint's concept of primary object-love.) For Balint, the basis of the infant-parent relationship is a mutual 'interdependence of the two'. Each 'partner' seeks out a 'harmonious relationship'. If either is not satisfied, then the relationship is under strain (Balint, 1937, p. 85). Recent developments in the theory of infancy would seem to confirm Balint's thesis.

Balint observed that, despite disagreement, both the Viennese Freudians and the English object-relations analysts started with the same view of the infant – namely, that he is greedy, insatiable, hostile, generally discontented and ambivalent. Quoting Joan Riviere, a prominent member of Klein's circle, Balint points out that 'the Londoners' (i.e. members of the British object-relations school of analysis) stress the 'sadistic' and 'cannibalistic' quality of the oral object-relation (1937, pp. 76–7). The oral, sadistic impulses which characterise the earliest psychical development have two sources: sadistic impulses arise either from within as manifestations of the death instinct, or in reaction to the delay of gratification from without. Since these feelings are intolerable, the infant projects them outwards onto external objects, particularly the mother. A vicious circle begins, a 'kind of paranoia develops' since 'everywhere and in everything he [the infant] sees bad objects' (1937, p. 77). Mental content in the earliest months consists mainly of phantasies of methods of absorbing or expelling good and bad objects. Impulses towards tender love develop later and as a consequence of guilt and remorse. Thus, both the Viennese and the English schools postulate a state of primary negativity towards the world. The difference is that, according to the English school, this attitude is not undirected, non-specific, or objectless.

Balint looked at the 'narcissistic' wishes described by Freud and the English analysts as they arose in his analytic practice. He noticed that, at a certain point in analytic work, many patients began to express their wishes for various primitive gratifications. When these wishes were frustrated, phenomena appeared which corresponded to the conception of the infant put forward by the London analysts: namely, loss of security, feelings of worthlessness, despair, disappointment, mistrust, which were mixed with venomous aggression and the wildest sadistic phantasies. The expression of these feelings was then followed by fears of retaliation and the most complete contrition. On the other hand, when Balint reportedly responded to these wishes, by permitting their satisfaction, almost manic states would break out which were soon followed by despair, hatred and fears of retaliation at the first sign of dissatisfaction. Neither way of responding seemed appropriate or therapeutic (pp. 80–1).

Balint then asked himself,

> What are these dangerous wishes like in reality? Rather innocent and naive, one would say. A kind word from the analyst, the permission to call him by his first name or be called by him by one's first name; to be able to see him also outside the analytical session, to borrow something or to get a present from him, even if it be quite insignificant, etc. Very often these wishes do not go farther than to be able to touch the analyst, to cling to him, or to be touched or stroked by him. (p. 81)

Balint confessed that it took him a long time to notice two

essential qualities of these wishes. First, they were always directed towards an object and, second, they never went beyond the level of 'fore-pleasure'. The first observation meant that only someone in the external world could satisfy the wishes and, therefore, that auto-erotic narcissistic satisfaction was insufficient. The second meant that, when satisfaction arrived at the right moment and with the right intensity, it caused reactions which were observable only with difficulty, because the experience of gratification happened so quietly. Balint described this feeling of pleasure as 'a tranquil, quiet sense of well-being' (p. 81). He concluded that vehement, stormy and noisy reactions were not primary; they had a history. The Londoners, however, studied only the vehement reactions *after* frustration; the experience of the tranquil, quiet sense of well-being after proper satisfaction escaped their attention. What presented itself as loud and forceful was valued and what happened quietly was thought unimportant.

Thus, for Balint, the earliest phase of extra-uterine mental life is not narcissistic, it is object-related but passive: 'I shall be loved and satisfied, without being under any obligation to give anything in return.' So-called primary narcissism, self-love and self-gratification, is a detour and a protection against the bad or reluctant object. Another detour is active object-love – namely, that I 'love and gratify' my 'partner, i.e. . . . conform to his wishes, in order to be loved and gratified by him in return' (p. 82).

Anticipating Bowlby's ethological studies of attachment and his evolutionary viewpoint, Balint was perhaps the first psychoanalyst to note the importance of clinging and crying in the ontogeny of attachment. The primary goal of birth is proximity-seeking. Balint also thought that clinging was the common precursor of a large number of object-relations and that it led to touching, stroking, caressing and tenderness in normal sexuality. He observed that newly born babies tend to cry more in the first few weeks of life than later. However, picking up the child usually results in the cessation of crying. This is not because the mother serves as a defence or stimulus barrier against instinctual excitement or external impingement, but because the crying *is* the expression of the desire for physical contact. The acceptance of this basic desire means the acceptance of an object-relation and is, therefore, a serious challenge to the primary narcissism hypothesis. Since primary narcissism is by definition a state without any object-relation, it follows that all signs of love must be ascribed to oral erotism. For Balint, oral erotism and the need for physical contact as demonstrated by crying and clinging are simply features of primary object-love. The secondary and vehement reactions to frustration studied by the English school are specific responses to the premature severance of the intimate, interdependent object-relation between mother and infant; they reflect child-rearing practices which prevailed in some sectors of European society.

The main cause of 'the confusion of tongues between Vienna and London' (p. 86) was attributed by Balint to the primary narcissism hypothesis. Balint's pronouncement is still relevant today, particularly in the United States where the polarisation of analytic beliefs is most extreme. Primary narcissism 'is a very curious notion, full of meaning and yet very poor' (p. 86). All its characteristics are negative and, as Freud himself observed, in its absolute form, the state is impossible. Primary narcissism is only possible within the mother-infant unit. The mother's state of responsiveness was also inadequately explained by the primary narcissism hypothesis. According to Freud, parental love is simply a transference of abandoned narcissism. Through their unconditional love of their infant, parents relive their own narcissistic wishes for total gratification. Balint gave the primary object-relation a biological basis in the 'instinctual interdependence' of mother and child. 'What is good for the one is right for the other' (p. 85). This biological interdependence of the dual unit makes sense when placed in an evolutionary context. In keeping with the ethological point of view, which his work anticipated, Balint also distinguished the development of instinctual object-relations from the development of instinctual aims. The aim of the relationship is not to satisfy or expel oral, anal or genital urges. Primary object-love is not oral, anal or genital. It is not linked to the erotogenic zones 'but is something on its own' (pp. 84–5).

Clinically, Balint found that the primary narcissism hypothesis had little to offer. The attributes of independence and indifference to the external world, which were thought to characterise the state of primary narcissism, do not characterise narcissistic people. In general, such people are hypersensitive and irritable and give the impression of 'an anxiously and painfully counter-balanced lability' (p. 88). Despite contrary evidence, Balint thought that psychoanalysts clung to the primary narcissism hypothesis because they were 'victims' (p. 89) of the fallacy that the logically simplest form is the most primitive. A mind that is amoeboid and which maintains no relation to the external world is the simplest. So long as analysts did not focus on the pre-oedipal problems, primary narcissism represented the simplest starting point for the theory of development; psychic growth consisted in the development of object-relations out of the amoeboid state. *'In my opinion, the time has come for us psycho-analysts to follow the biologists in facing the* end *of the amoeba myth'* (p. 90, my italics). Although clinical evidence seemed to support Balint's thesis, he anticipated a common counter-argument to primary object-relations which we still hear today: if the infant does not know of any external world and still less is able to discriminate objects in it, then surely he cannot build up a relation to objects which do not yet exist in his mind. This fact, however, does not argue against the psychological validity of the object-relations point of view. Furthermore, Balint commented, the authors who doubt the possibility of the infant's mental life seem to know 'absolutely firmly and safely what *cannot* exist in the infantile mind' (p. 89). How do we know for certain that the infant does not know anything at all of the external world?

John Bowlby

John Bowlby, now in his seventies, has spent forty years in pursuit of a positive answer to this question. Yes, indeed, the young infant is very much aware of the psychological and physical circumstances of his most intense preoccupation – his mother (or mother-figure). To her he is inordinately attached. His joys and sorrows are frighteningly contingent upon the tie which links them together. Since his early years in the British Navy, Bowlby's consuming interest has been the study of separation and, there-from, attachment. At twenty-one, prior to completing his psychiatric training, Bowlby went to teach at one of London's progressive schools in which he was first exposed to the problems of disturbed children. He began to see some of these problems of deprivation as the result of family difficulties in the early lives of the children. These early 'hunches' were supported and refined by further studies of post-war refugee children which culminated in a simple and readable book – *Child Care and the Growth of Love* (1951). In this work, the focus was on maternal deprivation. Its counterpart, to which Bowlby then turned, was maternal love and care. Bowlby became interested in the social and psychological conditions which underlie the normal process of attachment. At this point, he turned increasingly to the new ethological paradigm put forward by Lorenz, Tinbergen and others. Using this model, he published his first statement of attachment theory – 'The nature of the child's tie to his mother' (1958).

Over the past twenty years, Bowlby has expanded and refined the original thesis presented in 1958. In that paper, Bowlby postulated the existence of a primary affectional tie between the infant and the mother; this was a controversial thesis which was to challenge all previous theories which regarded attachment and socialisation as secondary developments. Bowlby spelt out the obvious – the infant is attached to his mother from the beginning of life. The infant does not learn *secondarily* that it is his mother who satisfies his physiological needs, he does not relate to her primarily through sucking at the breast and he does not resent his extrusion from the womb and crave to return therein.

Like Balint, Bowlby noticed that, in the difficult task of constructing a picture of the infant's cognitive world, it is easy to fall prey to two fallacies. The first is that, because an infant responds in a typically 'social' way, he is *aware* of the human characteristics of the object to which he is responding. In psychoanalysis, wariness of this assumption has sometimes fostered the contrary belief – namely, the theory of primary narcissism. Since the neonate is not aware of many specifically human characteristics, he cannot be thought to be socially responsive. The second possible fallacy is that, because an infant recognises a person as familiar, he must perceive that person as having a separate and permanent existence in time and space. Again, since the neonate is clearly incapable of such cognition, there is a tendency to deny the specificity of the infant's response to the familiar mother-figure. In the pre-object-related stage, it is proposed instead that the infant only responds to a familiar figure because he associates that figure with the alleviation of physical discomfort or primary anxiety and/or persecution.

Freed from the misconception that object-relatedness means the relation to an external, separate, whole object and from the belief that differential and specific responsiveness depends upon the understanding of separateness and permanence, Bowlby was able to focus upon the primacy of the affectional bond which existed between mother and child. He no longer sought reasons as to how the child became social or came to love his mother above all others.

Bowlby distinguishes four main phases in the development of attachment behaviour. (An excellent summary of these phases is given by Ainsworth (1969, pp. 1003–7.) *Phase 1, orientation and signals without discrimination of figure* (first few weeks). *Phase 2, orientation and signals directed towards one or more discriminated figures* (displayed by differential crying, smiling, vocalising and greeting). *Phase 3, maintenance of proximity to a discriminated figure by means of locomotion as well as by signals* (manifested by differential behaviours such as approaching, following, climbing upon, exploring, clinging to the mother in preference to others, and using her as a secure base from which to explore and as a haven of safety to which to return). Bowlby has focused upon this phase because in it the infant's behaviour has become organised on a goal-corrected basis. The infant maintains proximity to his mother by means 'of a more or less primitive cognitive map' (Ainsworth, 1969, p. 1007) which provides the framework within which the mother comes to be conceived as an object, independent and persistent in time and space. Mary Ainsworth, a close colleague of Bowlby's for twenty years and president of the American Society for Research in Child Development, comments that, at this stage, the infant's ' "attachment to his mother . . . is evident for all to see" ' whereas, previously, 'his discrimination and differential behaviour could scarcely indicate "attachment" ' (pp. 1006–7). *Phase 4, formation of a reciprocal relationship* or, in Bowlby's terms, 'goal-corrected partnership'. Until the child is able to understand his mother's set-goals, he is incompetent in his attempts to alter her plans to fit in with his own. The ability to change the mother's plans requires the infant to see things from another's point of view and not merely to adjust his set-goal to synchronise with hers.

The path mapped out of the development of attachment and its vicissitudes is, of course, contingent upon a specific definition of attachment and attachment behaviour. The attachment theorists have focused on proximity-seeking behaviours which are seen as the hallmark of attachment. Attachment behaviour, in Bowlby's formulation,

> is conceived as any form of behaviour that results in a person attaining or retaining proximity to some other differentiated and preferred individual, who is usually conceived as stronger and/or wiser. While especially evident during early childhood, attachment behaviour is held to characterize human beings from the cradle to the grave. (Bowlby, 1976, p. 203)

As a way of conceptualising proximity seeking, Bowlby emphasises seven features which contrast attachment theory with dependency theory. These are:

(a) Specificity.
(b) Duration. An attachment usually endures for a large part of the life-cycle.
(c) Engagement of emotion. Since many of the most intense emotions arise during the formation, maintenance, disruption and renewal of attachment relationships, the psychology and psychopathology of emotion is in large part the psychology and psychopathology of affectional bonds.
(d) Ontogeny. In the great majority of human infants attachment behaviour to a preferred figure develops during the first nine months of life and remains easily activated until near the end of the third year, after which it becomes gradually less readily activated.
(e) Learning. The key process in the development of an attachment is the learning to discriminate between the familiar and the strange. In contrast, reward and punishment play only a small part, as witnessed by the observation that strong attachments develop despite repeated punishment from the attachment figure.
(f) Organisation. Attachment becomes mediated by increasingly sophisticated behavioural systems which are organised cybernetically and incorporate cognitive maps of the environment and the self. Activating conditions of attachment are

strangeness, hunger, fatigue and anything frightening.
(g) Biological function. In a number of species, maintenance of proximity by an immature animal to a preferred adult is the rule. Thus suggests that attachment behaviour has survival value, the most likely function of which is protection mainly from predators.

Attachment behaviours are often contrasted with two other behavioural systems: care-taking and exploration. The interconnectedness of these three central behavioural systems is of great importance and interest, especially in the light of recent studies (to be described in chapter 4), in which the growth of attachment is linked to positive, social interaction. In Bowlby's view, care-giving is complementary to attachment behaviour whereas exploration is often antithetical to such behaviour. The roles of the care-giver are first, to be available and responsive when wanted and, second, to intervene judiciously in case of trouble. Nevertheless, Bowlby points out that children are curious and inquiring and their pursuit of inquiry usually leads them to move away from their attachment figure. Their explorations lead them to build up a coherent picture of their environment. However, exploration usually flourishes when a person feels that he has a secure base. Therefore, although attachment and exploratory *behaviours* may be antithetical, secure attachment and the growth of self-reliance, upon which exploration is contingent, are complementary. The capacity to form affectional bonds and to be self-reliant in adult life depends upon two crucial factors in a person's family life. First, the provision of a secure base through parental responsiveness to a child's attachment desires and, second, parental encouragement to explore from this base and to extend relationships with peers and other adults.

In his more recent formulations of attachment behaviour, Bowlby suggests that five main classes of behaviour should be considered in any attempt to assess the attachment behaviour of a child. Although two of these classes refer to proximity-seeking behaviour in situations of distress, two (c and e) refer to more positive interactions and one to exploratory behaviour (d). These are:

(a) behavior that initiates interaction, such as greeting, approaching, touching, embracing, calling, reaching, and

> smiling; (b) behavior in response to the mother's interactional initiatives that maintains interaction (the above behaviors plus watching); (c) behavior aimed to avoid separations, such as following, clinging, and crying; (d) exploratory behavior, as it is oriented with reference to the mother; and (e) withdrawal or fear behavior, especially as it is oriented with reference to the mother. (Ainsworth, 1969, p. 1005)

The harmonious quality of mother–infant interaction, which is built up out of communicational 'games' as well as synchronised proximity-maintaining patterns of attachment behaviour, is crucial to the arousal of a baby's 'interest' in the first weeks of life. Explorations can, of course, be part and parcel of the simplest care-taking functions. Analysts of varying orientations have observed that infants at the breast like to interrupt the business of feeding and, if mother allows, play at the breast or explore the mother's face and clothing. Ainsworth and Bell have correlated attachment behaviour of one-year-old children placed in a strange situation with the extent to which, as infants of three months, they had been permitted to be an *active* partner in the feeding situation (Ainsworth and Bell, 1970a, 1970b; Bell, 1970, pp. 291–311). Their observations suggest that mother–infant reciprocity and the mother's conception of the relationship as a *partnership*, even in the first months of life, affect the development of both attachment and exploration. These researchers further correlated ambivalence, indicating disharmony, in a strange situation with general ambivalence in the home environment. Ambivalent children tend to resist contact when picked up and to ask to be picked up when they are set down in the home environment and in the strange environment and, further, upon reunion with the mother after separation. They are also less exploratory in the home environment. Thus, although proximity-avoiding behaviour is not strictly incompatible with exploratory behaviour, Ainsworth and others found that most children did not explore constructively when avoiding contact. They tended to move around hyperactively or to alternate uncomfortably between avoiding and seeking contact. In the sense of resisting contact, they were more angry, aggressive and disobedient.

In the light of these findings, I picture an in between situation in which attachment and exploratory behaviours are complementary rather than incompatible. The mother is holding her infant and together they look outwards at some third person or toy. Or the infant is seated on the mother's knee and exploring the face or hands or movements of an unfamiliar person. We tend to think of those situations in which exploration of something in the environment necessitates that the child turn away from his base and towards the interesting object. With growth and maturity, this is most often the case. However, there are innumerable instances in the daily life of a young infant in which he can be held and yet turned towards the thing which catches his eye.

Bell, like Ainsworth, is a leading attachment theorist in the USA who has made a particular study of the *social* aspect of attachment behaviour. In Bell's study of the development of object constancy as it relates to infant-mother attachment, she noted that those infants who had an advanced sense of person-permanence had mothers who not only avoided even brief daily separations but also tended to go on frequent outings with their babies (1970, p. 309). These mothers provided their infants with the type of overlapping situation described above. In contrast, those infants who manifested ambivalent attachment towards their mothers and had a less well-developed sense of person constancy had mothers who rarely took their babies on outings and openly commented on negative aspects of the babies' temperaments. It seems that the enjoyable exploration of some third or novel element *with* another person generates a closer, more secure, attachment. Although the infant turns towards his mother and away from another person when afraid, lonely, ill, tired, etc., he may, at other times, seek proximity with her and simultaneously wish to explore something in the outside world. Mother and child may then face the world together, side by side, or hand in hand, or from the seat of the mother's knee. The ethologist, Niko Tinbergen has pointed out that *joining in* with a child in laughing at something else is itself bonding. When dealing with a toddler, it is important to squat so as to look at the world from the same level. At any age, he comments, 'laughing together at something or someone is one of the most strongly bonding behaviours known' (Tinbergen, 1972, p. 190). These observations serve to remind us that 'playing' is a fundamental part of life and that infants, as well as children, love to engage their mothers in such unbusiness-like activities.

In more recent formulations of attachment theory, it seems that there is a trend towards the investigation of the playful or exploratory contribution to the strength of the primary affectional bond. In this respect, there is a close link between this group of theorists and the interactional theorists to be discussed in the next chapter. In earlier formulations of the attachment view, proximity-seeking behaviours were stressed almost exclusively and the *growth* of attachment was linked to the development of the notion of person constancy. In my view, this has led to an underestimation of the infant's contribution to the strength of attachment during the first weeks and months of life. Bell, for instance, paraphrasing Ainsworth, Bowlby and Schaffer (another British attachment theorist), states that:

> an infant needs to have acquired at least an incipient awareness of the continuing existence of object absent to perception, and in particular of his mother as an object governed by the same physical laws, before he can become attached . . . It seems that, although an infant may be described as attached long before the symbolic processes characteristic of the final stage of object permanence have fully emerged, a primitive notion of permanence is a necessary precondition for the development of attachment. Evidence gathered so far suggests that this hypothesis is sound, since specific attachments emerge in the third quarter of the first year, at a time when Piaget anchors the beginnings of permanence. (Bell, 1970, p. 294)

It seems to me, however, that the infant's most primitive notion of permanence arises in the context of the mother's almost constant physical presence and holding, together with the increasingly familiar patterns of communication which develop between a particular mother and her child. At this stage, permanence means that the mother is around and available. The infant may be painfully aware of absence, and of the disruption of contact with one *specific* person, and yet still have no awareness of the continuing existence of the mother who is absent to his perception. Moreover, he is able to *recognise* his mother as a familiar person long before he has acquired a mental representation of her. A primitive conception of absence, the clear manifestation of a specific and intense attachment and a responsiveness to the familiar do not entail the concept of *two parallel continuities of existence* which is what object-permanence means. As long as the concept of attachment is anchored to the capacity to envisage the continued existence of objects or persons absent to perception, the existence of attachment prior to the third quarter of the first year remains obscured. This leads to an underestimation both of the infant's *competence* in eliciting responsiveness and of his *contribution* to mother-infant reciprocity in the first weeks of life.

The idea of a primary affectional bond and of an intense, loving relationship between mother and infant was (in the 1930s), and still is today, novel to the *psychoanalytic* theory of early infancy. In this chapter, I have drawn on the work of two outstanding figures in the history of psychoanalysis – Michael Balint and John Bowlby. Their view of infant–mother attachment can be seen as a development of one of Freud's ideas of a state of primary union between the infant and his surroundings (position 1) and as a variant of object-relations theory – a variant, however, which emphasises the positive, harmonious and interdependent, nature of the relationship.

4
Interactional synchrony and mutuality

Donald Winnicott

Donald Winnicott has been a pivotal figure in the development of child and family psychiatry and child psychoanalysis in Britain since the 1920s when he first started his career in paediatrics. As a member of the Middle-Group of psychoanalysts, neither wholly Freudian nor Kleinian, Winnicott's viewpoint is close to that of Balint and Bowlby in that he stresses the primacy of the mother–infant tie from the point of view of *both* mother and baby. Like Balint and Bowlby, he has made his psychoanalytic perspective accessible to the general public through his capacity to communicate with non-professionals as well as professionals who are not analysts, such as parents, nurses, midwives, social workers, general practitioners, paediatricians and teachers – that is, anyone who has entered the world of children. Like the above two authors, his written work has been addressed to both specialists and to the general public. His three small volumes (*The Child and the Family* (1957a), *The Child and the Outside World* (1957b), *The Family and Individual Development* (1965a)) are practical enough to have been broadcast and read by thousands, while his four volumes of collected papers (1958b, 1965b, 1971a, 1971b) form a major contribution to the specialised field of child psychoanalysis.

In his early paediatric practice, Winnicott dealt with children and their families who were not necessarily either physically or psychologically ill. Infants were observed in the immediate context of their families and, in particular, in interaction with their mothers. Like Bowlby, who also started his psychiatric career out in the field, Winnicott's experience gave him a keen eye for the environmental factor in child pathology. Again, like Bowlby, this 'field-experience' led Winnicott to a study of clinical illness or pathology and to a personal analysis as a necessary adjunct to the understanding of the inner life of man. In his later life, again somewhat parallel to Bowlby's interest in normal attachment, Winnicott became increasingly engrossed in that part of a normal child's life which *can* form the major focus of his day – namely, playing. His work in this area of play and creativeness is both original and revolutionary within the discipline of psycho-analysis. His focus on the normal, which is playing, led him to regard its absence as the hallmark of pathology. Some children, surprisingly enough, simply cannot play. Winnicott's thesis is that playing originates in the earliest to-and-fro relationship of mother and infant. Winnicott's acknowledgment of the relational contribution to the development of the inner world of the child did not obscure his remarkable insight into the 'phantasy' world of the child which, he realised, is only a personal, and therefore partial, reflection of the actual situation. His books, reporting his communications with the children who came to draw, play and talk in his consulting room, reflect his extraordinary skill in eliciting, and following, the intimate details of a child's thoughts and dreams (Winnicott, 1971a, 1971b).

In his 1970 paper on 'The mother–infant experience of mutuality', Winnicott observed that the recent study by psychoanalysts of very early mutual influences reflected a shift in attention from conflicts within the individual to the area of infant dependence where the environment cannot be ignored. Previously, the psychoanalyst 'was always fighting the battle for the individual against those who ascribed troubles to environmental influences' (1970, p. 246). In clinical practice, the psychoanalyst must concentrate on the one person whom he knows and on this person's contribution to the continuation of unsatisfactory relationships. However, when the findings which arise in the clinical situation are transferred to the psychoanalytic theory of infancy, the individual contribution is transcribed into drives and unconscious fantasies, erotic and aggressive or destructive and reparative, by which the infant is impelled from within. The fight for the individual has been won at the expense of the environmental contribution to his pattern of relationships. Winnicott reclaimed this factor, insisting that it had a respectable place in the discipline of psychoanalysis.

Like Bowlby, Winnicott concluded that the infant's absolute dependence on his environment requires us to conceptualise object-relationships in terms which do not imply 'the capacity to objectify' (1970, p. 247) – that is, the achievement of the concept of whole, separate persons out there existing in a parallel continuity to one's own existence. Winnicott states that 'the baby is a complex phenomenon that includes the baby's potential *plus* the environment' (1970, p. 248). Winnicott's thesis is that whatever the baby's *potential* towards integration, object-seeking, etc., the actualisation of normal attachment and independence depends upon the quality of mothering. Winnicott's earlier work is situated to some extent within Freud's framework. He talks of a three-month period of 'absolute dependence', which is complemented by the mother's 'primary maternal preoccupation', during which the securely held infant is barely aware of separateness. During the holding phase, 'primary process, primary identification, auto-erotism and primary narcissism are living realities' (Winnicott, 1960, p. 44). Later, influenced perhaps by Klein by whom he was supervised, Winnicott characterised the infant's object-relations in more active terms. In his later work, Winnicott took the step out of the Freudian account of the development of object-relating, which entailed the achievement of the capacity to objectify, into the contemporary framework of attachment theory and communication theory. All communication takes place in a context of relationships.

When Winnicott was trying to formulate his observations of mother–infant relationships made in his paediatric and early psychoanalytic practice, Klein had already proposed a theory of primary object-relating and a theory of communication *from the infant's point of view*. She conceptualised primitive communications in oral terms and described the baby's internal or phantasied relationship to the breast and the milk which flowed from, or was withheld by, it. However, although the breast-feeding model of early relationships and communication dominates Kleinian theory, Melanie Klein observed that an infant as young as three weeks may 'show unmistakable signs of love and of a developing interest in the mother' (Klein, 1952, p. 239). Klein *likened* the baby's interest to 'a loving conversation between mother and baby' (Klein, 1952, pp. 239–40) and commented that such behaviour indicated that gratification was as much related to the object which gives the food as to the food itself. Winnicott, benefiting from his Freudian background, his work with Klein, and his observations of a large number of infants and mothers, was able to state that the behaviour observed by Klein was not just *like*, but simply *was*, a loving conversation. Although Klein's theory of infant object-relations exploded the amoeba myth, any desire on the baby's part to engage harmoniously with another person was allotted a secondary place.

Winnicott states that, whereas all babies take in food, communication between baby and mother depends upon mutuality. In the language of communication theory (of which Winnicott seemed unaware), we would say that, since everything is communication, including zero messages such as a mother's lack of responsiveness, the experience of mutuality develops out of a particular type of interaction – namely, a harmonious and stimulating dialogue. In Winnicott's view, the experience of mutuality depends upon the mother's capacity 'to make real what the baby is ready to reach out for, to discover, to create' (Winnicott, 1970, p. 250). The mother teaches the baby mutuality by her adaptation and responsiveness. She brings to the situation her previous experiences of mutuality which she herself learned both as a baby and through her own experiences of baby-care. The baby, on the other hand, 'is being a baby for the first time' (p. 251) and has received no such instructions. All he brings is 'the sum of the inherited features and inborn tendencies toward growth and development' (p. 251). Winnicott stops short of the statement, made by the interactionists, that the baby also brings a tendency to *initiate* communication with his care-giver and to seek to harmonise his interactions with her.

To illustrate what an experience of mutuality might mean for a mother in communication with a baby of only a few days or weeks of age, Winnicott describes the rhythm of rocking as an aspect of holding. Here, instinctual drives are not particularly involved. The significant phenomena are 'the crude evidences of life, such as the heartbeat, breathing movements, breath warmth, movements that indicate a need for change of position, etc.' (p. 253). A mother may synchronise her rocking and walking with the baby's breathing. She might sing or hum a song that fits with the rocking rhythm. She finds just the right moment, non-interruptive, to put her baby down. He continues to breathe peacefully when the background rhythm has ceased. All this might sound like hard work or seem idealised, but Winnicott's point is that most mothers make these minute adjustments all the time without much thought. Indeed, a mother may only become aware of the need for, and task of, adjustment when something goes wrong – i.e. when there is negative feedback in the mother-infant system of communication.

In his analytic work, Winnicott was attuned to the transference of early experiences in the holding situation. In the analytic transference of primitive, non-verbal communications, the analyst may become painfully aware that a shift in his attention or a movement in his chair is felt by the patient as a failure to hold. 'The mind has dropped the patient' (p. 252). Winnicott observes that these cases put a strain on the analyst. There are long periods of quiescence (cf. Balint) and the room temperature may need to be higher than normal. Like Balint, Winnicott notes that these primitive or fundamental interactions are of 'the nature of silent communications; that is to say, the communication only becomes noisy when it fails' (p. 253). Winnicott's concept of holding includes putting the baby down when the moment comes for an impersonal experience of being held – that is, when the baby wishes to not interact without necessarily desiring to be alone. The silent communication is one of *reliability*, which protects the baby from the confusional states which occur when his line of life is broken up and he has to *react*. Without the experience of holding, the baby feels dropped and carries with him an experience of 'unthinkable or archaic anxiety' (p. 255). The baby becomes keenly aware of holding when it is absent or fails or is arhythmic and dissonant.

Winnicott's observations of the history of the theory of infant development in psychoanalysis are complemented by the following summary of changes in the field of infant psychology. 'In the course of this century, the newborn child has, first of all, had to convince us that he is not a vegetable, that he requires something more than just food and water; and he has succeeded in convincing us that he is a highly intelligent animal' (Bower, 1977, p. 27).

Winnicott, who died in 1971, might have been happy to find that his novel, sometimes disputed, ideas on the importance of mother–infant play have been supported by some of the psychological and paediatric research published in the last decade. Jerome Bruner is perhaps the most well-known of this group of psychologists whose research is focused on the cognitive and learning capacities of infants and children.

Thomas Bower

Thomas Bower, a professor of psychology at the University of Edinburgh, now an important centre of research on infant development, is an unusually lucid exponent of the intricate experiments which he and others have devised in support of their picture of the infant. Mutuality and play form a central theme in their theoretical framework. In Bower's view, the newborn emerges from the completely safe, stable and tranquil world of the womb into the world of conflicts and contradictions which is the normal psychological environment to which the infant primarily relates. I doubt whether intra-uterine life is as conflict-free, tranquil and safe as Bower describes. However, the important point is that the newborn begins to learn from the minute he emerges from the womb and, moreover, that he seeks involvement in his new environment rather than craving, as Freud maintained, the amoeboid state sustained in the womb.

Where Winnicott emphasised the communication which occurs in the quiet holding relationship between mother and infant, Bower's work is biased towards a study of the neonate's learning capacities and cognitive and communicational skills, all of which are clearly demonstrated by the movements and sounds that he directs both towards his specific communicational partner and towards the outside world. Bower produces experimental evidence to show that social behaviour and problem-solving behaviour are primary. The baby is seen by Bower as an active initiator, who brings an expectation of dialogue and play to his new situation. The concept of 'interactional synchrony' is more refined than the less specific concept of 'mutuality'. In line with the new emphasis on the infant's contribution, Bower gives a slightly different account of the mother's contribution to synchronous exchanges. He points out that, if mothers are strangers to their babies, the baby is an equally puzzling stranger to his mother. However experienced, a mother must learn to communicate with her baby so that the learning is a two-way process. The difference is that the mother brings more preconceptions to the situation which greatly affect the learning process. Winnicott makes a similar point with reference to both student analysis and new mothers. A student analyst sometimes does better analysis than he will do in a few years' time when he knows more. Similarly, mothers who have had several children begin to be so good 'at the technique of mothering that they do all the right things at the right moments, and then the infant who has begun to become separate from the mother has no means of gaining control of all the good things that are going on' (Winnicott, 1960, p. 51). To put the point another way, to each baby his mother is unique and unknown whereas, to a mother, a new baby may be just another baby.

Here are some of the experiments which Bower uses to support his views on neonatal learning, social behaviour and problem-solving.

1 The learning ability of newborns. Bower describes a very simple learning experiment 'in which newborn babies were placed in cribs with a special recording device that recorded the extent and direction of their head movements. At the sound of a tone, if the baby turned his head to the right he received a sweet-tasting solution in his mouth. If a buzzer sounded, the baby had to turn his head to the left to receive the sweet solution. It took only a few trials for these newborns to reach a state of perfect discrimination . . . without any confusion' (Bower, 1977, pp. 16–17). What is more, when the situation was reversed so that the response appropriate to the tone was now appropriate to the buzzer and vice versa, the babies who were no more than hours old were able to learn in about ten trials. They had to unlearn the first task in order to learn the second one. Bower enumerates various abilities demonstrated by this experiment besides the simple capacity for learning itself. The baby must be able to tell the *difference* between the sounds of a tone and a buzzer and between a head movement to the right and a head movement to the left. He must be able to make a *link* between tone, head movement, and sweet taste and between buzzer, head movement, and sweet taste. To do this, he must be able to *connect* three events that are separated in time. Furthermore, in order to reverse

the discriminaton, the baby must be able to *disconnect* the events that he had related and form a completely new set of connections.

The newborn has many perceptual, motor and social skills. He even has some intersensory co-ordination, as is demonstrated by his expectations that a sound is associated with the appearance of something to look at and that an approaching object will probably be tangible. An infant in the first week of life will defend himself from an approaching object by pulling his head back and interposing his hands between his face and the object. Bower thinks that such ready learning in the first few hours after birth should caution us against quick acceptance of any statement that an ability is innate or unlearned unless we can rule out any opportunity the baby might have had to form the connections. 'The newborn's ability to learn is so astonishing that it would need only the slightest exposure for any connection to be learned' (1977, p. 17).

2 The social abilities of newborns. Bower comments upon the extensive literature which exists on processes of socialisation – that is, 'how the baby comes to be socialized, how he comes to realize that he is a human being, how he comes to have special sets of responses to people that are not elicited by anything else in his environment'. In Bower's view, which is also my own, much of this effort has been wasted 'because right from the moment of birth the baby realizes he is a human being and has specific responses elicited only by other human beings' (p. 28). A spectacular demonstration of this is the fact that babies less than a week old will *imitate* other people.

> If the baby's mother, or some other adult, sticks out her tongue at the baby, within a relatively short time the baby will begin to stick his tongue back out at her. Suppose she then stops sticking her tongue out and begins to flutter her eyelashes; the baby will flutter his eyelashes back. If she then starts to open and close her mouth, for example, the baby will begin to open his mouth in synchrony. Of course, the baby will also stick out his tongue, flutter his eyelashes, and open his mouth spontaneously, but he does it to a far greater extent if there is an adult model present. (p. 28)

Bower remarks upon the amazing intersensory mapping which must go on for the baby to be able to look at an adult sticking out her tongue and then transform this information so that he knows, in this social situation, that he should stick his tongue out in return. An astonishing amount of built-in intersensory co-ordination is implied in the newborn's ability to imitate. All these capacities seem to have a *social* purpose. The baby seems to engage in imitation as a social game and for pure enjoyment. The baby does not have to be given anything, such as food, in order to get him to engage in the imitation game. He finds pleasure in human company itself and not as a result of associating adults with food or relief from pain.

A related social behaviour displayed by newborns is described by Bower as 'interactional synchrony'. This terms refers to a form of behaviour which is characteristic of all human communication – the body movements and actions which accompany speech. Kinesic analysis reveals that the closer the synchrony of movements between two adults, the closer the rapport between them. All these movements convey *meaning* which may be at variance with communication at the verbal level. Condon and Sander conducted a study of infants about twelve hours old (Condon and Sander, 1974). The infants were presented with tape recordings of spoken English, isolated vowel sounds, regular tapping noises, and spoken Chinese, as well as with a straightforward adult speaker. Whereas the tapping and isolated vowel sounds produced no response, the babies who were born in the north-east USA displayed synchrony with Chinese as well as standard American English. These findings indicate that the newborn is far from a social isolate. 'Right from the beginning, he participates immediately and deeply in communication' (p. 35). From the very beginning, the newborn will use his extraordinary learning and perceptual abilities to serve his social needs and social wishes. In the first days of life, the baby forms social attachments, as demonstrated by studies which show that babies protest strongly when a substitute care-taker is provided after only a few days of care by one person.

These findings contradict the primary narcissism/auto-erotism thesis in which speech has a function of unburdening the infant of tension. The newborn, unlike the adult, picks up the segments or units of human speech in order to move in precise rhythm with them. An adult is often incapable of this. He tends to experience a foreign language as a meaningless flow of sounds in much the same way as people have regarding the meaningless babbling of a young infant. Bower points out that the newborn is prepared to participate in all possible linguistic communities. This amazing repertoire becomes restricted, after the first six months, to the particular language community in which the baby lives. Studies of the noise-making aspects of language completely obscure the communicational capacities of babies and their desire for 'togetherness' which is demonstrated by their enjoyment of mutual imitation games and interactional synchrony.

3 Problem-solving in newborns. Studies of smiling have demonstrated that babies will smile from 'intellectual pleasure' (Bower, 1977, p. 46) as well as social pleasure. When a baby discovers a contingency between some action of his own and its predictable effect on the world, he may smile vigorously. The pleasure, unrelated to food or social reward, seems to reflect the discovery of something about the causal structure of the world and his own control over it. A newborn may learn in order to obtain a sweet taste, but many babies are equally happy to learn in order to switch on a projector, make a mobile move, or make an adult jump up in a game of peek-a-boo. The Czech psychologist Papousek discovered that the actual characteristics of the event which the baby managed to produce were quite unimportant. The important element was the *relationship* between a given behaviour and a given event in the external world. Papousek also noted that babies would usually stop performing once they had discovered the connection; however, if the contingency was changed, as for example when a light would come on if the baby turned his head to the right instead of to the left, there would be a rapid burst of activity until the baby figured out the movement required to switch on the light. Again, there would be vigorous smiling and cooing and then a diminution of activity until the problem was made more complex again (Bower, 1977, pp. 42–4).

In another experiment, two groups of babies were given identical mobiles except that one group was given control over the movement of the mobiles whereas the second group had no such control. The group of babies who could set their mobiles in motion by moving their cribs smiled and cooed while they were controlling the mobiles. The other group attended to the mobiles but did not coo or smile to any significant extent (Bower, 1977, p. 44).

The conclusion which may be drawn from this research is that problem-solving in itself, like communication, is motivating and pleasurable to babies. Again, we do not have to look for ways to make babies learn or acquire knowledge just as we do not have to look for ways to make babies socialised and attached to specific others. Tinbergen has also stated that there are specific behaviour patterns, the exclusive function of which is to create the opportunity to learn certain things (Tinbergen, 1964, p. 167).

4 Communication and the development of separation and stranger anxiety. In keeping with Bower's claims about the strength of attachment in newborns, he observes that a baby of only two weeks of age may show some aversion when a stranger speaks to him. Similarly, a baby of this age may become upset if a stranger looks after him in his mother's absence. Bower outlines a standard pattern in the development of stranger and separation anxiety as these two separate phenomena relate to attachment. The standard pattern of development is *from single to multiple attachments*. As the baby grows older, he forms more and more attachments and the departure of any of these people can lead to protest. In a study of separation anxiety at eighteen months by Schaffer and Emerson (1964), only 13 per cent of the babies in the sample had one target for their separation anxiety and as many as one-third of the babies protested at the departure of five individuals. Schaffer (1971) suggests that the characteristic that determines whether or not a particular adult will become the object of the baby's separation anxiety is the *social attentiveness of the adult to the baby*. Physical care is less important than social interaction.

Bower questions the link made by Spitz between *stranger* fear and *separation* anxiety. In Spitz's view, the sight of the stranger reminds the child that his mother is not there. However, although there is usually an absence of stranger fear when a child is on his mother's lap, Bower has observed a similar absence of stranger fear when a baby is in a strange environment with his mother completely absent. If a baby is in a strange and novel environment, particularly in the open air, he may even approach a stranger. The most extreme reaction to a stranger usually occurs when an infant is approached by a stranger when his mother is *present*, but not holding him.

Bower, developing Schaffer's view of *separation* anxiety, puts forward a communicational explanation of *stranger* anxiety as it relates to attachment formation. Using the concept of interactional synchrony, Bower points out that each baby and mother develop a specific communicational style. When the mother leaves the baby with a stranger, the baby loses his 'communicational partner' and is left with someone who does not speak the same 'language' (Bower, 1977, p. 56). The stranger usually cannot respond to the baby's particular social gestures, social invitations, and social ploys so that, in effect, the baby is left alone. 'He is isolated from other adults by the very development of the communication routines he shares with his mother' (p. 56). Bower's point is that, although the *newborn* is prepared to interact with anyone in any language community, his propensity to form close, social attachments and to learn to synchronise with the most available and attentive person around (usually his mother) leads him to expect precise patterns of interchange and to expect newcomers to respond appropriately.

According to this view, we would expect that stranger anxiety, combined with separation from familiar figures, would diminish with developments in the child's range of communicational skills. A child, who has *confined* his amazing neonatal repertoire to the communicational games of the most prominent figures in his environment, must thereafter *expand* his skills so that he may again communicate with anyone. Thus, a child whose communication is finely attuned to his mother will usually experience more intense separation anxiety but, with the acquisition of speech, his anxieties may again diminish. Just as the inability to communicate in a world of strangers is responsible for the rise of separation anxiety, the mastery of communicational skills is responsible for its decline (p. 58). Thus, both stranger anxiety and separation anxiety rise and fall with the contraction and expansion of the child's communicational skills. Bower makes the interesting point that an eight-month-old baby will only show stranger fear when a stranger makes an overt attempt to communicate with the baby. As long as the stranger makes no particular attempt to interact, the baby will usually show no particular aversion. 'From the baby's standpoint, he is being approached by someone much larger than he is, who is addressing him in a foreign tongue, obviously expecting to be understood. It is not surprising that such a situation is fear provoking' (p. 59). In an experiment with babies of only three months of age, Wahler (1967) found that the babies.smiled *more* at the stranger *before* he tried to interact with them. Instead of being a source of pleasure, the stranger's overtures were simply a source of puzzlement. The stranger was not using the customary communicational routines. Bower remarks that babies of this age will usually show puzzlement rather than the more extreme fear manifested a few months later (1977, p. 59).

Bower's conclusion is that a baby must develop a certain level of *communicational* ability in order to form the kind of attachment evidenced by stranger and separation anxiety. Bower contrasts his view not only with traditional psychoanalytic and learning theory explanations of the growth of attachment but also with the ethological view. Rather than a critical period for attachment formation, as in imprinting, it is the ability to learn which is critical. Since communicational skills are *learned*, it is possible for a baby to acquire this learning at any point, even if it becomes more difficult as he gets older. Stranger anxiety not only demonstrates the achievement of true object-relations or attachment proper as is usually thought, but also that the baby lacks the communicational skills to converse with unfamiliar persons. The elaborate and specific communicational game devised by himself and his mother precludes him from more varied social exchanges.

The theme of the book *The Effect of the Infant on its Caregiver* (1974), edited by Michael Lewis and Leonard Rosenblum, is 'the impact of the infant as *a source of* the formation, regulation and, indeed, even the malevolent distortion, of the caregiver's behaviour' (p. ix). Contrary to the belief of the primary fusion theorists, these authors state that, even at birth, the infant is no 'mere passive recipient of stimulation from those around him, ready to be molded like clay on the potters wheel' (p. ix). The contributors to this volume, whom I take as representative of the interactionist point of view, wish to capture the dynamic elements of the developmental system of infancy through 'a dyadic study'. However, as with many interactionist studies, a key issue is the delineation of the *individual contribution*.

When questions of the individual contribution arise, the interactionist or 'flow' model suffers from difficulties which arise when systems theory is applied to individual human beings. For instance, the point of *entry* into the flow system may mislead a researcher into thinking that a particular behaviour is an initiator.

On the most general level, the interactionists believe that a dyadic relationship cannot be understood by a study of elements in isolation. However, on the individual level, it is extremely difficult to specify which constructs may be deemed sufficiently stable and hard as to say that this *particular* baby or mother brought this particular characteristic to the relationship. One can think of physical characteristics such as arousal level, sexual differences, etc., and mental or personality characteristics such as happiness or liveliness. For instance, 'an "optimistic" mother may interpret the withdrawal of infant gaze as an interest in something else, whereas another mother might interpret this to mean that the infant is tired of looking at her' (p. xviii).

Obviously the plan, strategy or ideology of the adult member of the dyad is more easily studied than that of the infant. A conceptualisation of 'infant ideology' is totally lacking. But even adult ideology is full of ambiguity. Consider the term 'responsiveness'. Value judgments are involved. One mother may 'respond to an infant's cry with vocalisation, holding, and rocking' whereas another may respond by 'just looking at' the infant. Investigation of their ideologies reveals that one mother believes that the infant should just cry it out so that he learns that he cannot have what he wants all the time and that the other mother believes the infant should be protected from a cold world as long as possible. 'Both parents seek to teach their infants, and both are responsive, but their ideologies result in different behaviours' (Lewis and Rosenblum, 1974, p. xx).

In discussing mother–infant relationships, Richard Bell (1974) makes a valuable distinction between aversive and appetitive behavioural systems. Aversive behaviours include providing life support and protection. The parent acts to *avoid* undesirable outcomes. This system has been the main focus of study by those psychologists and psychoanalysts who emphasise the need-satisfying aspect of infant attachment. The parent modulates the infant's anxiety, satisfies his hunger and keeps him warm and safe. Appetitive behaviours involve mutual, reciprocal social interactions in which both parents and offspring behave so as to produce or maintain the behaviour of the other. This system features complementarity, reciprocity and play (p. 2). Bell observes that, when care-giving demands are reduced, spontaneous play interactions are much more likely to occur. To illustrate, Bell points out that a common case of colic maximises caregiving interactions and minimises social interactions (p. 8). This observation correlates with the view of Ainsworth and Bowlby that proximity-seeking behaviours and exploratory behaviours are generally mutually exclusive and also with the important distinction drawn by Winnicott between playing and 'fantasying'. Winnicott's view of play is that it is not merely a *representation* of a child's phantasies about the care-giving aspects of the relationship such as feeding, defaecating, etc. Playing is 'a thing in itself', which flourishes when more circumscribed, need-oriented, interactions are in abeyance. This observation holds for both parent and child. When an infant's responses have positive value for the parents, their appetitive behaviours are usually generated and they seek to maintain and renew playful contact.

Bell considers that proximity is a necessary, but not a sufficient, condition of socialisation (p. 9). Attachment behaviours, such as smiling and vocalisation, maintain a mother in social interaction and facilitate play and novelty. When secure, both mother and infant respond well to novelty, which in turn increases attentiveness. Bell points out that a mother who maintains a care-giving system may not know much about her infant, whereas a mother who functions both as a care-giver and as a partner in social interaction is likely to be more aware of the novel behaviours showing up in each period. The push towards novelty is particularly visible in an infant's increasing interest in peer interaction. Peers generally provide more activity and variety in stimulation.

Bell makes an interesting distinction between maturity and competence (p. 14). In most psychoanalytic studies, these qualities are thought to be interchangeable. However, the parent, who is obviously more mature and capable of intentional behaviour, may nevertheless not be as competent as the infant in eliciting a certain level of responsiveness. The neonate brings a set of highly effective behaviours to the interaction which are extremely compelling in bringing about support and protection. Most people comment that they find an infant's cries particularly difficult to ignore and, if intolerable, have to remove themselves from earshot.

Interactional synchrony and mutuality

Terry Brazelton

A major exponent of the interactionist view is Terry Brazelton. Like Winnicott, Brazelton is a paediatrician. Through a series of fascinating and simple volumes illustrating infant development, Brazelton's research is influencing parents and child care professionals throughout the USA (Brazelton, 1969). In *The Effect of the Infant on its Caregiver* (Lewis and Rosenblum, 1974), Brazelton describes the cyclical, rhythmic nature of mother–infant interaction. There is an *attention–withdrawal cycle* which cuts across different behavioural patterns such as feeding, changing, etc. Brazelton, Koslowski and Main conducted a study of five white middle-class mothers with normal full-term infants who were seen once weekly at the Harvard Center for Cognitive Studies. The development of interactional behaviour was studied from birth to four months of age. Brazelton also compared the infant's interaction with his mother to his behaviour with an object. In relation to an object, the switch from attention to disruption was much more sudden. The state of intense, rapt attention would build up to a peak which was suddenly disrupted by the infant turning away from the object or becoming active and fussy. In relation to the mother's interactive responsiveness, both build-up and decrease were gradual.

Brazelton divides a period of interaction into seven segments:

- I) *Initiation* when the infant begins to look at his mother with dull eyes and a relaxed face and slowly moving limbs.
- II) *Orientation* in which the baby looks towards his mother with brightened eyes and face and with his extremities extended towards her.
- III) As the mother responds, the infant assumes a state of *attention* in which he alternatively extends and receives cues.
- IV) *Acceleration* in which his body activity increases and often builds up to a vocalisation.
- V) *Peak of excitement* in which behaviour may be jerky and intense.
- VI) *Deceleration* in which the baby's bright look dims, his eyes dull down and seem to lid over and he becomes

more relaxed with fading vocalisations. Yawning and blinking may increase and reaching out is replaced by holding onto himself.

VII) *Withdrawal* or turning away in which the baby has a more glazed or dull expression and his eyes and face are not oriented towards the mother. If he builds up to an intense looking-away state, he may begin to focus on an object in the room. If the interaction has not gone well, more intense withdrawal and rejection may occur. The infant may actively withdraw or push at the object or he may withdraw into sleep or start to fuss and cry. (Brazelton, Koslowski and Main, 1974, pp. 56–9)

Brazelton *et al.* found that the most important rule for maintaining interaction was a mother's sensitivity to her infant's capacity for attention. The most prolonged interaction was maintained by short and smooth periods of attention and withdrawal. Brazelton postulates that the homeostatic model which underlies the neonate's physiological repertoire may also regulate his communicational system. A mother may respond by adjusting her rhythm to her baby's and by adding her cues only when the infant demonstrates receptiveness; or she may not respond to the baby's rhythm and continue with a steady bombardment; or she may also establish her own rhythm to regulate his. The first type of response increases the interaction, the second rapidly dulls the infant's attention and increases his active withdrawal, the third results in out-of-phase, unsatisfying periods of interaction. A crucial feature is the mother's allowing for reciprocity, particularly when this is manifested by the cyclic turning away of the baby from her (pp. 66–7). If the mother can allow her engagement to subside as the infant decreases his attention, then he is much more likely to look back and to build up intense interaction again.

Brazelton *et al.* also found that the 'holding' environment provided by the mother was crucial; in this environment, Brazelton includes the mother's reduction of 'interfering' behaviour such as hunger, wetness, sleeplessness, etc. These states are called interfering in that they often interrupt ongoing social interaction. Like Winnicott, Brazelton believes that mothers have very different ways of 'holding' their infants; a mother may hold with her arms, her face, her gestures, her voice or by caressing, smiling, rocking, patting etc. (p. 70). Mothers also vary in their flexibility and capacity to substitute one holding behaviour for another. Brazelton observed that flexibility in the nuances of behavioural patterns was necessary for the maintenance of optimal interaction. Mothers vary in their capacity both to substitute behaviours and to qualify a specific behaviour by a change, for instance, in force (e.g. of patting), tempo (e.g. rocking) and distance (e.g. kissing or nodding) (p. 72).

Brazelton thinks that the attachment model may be too simple since the rules governing interaction are extremely complex. The interdependency of *rhythms* may be at the root of mother–infant attachment as well as such factors as proximity and reliability (p. 74). In the early weeks, the mother's capacity for learning has a great deal of influence on the interaction which develops. One of the most important rules which the mother has to learn is her baby's capacity for attention. Also, she must learn which of the behaviours set up an expectancy for interaction, which 'hold' him, which echo his responses, etc. All these maternal behaviours, demonstrating responsiveness, may appear to be unlearned: yet cases of failure demonstrate that a kind of rule-learning is involved. The rules for interaction are in constant change. As Winnicott states, an infant may only be aware of his holding when it fails. The adoption of a particular rule is the outcome of a large number of restraints. Imitation and the enlargement of the baby's communications are also of consequence since it is through complexity and novelty that the baby *learns to learn*.

Thus, on the interactionist view, the interdependence of rhythms leads to positive attachment as well as to harmonious communication. These authors observe that the strength and interdependence of the dyad is directly related to the synchrony of interaction and to the smoothness of adjustment called forth by the activities of the growing infant.[1] As the infant learns how to master his gross physiological needs, he frees his attention for learning about the external world.

In my view, the interactionists add a valuable dimension to the development of both object-relations theory and attachment theory. The distinction between the caretaking and the social aspects of infant relationships, together with the observation that play and attention to novelty (the appetitive system) flourish when caretaking behaviours (the aversive system) are reduced, brings an entirely new perspective into the psychoanalytic theory of infant development and the origins of communication. In the discipline of psychoanalysis, Winnicott is alone in his belief that playing is at the root of the capacity to communicate and to enjoy life.

In the preceding four chapters, I have attempted to outline various representations of the young infant. Using the work of key figures in the disciplines of psychoanalysis, child ethology and developmental psychology, I present a picture which changes in outline and detail from blurred to sharp. Moving from left to right on my spectrum, we start with an ill-defined, murky picture in which the infant is barely aware of himself or his surroundings; his mother is almost invisible. In position two, we envisage a lively, mentally complex infant who is driven to relate to his 'internal' mother or 'phantasy' mother (or her breast) because of the persecutory forces he feels both within and without. In position three, the infant is again active, but he is positively linked to his mother in a mutual affectional system. In position four, the infant is portrayed as not only active and positive, but also as competent to engage other people in the most intense, intimate and interesting dialogue with himself. The infant jumps into focus and out at us, demanding not only our care and sympathy, but also our enjoyment and laughter.

I suggest that the early mother–infant relationship should not be described as 'narcissistic' unless one interprets the term, and the myth after which it is named, in a relational context. If this earliest type of intense, reflective (i.e. mirroring, echoing and imitating) relationship does not change so as to permit differentiation, various narcissistic pathologies ensue. One of these is described in the mythological account of the tragic deaths of the beautiful youth Narcissus and the talkative nymph Echo.

5
Narcissus: an 'average' history

Let us now turn to the myth and read of the birth of the hero, Narcissus, and the unfolding relationship between him and his mother, Leiriope. In the words Freud used to describe his reconstruction of the Oedipus legend (Freud, 1939), the following account is presented as an 'average' story of Narcissus' short life. We are told that Leiriope gave birth to 'a child with whom one could have fallen in love even in his cradle, and she called him Narcissus' (Ovid, 1955, p. 83). Through the naming of her child, Leiriope already announces some of her expectations. Graves tells us that the narcissus was also called 'leirion' (Graves, 1955, p. 288). The leirion was a three-petalled blue fleur-de-lys or iris which was sacred to the Triple-Goddess and worn as a chaplet when the Three Solemn Ones, or Erinnyes, were being placated. It flowers in the late autumn, shortly before the 'poet's narcissus', which, Graves says, is perhaps why Leiriope has been described as Narcissus' mother. Leiriope means literally the face of (-ope) the leirion. It appears, therefore, that the narcissus flower either had another name, the leirion, or it closely superseded the flowering of the leirion. We may infer from Leiriope's choice of a name that a child represented a strong wish for closeness and even for the birth of a version of herself.

Graves also tells us that the narcissus flower was used as a placebo while the oil of the narcissus was a well-known narcotic. For some mothers, a 'perfect' baby is a pleasing baby who sleeps well, is easy to soothe and who in turn soothes his mother. He functions as a placebo. A mother may fear the demands of an alert baby, particularly if she has been brought up to believe that babies need to sleep a lot during the first months. Mothers who were brought up on the strict schedule feeding and sleeping of the 1930s and 1940s in the UK and the USA would not expect that a baby could enjoy a rhythmic alternation between quiet and social interaction.

During my psychoanalytic training, I visited a 'very good' and 'placid' baby. When I arrived to observe each week, the mother told me that her baby was upstairs asleep. Several times, I climbed up the four floors to the nursery where I would find that the baby was lying noiselessly in her cot completely awake. It amazed me that such a young baby could be so amenable as to lie alone for hours. Although this baby was quite alert and in no way insensible, the atmosphere in the room was one of loneliness. I would sit down beside Tanya's cot. She would look towards me and then back to her immediate cot-environment. In turn, I would look at her and sometimes lean over and try to engage her with smiles, noises and, later, toys. When I tried to join in her 'space', I felt that we were up in the clouds in a no-man's land of stillness and quiet.

Tanya lived very much in a world of her own, but she could not be called a 'narcissistic' little girl. She may well have grown up to be an Echo. Her mother became extremely attached to an Irish setter. Tanya's silence and compliance complemented the intrusive, bouncy and demanding behaviour of the dog. The mother spent quite a lot of time and energy shouting, slapping and whipping him. As he grew bigger, the two of them engaged in all-in wrestling matches, in which he stood up on his hind legs with his front paws on her shoulders, snorting and licking her face. When Tanya ate solid foods and drank from a cup, which she accomplished very early, Hercules immediately sipped at the cup, and licked up the purée and custard from her bowl. Tanya's mother intervened in a giggling-teasing kind of way. She constantly remarked on Hercules' jealousy but seemed to be unaware of the provocation to which Tanya was subjected. Tanya was always just behind, and secondary to, Hercules. One day, Mother asked me on arrival whether she had told me about Tanya's dreadful cough. 'Well, she had this awful cough and I took her round to lots of doctors, I even had her X-rayed and then one day Hercules barked and I realised that Tanya was imitating him. My friends says the dog is a nanny-substitute. I said I don't know about that, but he certainly is a constant in her life. He is so mean to her and yet she seems to like him.' There was a great similarity between Hercules' and Tanya's vocalisations. She modelled her crawling quite obviously on Hercules, whom she followed around the room. After eighteen months, the family moved away, Hercules was sent to a dog's corrective home, and I was unable to observe Tanya's further development. My point in relating these incidents is that a baby, who is born to please and who is not seen as a developing centre of initiative, may develop placatory and echolalic qualities.

Narcissus' fate was to be pleasing (especially to the eye) and to be pleased. The mother of a narcissistic person may have had an unusual difficulty in separating herself from her baby's distress. She may have over-fed her baby in order to placate him as quickly as possible. All 'good-enough' mothers try to avoid distress during the early months. Some will continue to devote their lives to pacification, while others will gradually tolerate a certain level of distress as an essential part of the process of differentiation. The excessively pleasing mother–baby relationship will tend to break down irrevocably. Either things go perfectly smoothly, or they are intolerably rough. The child's temper tantrums can be 'panic tantrums' at the unbearable experience of separateness. Neither the child nor the parent(s) realise that it is not the love of the other which is lost forever, but the narcissistic relationship of mutual placation which cannot hold up and weather the storms of growing up and of individuation.

In the first paragraph of the myth, we are also told that everyone was in love with Narcissus 'even in his cradle'. This observation is central to my interpretation of narcissism. Narcissism does not refer to some primary 'cathexis' (i.e. energetic involvement) of the self. Narcissus falls in love with *his own image*. Narcissism has to do with looking and with reflection, with the eyes and the mirror. The first image or outline to which the human infant orientates visually is the human face. Normally, the infant further selects out the face of the mother. As he comes to familiarise himself with its contours, what does he find there? The mother's face reflects how she sees her baby. This reflection may mirror either the baby's or the mother's own feelings and mood or, optimally, the interaction or overlap between these two.

Freud used the term 'primary narcissism' to refer to the intrapsychic state of the infant. He assumed that the baby's omnipotence and needs rendered him relatively inflexible and unadaptable in comparison to his parents. However, unlike his parents, the infant is growing into being human and he is capable of doing this in an *infinite* number of ways. The mother aids the child's actualisation of his potential adaptations so that he becomes the child of a particular mother. The child responds to her unique needs and moods which have taken a *lifetime* in which to evolve. Long before Narcissus could use his eyes to see his own reflection and to fall in love with himself, others were in love with him. You will often find that the adult Narcissus, whom you see in therapy, was adored by his mother. He has suffered from having a 'doting' mother whom, inevitably, he has scorned. As a poorly individuated adult, his problem is that he can never find anyone who is as 'doting' as he expects, but who is not also besotted and, therefore, inferior in his eyes. The overwhelming effect of unconditional admiration and adoration can become painfully obvious during adolescence when a young person is sickened and infuriated by his mother's worshipful preoccupation.

We are told that Leiriope was the first to test the reliability of the blind seer, Teiresias. Like many mothers, Leiriope wishes that her son will have some unique and portentous future. An interesting aside to this tale is the history of the soothsayer, in particular, the circumstances which surrounded his gift of prophecy. Teiresias is a blind seer, who has been unsighted as a punishment for his view of a lovers' dispute. The interloper in a godly dyad meets the same fate – loss of sight – as may befall a young child whose curiosity is felt to intrude into the forbidden parental union. This is the moral which Freud drew from the story of Oedipus in which Teiresias again plays a telling role. When the curiosity of a young child is not met, satisfied or modified with tact or explanation, it may atrophy. A sense of either disgust, apathy, or phobia towards the act of knowing will develop or, sometimes, an irresoluble suspiciousness about the unfamiliar or dissonant. The histories of some 'autistic' children and children with 'learning problems' often include unusual precocity. Like Teiresias, their loss of normal sight is recompensed by the development of extraordinary sensibilities.

Freud's own life was blessed with such prophecies. He was

born with a caul which was believed to ensure future happiness. Freud wrote of the impression made upon him by his mother's pride and love. ' "A man who has been the indisputable favourite of his mother keeps for life the feeling of a conqueror, the confidence of success that often induces real success" ' (Jones, 1961, p. 6). In contrast to the picture of Narcissus which I have drawn, the love and pride Freud received from his mother included her wish for his success and victory. If her love emanated confidence in his unique capabilities, it freed him from the type of parasitic symbiosis I portrayed in my imagined picture of the relationship between Leiriope and Narcissus. Ernest Jones relates how 'when one day an old woman whom the young mother encountered by chance in a pastry shop fortified this [belief] by informing her that she had brought a great man into the world, the proud and happy mother believed firmly in the prediction.' Jones tells us that Freud was not to don the hero's garb so easily. Freud wrote: ' "Such prophecies must be made very often; there are so many happy and expectant mothers, and so many old peasant women and other old women who, since their mundane powers have deserted them, turn their eyes towards the future; and the prophetess is not likely to suffer for her prophecies" ' (Jones, 1961, p. 5).

However, when at the age of eleven, the story was strengthened by a new prophecy, Freud was willing to be slightly impressed:

> 'One evening, at a restaurant in the Prater, where my parents were accustomed to take me when I was eleven or twelve years of age, we noticed a man who was going from table to table, and for a small sum, improvising verses upon any subject given to him. I was sent to bring the poet to our table, and he showed his gratitude. Before asking for a subject he threw off a few rhymes about myself, and told us that if he could trust his inspiration I should probably one day become a "Minister". I can still distinctly remember the impression produced by this second prophecy.' (Jones, 1961, p.5)

Jones goes on to say how Freud made an early identification with Hannibal, and had boyish phantasies of military distinction which later gave place to the ambition of being a culture hero; when he dreamed that some day he would be commemorated by a portrait bust in the Aula of the University, the inscription that he hoped would be thought appropriate to him was the line from Oedipus the King: 'Who solved the riddle of the Sphinx and was a man most mighty.'

To Leiriope's question to the soothsayer, Will he 'live to a ripe old age?, the answer comes Yes, 'provided that he never know himself' (Graves, 1955, p. 286). As in the Oedipus story, we have an answer which, like many a riddle and the cryptic words of the Oracle, seems to be 'nothing but empty words'. Freud's scepticism reflects the view that riddles and prophecy are nonsensical.

However, in the Narcissus myth, we are told that the prophecy was justified by the outcome of events: 'the strange madness which afflicted the boy and the nature of his death proved its truth' (Ovid, 1955, p. 83). In my analysis of this myth, Teiresias' answer contains a diagnosis of the particular affliction which befell Narcissus and which I take to be a characteristic of narcissism. Just as Oedipus suffers from knowing too much about himself, so Narcissus cannot survive the first taste of knowledge. For Narcissus, to be is to not know. So-called 'narcissistic' children do not reach the oedipal stage at the onset of which the child embarks on the quest for knowledge or, as Freud put it, 'the first grand problem of life' (Freud, 1908, p. 212). Their existence depends on the closeness of a two-person relationship which shuts out otherness, the third term, the intrusion of anything (or anyone) new and different. Difference cannot be found *in* one thing, nor can it occur *in* or *between* two things. Difference is the contrast between two things. It can only arise if there is another point of view or reference point outside the two things. It is only from such a vantage point that any information about them, which entails comparison between them, may arise.

In the myths of Narcissus and Oedipus, we watch a drama move from an auspicious beginning to a tragic end. Each man ceases to be a hero and comes to exist as a representation, as an 'object' completed and fixed. The will and strength of each, which at first seems considerable, is insufficient to combat the forces which pull each man away from the contingencies of life towards a death which is both untimely and foreseen. Life turns into tragedy when change is no longer possible. Thus, it is not surprising that Freud's mind was drawn to tragedy when he set about the formidable task of undoing the fixations of his patients by the investigation, and reconstruction, of their early history. The neurotic lives out a representation – a picture fixed in time – of what went on before. The tragedy in each case is the transformation of a life into an artifact. At a certain point, living stopped and life became partial. The task of the analysis is to replace representation by action so that the person no longer thinks of himself as an object completed but as an agent in an unfolding drama. Instead of 'I knew that would happen', one wants to exclaim 'I never would have expected that to happen, even in my wildest dreams' – the wildest dreams are nearly always part of the person's fixation.

Narcissus is a grown man who has missed out on the act which normally brings the age of narcissism to a close. With the act of grasping, the infant is freed to begin on his search to find the optimal distance between himself and his 'object', which is the primary task of the individuation process. Narcissus' life ends in tragedy because of omission. He is unable to grasp the image he loves so dear. His 'problem' is over an unattainable proximity. He grasps in vain. We might say that Narcissus does not know what an 'object' is. The act of grasping is essential to the young child's comprehension of externality, or 'objectness', itself. The met grasp challenges the child's expectations and projections; it may fit or enlarge them.

In many of the narcissistic relationships which I have seen and read about, the history of the Narcissus has revealed an exclusive and possessive closeness with one parent, usually the mother, and an excluding or remote relationship with the other. There is no external dyad to be excluded from or to be curious about. In many cases, either the father has been physically absent or he has been preoccupied or passive. To the child, one parent just does not seem to figure. Baby and parent form the couple. No member of the triad is able to make the transition from the 'nursing couple' to the sexual couple, which demands a tolerance of exclusion.

Narcissus, the object of prophecy of the blind seer who had been both man and woman, enters adolescence, as we might expect: with 'a stubborn pride in his own beauty', his path 'strewn with heartlessly rejected lovers of both sexes' (Graves, 1955, p. 286). In adolescence, narcissism or echolalia, which have been latent, may come to a head. The teenage love affair may reproduce many features of the early relationship between infant and mother. Until recently, adolescents, along with narcissistic patients of all ages, were thought by some analysts to be unamenable to psychoanalytic treatment. Some analysts now have changed their opinion with respect to narcissistic disorders; in turn, this change has affected attitudes towards the treatment of adolescents (Goldberg, 1972, pp. 3–7). These analysts recognise that the narcissistic type of relationship has a place in normal, pre-oedipal development but that, under certain inter-personal circumstances, relationships of this type may give rise to specific disorders – in particular, those surrounding separation and individuation. Understanding of the early two-person relationship leads to an understanding of its potential pathologies, many of which seem to erupt at the onset of adolescence.

During adolescence, there is usually a revival of narcissistic features because the adolescent is involved in a struggle for separateness and individuation which often takes the form of a preoccupation with his 'identity' or his 'image'. It may be the adolescent's ideas or preconceptions about identity which cause him trouble, quite apart from any specific identity he may wish to avoid or emulate. His day-to-day struggle for individuation involves quite new experiences of separateness in terms of both physical space and thought. The adolescent, unlike the infant, has the capacity to distance himself from his parents. He knows that departure from home is imminent and essential. Acute anxieties and ambivalence over this future event often interfere with his capacities to *think about* detachment. Phobias and acts of delinquency are common. The adolescent feels that he must stay within, or go outside, fixed boundaries. He may want to sever all ties, to cut, obliterate or break in. He may try to blot out his parents through an angry departure or an enforced exile (say through delinquent acts), or through ascetic withdrawal in which hostility and confrontation are redirected or disowned. However, if repetitive 'acting-out' is to be avoided, independent actions must be matched with independence of thought. When a young person gets involved in 'acting out' the leap, he defies the law, he skips school, hoodwinks authority or seeks the supernatural, which he wrongly conceives to be a place. Psychoanalysis often seems to be ineffective because the adolescent will not attend. The adolescent is not able to use the analytic approach to the extent that he cannot make a leap in consciousness but only in action. He may sometimes be right, since analysis at this point in life is useful only if it does not pre-empt the adolescent's acute awareness of the vast unknown and of the necessity to find out through *his own experience*.

Thus, in adolescence, there is a general propensity towards concrete thinking. The adolescent's need to define himself may circumvent his ability to use co-operation or reciprocity. He wants to free himself from all influence and yet may find that he cannot get his parents out of his mind, or his hair or from under his skin. Moreover, the adolescent's very preoccupation with his image, with how he looks to others, tends to deflect him from his need to be free of the judgment of others. In part, Narcissus does not live to a ripe old age because he is trapped by the pleasing image fabricated by those who first looked at him in his cradle.

Winnicott has written about the confrontation and challenge which is crucial to an adolescent's detachment from familiar figures. The adolescent feels that personal victory can be won only at the expense of someone else. Someone has to be killed (Winnicott, 1971a, p. 144). How are parents to take the adolescent's battle seriously when it seems to invoke a fight to the death? No one should expect an adolescent simply to accept 'adult', detached ways of thinking. Everything in the adult world must be *found*, and that which is found must seem to be a unique, personal *discovery*. Action and imagination must precede reflection. Parents may feel literally terrorised by their awareness that a murder is brewing. The adolescent's defiance is no raucous scream which can be suffocated quickly or removed out of sight and earshot. The adolescent is also at the height of his learning capacities. He has the ability to think profoundly and incisively. He is ruthlessly curious. Censorship is ridiculous and only invites further challenge. The adolescent's comeback to criticism is sharp, and parents may feel intellectually inferior and even resent the opportunities which they have made available. Challenge may also be avoided when over-empathic parents try too hard to join in or understand a world of which they may not be a part. There is an intrinsic contradiction – supported independence – in the situation, which can be exploited for growth or fixation. The support of independence at this stage is as important as it was to the toddler who wanders off using his mother as 'a beacon of orientation' (Mahler *et al.*, 1975, p. 7). Often, the child seems to become adolescent overnight. A week at a school camp may play this trick on parents and child alike. A well-meaning parent may deal with the shock by saying, 'O.K., kid, you're on your own now.' But the adolescent does not just want to be all on his own. Neither does he want to run back to mummy's lap. The adolescent needs a familiar place where he may return and relax unattended. Relaxation means a respite both from the relentless adventure and challenge of entry into the adult world and from the gang of thrusting, fickle and yet fiercely loyal, young adults to whom he is also attached.

In adolescence, interest in sexual distinction revives. In the Greek myth, we read that Narcissus' path was strewn with heartlessly rejected lovers of both sexes. As Freud said, bisexuality is a feature of normal relationships. However, a lack of sexual discrimination is more common when admiration and the need for mirroring play a large part in relationships. In adolescence, the issue of appearance and the concomitant attitudes of admiration and disgust are particularly extreme. A girl will dress to evoke the envy and admiration of girlfriends as much as to please boys. Competitiveness is essential to adolescent striving. If the challenge of sexuality and sexual distinction is avoided, the young person may falter and, like Narcissus, settle for the admiring gaze of either sex.

It is not surprising that, in Freud's day, narcissism was considered to be particularly characteristic of women. Since many women existed solely in the eyes of men and in the expectation of men's praise or disapproval, they tended to be excessively preoccupied with their image and to engage in a kind of 'mirror transference' with the loved person. Freud wrote: 'Women, especially if they grow up with good looks, develop a certain self-contentment which compensates them for the social restrictions that are imposed upon them in their choice of object' (Freud, 1914, pp. 88–9). Men, who were thought to be narcissistic, were usually described as 'feminine-minded'. That narcissistic men should have been regarded as feminine-minded is a reflection of Victorian ideas about femininity and masculinity.

Because of the enormous and obvious physical changes at puberty, girls may manifest a greater preoccupation with their appearance than boys. Womanhood is demarcated, for some, by the onset of menstruation. Late menstruation will sometimes coincide with a gangly, neuter appearance. It was important to several teenagers of this type whom I saw in therapy that they could pass off as either a girl or a boy. One thirteen-year-old girl I saw in therapy deliberately had her hair styled short and wore unisex shoes, anoraks and trousers so that, at the drop of a hat, she felt able to play whichever sex was to her immediate advantage. There was no father in the home and Sharon's appearance changed dramatically once she was granted her wish to leave home and go to a boarding school. She immediately grew her hair long, wore fashionable trousers and became extremely clothes-conscious in a very individual, not quite fashionable, way. School freed her from a kind of asexual symbiosis.

Doreen was referred to therapy at twelve years of age because of school phobia. Like Sharon, she was tall and gangly, but she dressed, or was dressed, like a nice little girl of eight or nine. This reflected the particular kind of closeness between herself and her mother which was the basis of her school phobia. Although her father was at home and in many ways a quite active, and at times aggressive, man, he had been pushed out from the close mother-baby huddle between Doreen and her mother. This twosome was threatened by Doreen's entry into a large, anonymous, comprehensive school. Sharon, on the other hand, fought dependence with tooth and nail. The last thing Sharon wanted was to be her mother's little baby girl. But she also did not want to grow up to be a woman, like mother. She would rather be a boy. Femininity was equated with softness, 'mushiness' and lack of definition. However, without the intervention of a father, she and her mother were trapped in harsh, hateful exchanges, through which each sought to establish her difference. They seemed to be engaged in a fight to the death. Doreen and her mother were terrified of any difference. Father was excluded at all costs. The intervention of therapy as a third term was extremely difficult and laborious. However, when Doreen and her parents did begin to differentiate themselves, Doreen did sometimes have the satisfaction and frustration of confronting two parents who were united.

At the point when open warfare and hatred were at their height during a summer holiday, Sharon's mother died from a brain tumour. Sharon now holds a reality-tested belief that individuation involves a fight to the death. For her, freedom was won through the death of her mother. In the concrete style of thinking which had characterised all communication between Sharon and her mother, this outcome was tantamount to murder. Characteristically, Sharon was quite unable to think about her mother's death and to mourn her loss. The murder should have taken place *in phantasy*.[1]

When the adolescent wins too easily, he or she grows up with a peculiar idea of the nature of challenge. Victory has been easy enough for a fantasy to evolve that someone must have cheated. The adolescent feels that the adult is a puppet, his maturity and potency a mere façade. Although the gleeful adolescent may feel that he is the clever one, he also feels he has been tricked and deprived of something essential to his own growth. The primitive notion that one person's success is contingent upon someone else's downfall is reinforced. The belief that success is dangerous and vengeful is the undoing of many an adolescent's progress. When the confrontation is not met and thus taken seriously, the adolescent begins to believe that success *in any* field amounts to murder. The succeeding adolescent has to ride a very uncomfortable see-saw of triumph and guilt.

The narcissistic relationship is not always one of mutual admiration. Sometimes an attitude of 'negative narcissism' is adopted. Havelock Ellis has referred to the state of mind, which Abraham called 'negative narcissism' (Abraham, 1924, p. 456), as 'defective narcissism' (Ellis, 1927, pp. 129–53). He describes this state as an anxious self-dissatisfaction and constant preoccupation with the self. In this context, he quotes from Tolstoy's *Childhood, Boyhood and Youth:*

> Apart from my studies my occupations . . . included solitary and incoherent reveries . . . aimless, thoughtless wandering through all the rooms of the house . . . and much looking at myself in the glass, from which, however, I always turned away with a heavy feeling of depression and even disgust. My outward appearance, I was convinced, was unsightly, and I could not even comfort myself with the usual consolation in such cases – I could not say that my face was expressive, intelligent or distinguished. There was nothing expressive in it – only the most ordinary coarse plain features; my small grey

> eyes were stupid rather than intelligent, especially when I looked at myself in the glass. (Tolstoy, 1964, p. 179)

A preoccupation with one's image in the context of acute interpersonal insecurity is the hallmark of narcissism. The image in the mirror is used as an antidote to feelings of fragmentation and insignificance. If the image reflected is a source of pleasure, as in the case of Narcissus, the person who is looking may be quite unaware of the sustaining power his image holds for him. But true self-confidence can never be given by a mirror or gained by a pleasing exterior. The child must free himself even from the admiring image of his mother. At this task, Narcissus fails.

6
Narcissus and Echo

Let us return to the story of Narcissus, this time to the meeting between Narcissus and the nymph, Echo. Sixteen years have passed. The adorable baby is now a handsome teenager, beloved by many. 'Among these lovers was the nymph Echo, who could no longer use her voice, except in foolish repetition of another's shout.' We may imagine that Echo is just the sort of woman whom the son of Leiriope would choose and spurn. In Chapter 5, I presented a picture of the baby Narcissus with his mother. In this chapter, I describe the kind of love-affair which can transpire when early symbiosis goes on too long. The exchange between Narcissus and Echo tells us what happens when a certain kind of baby becomes a teenager. For although Narcissus cannot tolerate separateness and difference in a relationship, the *folie à deux* created by perfect mirroring is also unbearable. He spurns his echo. The myth is, after all, about someone who, in the end, desperately wants to become separated from his illusions and, in particular, his fascination with his own image. The link between Narcissus and his love is like a rubber band or bow-string which never snaps. Over and over again, Narcissus turns his back on his lover. But, in so doing, he turns him or her into his follower, his shadow. He tries to go forward, to put all behind him, but always through the very act of trying to bend the world his way, he springs back to face the same old boring, empty face. He is drawn back to the shadow. Unknowing, since knowledge demands difference and a third term, he is forced to repeat the engulfing twosome.

Echo is also arrested. Like Teiresias, the blind seer, Echo's sensory powers have been curtailed as a punishment for her intrusion into a marriage of the gods. In the myth, a picture is painted of a young, precocious and provocative nymph, who displays all the initiative and daring we associate with an oedipal child or a healthy adolescent. But it seems, partisanship and deception are ultimately punishable by the loss of the resourceful power – in Echo's case, her voice. Like Teiresias, Echo interferes in the 'parental' marriage between Hera and Zeus by her deliberate aiding and abetting of Zeus' adultery. She joins in the triad in a way which is impermissible. She is punished severely and suffers a complete loss of initiative, retaining only the power to repeat.

We are all echolalic to some extent. We learn by imitation and through identification with those whom we love and admire. We tend to repeat when we like, but do not fully comprehend, the sound of what we hear. Echolalia, like narcissism, has been investigated principally from the point of view of individual pathology rather than as a pathology of relationship. Some psychoanalysts have studied echolalia as it forms part of the autistic syndrome. Like the 'autistic armour', which is made up of 'bits of the strong invulnerable father', echolalic children pick words from external objects and 'hide themselves behind a façade of parrotted words and phrases'. They do this to hide the heartbreak of too abrupt disillusionment. 'The artificial voice of the echolalic is a mockery of the real thing' (Tustin, 1972, p. 48).

I put forward the tentative hypothesis that echolalia may be a precursor of narcissism. In ontogenetic development, auditory orientation is sometimes thought to precede visual discrimination. Before the baby is captivated by the visual image of the human face, he orientates towards the human voice, particularly one which is soft and high-pitched (Bowlby, 1969, p. 274).

He further discriminates his mother's voice. The baby's vocalisations – the range and quantity of his babblings – are dependent upon the range of sounds which surround him, the specific responses which are made to his own vocalisations and the vocal approaches addressed specifically to him. By the second half of the first year, the tendency to select the intonations and inflections of his companions is marked.

Since the initial orientation towards auditory phenomena is rapidly supplemented by interest in visual phenomena, it is not surprising that the primitive preoccupation with the human voice soon declines and is supplanted by an apparent predilection for visual stimuli. However, when visual interest is not encouraged, we may imagine that the child will easily become fixated on sounds, as is the case with many autistic children. If the baby is to take pleasure in looking, the mother herself must respond with delight to *being seen* by him. It is not enough that, like Leiriope, she likes to look at him.

In his book *Awakenings*, Oliver Sacks (1973) has written most poignantly of the echolalia and palilalia – i.e. the repetition of one's own words – which characterise the vocalisations of post-encephalitic patients suffering from parkinsonism. Echo-praxia and palipraxia – i.e. forced repetitions of movements or actions – are also common characteristics of catatonia and autism. Sacks traces various correlations between the personality characteristics of his patients and their typical post-encephalitic behaviours and postures.

The precursors of parkinsonism, catatonia and autism are different and unique. But the sufferers of these syndromes share a similar fate: they are locked in a world of total self-reference. Any move which is made generates an infinity of paradoxes and convolutions. There is no move or word which can make a difference. In this self-reflective world, action is impossible. A poignant illustration of two overlapping, self-referring systems can be found in the passage in the myth where the first meeting between Narcissus and Echo is described. Echo, the follower, attempts to initiate dialogue and action. An excruciating monologue ensues. Talkative, but completely echolalic, 'she always answers back'. Narcissus calls out 'Is anyone here?' 'Here', she answers. 'Come,' cries out Narcissus. 'Come', the voice replies. 'Let us come together here', invites Narcissus. At last Echo hears the invitation for which she has waited so long. 'Let us come together here', she joyfully replies and rushes out to embrace him (Graves, 1955, p. 287). But when Narcissus hears Echo's total response to his invitation, he spurns her. His vision of being in love does not include the capacity to love.

In his paper 'On the incapacity to love', Arnold Goldberg (1972) writes of his work with adolescent patients between seventeen and twenty-two years of age. The chief complaint of all of the young people he saw in therapy was an 'incapacity to love anyone else or to fall in love' (p. 3). A feature which emerges from the histories of the three cases that Goldberg reports in his paper is the lack of communication between the patient and his father. This is a major component in the perseveration of the primary two-person narcissistic relationship.

The first case Goldberg presents is of a twenty-year-old student, who had 'an emotional and talkative' mother and 'a controlled, taciturn, and self-sufficient' father with whom the patient had had occasional, scheduled 'half-hearted talks'. The second case, a twenty-one-year-old musician, was the only child of 'an extremely doting and anxious mother' and 'a passive and quiet father'. The third case, a seventeen-year-old homosexual college freshman, was described by the referring psychiatrist as 'darling'. As a child, this young man was 'the apple of his parents' eye'. Goldberg describes how the adolescent who cannot fall in love suffers from the feeling of having been cheated. He is missing something. Perhaps, the child of a doting parent lacks the experience of fighting for, and winning, the love and admiration of another person. Like the youthful Narcissus, he tends to take the positive responses of other people *for granted*. Narcissus does not know how to *make* a relationship; either *it* works or it fails. Each time, the youthful Narcissus thinks 'This one will be just the girl for me, just what I've been looking for, the real woman at last.' But on sight, or at first touch, she becomes nakedly apparent – just another like the rest. Instantly, her shape, skin, smell, sound, etc. force themselves upon his senses and all his ideas crumble. She becomes the object of his dissatisfaction. Thus, he is driven further into the maze of his fruitless searching. Each disappointment serves to exacerbate his conviction that it is just because they have all been the same up till now that the next one is absolutely bound to be different. Narcissus does not *learn* from experience; experience reinforces his deepest convictions.

In response to Narcissus' expression of repulsion – 'I will die before you ever lie with me' – Echo pleads 'Lie with me' (Graves, 1955, p. 287). Like all echoes, she drives Narcissus deeper into the whirlpool of his pride and his delusions of self-reference. Every time she speaks, she validates his belief in his irresistible attraction for, and justifiable disparagement of, women. What else could he feel but revulsion towards someone who is so blindly and idiotically attracted? After all, the blind follower or shadow must be foolish since he or she has no mind of his/her own. Echo's speeches can be compared with a two-year-old who repeats triumphantly the last syllables of words or the last parts of sentences. The youngest child in a family, who tries to join in with his elder brothers and sisters, may use the words and phrases he hears as precious acquisitions to gain entry into their world. However, these debuts may only arouse the scorn and ridicule of those he seeks to impress; 'copycat, copycat', they scoff mercilessly. Like Echo, the child in this position in the family can easily take on the role of the despised follower. But even Narcissus, the leader, who appears to initiate, is little more than a shadow. Echo has been captivated by the voice of another of which she is a mere reflection. Echo and Narcissus fit together perfectly; neither is able to initiate and sustain *dialogue*. Both are consequences. This is what Narcissus finds out when he comes to know himself. In order to find himself and so live to a ripe old age, he would have to love another – to find out, first what an *other* means. How much closer to the exit (out of illusionment) was Oedipus when he fell in love with Jocasta and took her as his wife to bed.

Like the young infant, who is fascinated by the human face which he cannot yet reach or touch at will, the youthful Narcissus is fascinated by the appearance of the other which he has not yet touched. Interaction proves fatal. The image dissolves. The image, the promise of love, is all that Narcissus is allowed. Although the youth whose path is littered with heartlessly rejected lovers tends to arouse our hostility so that his partner may escape our notice and judgment, Echo's malleability is equally distracting and, indeed, provocative. Not a note of dissonance can be traced in Echo's voice. She offers nothing which might correct Narcissus' ever-expanding delusions of grandeur. Rejection is the inevitable fate which befalls a person who is unable to take the initiative to correct runaways in a system of communication. In many relationships, we find an Echo who is outcast and a Narcissus who casts out. As in the myth, Echo's love remains 'firmly rooted in her heart, and was increased by the pain of having been rejected' (Ovid, 1955, p. 84). She maintains the belief that rejection is a necessary ingredient to love. But her masochistic fidelity only reaffirms Narcissus in his view that she is no more than a mirror and a pathetic creature. In turn, through loss of self-esteem, Echo is engulfed by melancholia. She falls prey to fits of unmitigated anxiety and to self-absorbed, compulsive ruminations. 'Her anxious thoughts kept her awake, and made her pitifully thin . . . . Since then, she hides in the woods and though never seen in the mountains, is heard there by all: for her voice is the only part of her that still lives' (Ovid, 1955, p. 84). Like many melancholics, in a state of prolonged mourning, her anxiety renders her insomniac which further exacerbates the repetitiveness of her thoughts. Without the break of sleep and the shift in consciousness of dreams, Echo's life folds into one endless nightmare.

Narcissus, on the other hand, appears to be almost indifferent to anxiety. Like some autistic children, he does not seem to feel pain. Since both self-examination and the voice of criticism are unfamiliar to him, there is little cause for anxiety. Narcissus has never been rejected, his life-style has never been called in question. By a twist of his head, an aversion of his eyes and the turning of his back, a displeasing scene is dismissed.

One day, Narcissus over-reached himself. At last, something happened. Ameinius put a stop to the 'game'. Narcissus sent a sword to Ameinius, his most insistent suitor. Ameinius then killed himself on Narcissus' threshold, calling on the gods to take revenge on Narcissus for his treatment both of his admirers and of the spirits of the waters and the woods: ' "May he himself fall in love with another, as we have done with him: May he too be unable to gain his loved one?" ' (Ovid, 1955, p. 85). Artemis granted his prayer. He made Narcissus fall in love, though denying him love's consummation.

Through Artemis' action, Narcissus is brought to the threshold of the self-knowledge which will prove fatal to him. He falls in love with his own reflection. 'At Donacon in Thespia he came upon a spring, clear as silver, and never yet disturbed by cattle, birds, wild beasts, or even by branches dropping off the trees that shaded it; and as he cast himself down, exhausted, on the grassy verge to slake his thirst, he fell in love with his own reflection' (Graves, 1955, p. 287). Alone at last, his companions *left behind*, his admirers spurned, Ameinius dead and Echo bodyless, he gazes into the primal mirror. Narcissus' first mirror is as smooth as glass – a clear pool, rippleless, never yet disturbed by man nor beast nor tree. As in his cradle, the message transmitted to his eyes from the pattern on the surface of the pool is love at first sight.

> While he sought to quench his thirst, another thirst grew in him, and as he drank, he was enchanted by the beautiful reflection that he saw. He fell in love with an insubstantial hope, mistaking a mere shadow for a real body . . . As he lay on the bank, he gazed at the twin stars that were his eyes, at his flowing locks, worthy of Bacchus or Apollo, his smooth cheeks, his ivory neck, his lovely face where a rosy flush stained the snowy whiteness of his complexion, *admiring all the features for which he was himself admired*. (Ovid, 1955, p. 85; my italics)

As in his previous love affairs, Narcissus at first is enraptured by the image which appears to reveal the presence of an *independent* being. But this person is as insubstantial as Echo. Again, the primary circuit of communication, in which there is neither subject nor object, is reproduced. He admires all the features for which he was himself admired. He looks on the image with the eyes of the admirer, the eyes which he first saw look at him, the eyes of admiration. As I pointed out, it is misleading to say that Narcissus falls in love with himself. The myth tells us quite clearly that he falls in love with the image he sees in the mirror.

The element of the mirror is important to my interpretation of the myth, since it suggests the particular stage in the process of early differentiation at which Narcissus is arrested. His relation to the mirror-image indicates the emergence of identity formation. The mirror is ambiguous; it is both a third term and a symbiotic object. The mirror is 'magic' – both me and not-me – as the evil stepmother of Snow White knew. It contains the possibility of realisation and delusion, of being and annihilation, of separateness and fusion. Long before the infant is able to define his own identity through action, he learns about the '*theme*' of identity – the outline – from his mother (Lichtenstein, 1964, p. 54). Like Narcissus, the child first looks at his own image from the outside in. The first face which appears to the child in the mirror of his mother's face is the *mother's* image of her child (Winnicott, 1967) – in the case of Narcissus, the specific image is of an admiring face. This same outline is replicated when Narcissus looks in the pool, the first real mirror, of which the faces of Leiriope and of his other suitors were precursors.

During early development, the mirroring relationship with the mother has the potentiality to enforce or destroy an outline. The contours should be neither too hard nor too blurred. It is crucial to the child's emerging identity that the mother is not too set in the way she sees her child and that she is also able to modify her preconceptions into apperceptions and perceptions. The mirroring experience is a transitional experience. The more an adult is addicted to the mirroring relation, the less secure is his sense of both individuation and relationship. The mirror will never give him back what he wants. It will never show more than he can see. The delineation for which the looker so desperately searches can only emerge from the foundation of a secure *relationship* between two or more people.

In the passage which follows in Ovid's version of the myth, we read about Narcissus' confusion over the states of the image, and his abortive attempts to make active contact with the 'person' he sees in the pool. He is 'fired by the sight' and 'often plunge(d) his arms deep in the waters, as he tried to clasp the neck he saw' (Ovid, 1955, p. 85). When the baby has achieved visual convergence and co-ordination with his grasp, he becomes fascinated and thrilled at the sight of himself in the mirror. Originally, perhaps, he takes this vision to be another person and he stretches forward, crowing and clutching at the contours he sees. But over and over again, his fingertips slither across the slippery surface. His mother will probably help him out in the complex process of differentiating the image from the person reflected. When the baby looks in the mirror, the mother may point at the image and say 'baby' – or the baby's name – and then, pointing towards his actual body, she may touch him and again repeat his name. Or she might place herself in the frame of the mirror and, pointing both to the image and to herself, she might say 'Mummy' or her own name. This enables the baby to *compare* two images of the *same* person. First, the baby may look in the mirror and then turn his eyes away from the image and look across at his mother's face beside him. He will do this many, many times before he can begin to figure it out. Soon, he will be able to point with her. He may try to look behind the mirror. He may examine the back very carefully and pick at the sides and try to prise back and front apart. Like Narcissus at the pool, he looks for the body behind the reflection.

Even a seven-year-old, who understands the mirror, continues to be captivated by the sight of himself in a shop window, a car bumper or a puddle. The mirror remains a mystery throughout life. During adolescence, mirrors are found everywhere – on ceilings, table tops, knives, glasses, desk tops; every available surface in an adolescent's room is covered with pictures – of himself, his friends, idols and pin-ups. This behaviour may seem conceited and self-absorbed and yet it is unfair to make a negative judgment of vanity at this stage. Parental attitudes are vital to the resolution of this preoccupation. The teenager searches in the mirror, he asks Who, What and How am I? If attractive, he (or she) may preen him (or her) self and return to the mirror and look again and again as if, thereby, he (or she) might stamp the desirable image on his (or her) face forever. Like Tolstoy, on ugly days, the young person will go back again and again to see if the image has shifted a little – to check whether the nose might be a little straighter, the lips a little fuller, the cheeks rounder, the eyelashes longer, etc.

The 'heartless' Narcissus looks in the pool and asks no questions. He looks with the same eyes which once beheld him. The inquiring adolescent looks in the mirror in order to forgo the appraisal of his parents. He looks with new eyes, with the eyes of fashion, perhaps. If he is to accept any judgment or trend, it will be the very latest, certainly nothing handed down. Narcissus simply gazes. No gap or dissonance disturbs the flow. But the delight of the first look does not last. Like a young baby, Narcissus becomes fixed on the image. He stares into it as if he might drain it in through the holes of his eyes. But the stare is ineffective. He is propelled into more desperate and futile attempts at incorporation. He tries to catch a picture in his arms. Like the echolalic who catches words, the narcissist picks off looks and features and moulds these into desirable images. But possession of this type never leads to a sense of belonging. Narcissus' distress is all the greater because no mighty ocean separates him from his love; only a little water keeps them apart. Narcissus tries to break through the wall between him and the 'external' object. It seems to be no more than a transparent membrane. He can see through and yet he cannot cross over. It is so fine, and yet as impermeable as his own skin. Moreover, the separation is all the more unacceptable because his love 'himself' desires to be embraced: 'for whenever I lean forward to kiss the clear waters he lifts up his face to mine and strives to reach me' (Ovid, 1955, p.86).

The mother of a friend of mine lived for several years in this sort of relationship to a photograph. She placed several photos of her dead husband at corners in the house and also on the walls facing the entrances to certain rooms. Thus, she felt herself to be seen by him at all times. She told my friend, Mary, that his features changed according to his moods which, in turn reflected his responses to her daily activities. He was angry, pleased, kindly, etc. She would kiss him, embrace the frame, murmur into the mouth, apologise, etc. It did not seem to bother her that this image was no more than a projection of her own thoughts and moods; nor that, as with Narcissus, her kisses reached no one. Mary came to regard these photos in a similar fashion.

In the myth, however, Narcissus becomes aware of his delusion. How could he endure both to possess and yet not to possess? Narcissus wonders what is wrong with him. 'Certainly . . . not my looks or age.' The nymphs have reassured him on that score. Moreover, the image itself is amorous:

> When I stretch out my arms to you, you stretch yours towards me in return: you laugh when I do, and often I have marked your tears when I was weeping. You answer my signs with nods, and, as far as I can guess from the movement of your lovely lips, reply to me in words that never reach my ears. (Ovid, 1955, p. 86)

This tragic overture could as well be addressed to Echo or to Leiriope – to the mother or lover, who is always at hand at the right moment, who hands things before they are asked for, who anticipates every wish, who cries when Narcissus cries. The baby needs to be able to call for the mother who is *not there*. He must be able to protest, when she does not come immediately, and to learn that he can control her sometimes but not always. Narcissus realises that it is his self-sufficiency which renders him utterly deficient. 'My very plenty makes me poor.' Freud remarked that, although a strong egoism is a protection against falling ill, we must begin to fall in love in order that we do *not* fall ill (Freud, 1914, p. 85). However, when advantage through illness is pronounced, and no substitute for it can be found in reality, Freud thought the physician could not look forward very hopefully to influencing the illness through therapy. Some people, who emerge from a long period of absorption in illness, die 'naturally' or commit suicide. Sacks describes how the 'wonder' drug, L-Dopa, can precipitate death (Sacks, 1973). Suddenly the person's protective armour is in shreds as he or she seems to 'explode' into health. But this 'awakening' is often followed by a period of 'tribulation' (Sacks, 1973) because the person's day-to-day life cannot reproduce the initial period of bliss and promise. Reality does not supply the necessary substitute for the illness. Reality is disappointing and harsh. Similarly, a child, who has lost his autistic shell, needs a therapist who is able to withstand the child's volcanic eruptions and disappointments. The therapist must also endure repeated retreats into the painless fog or brittle shell of the autism (the illness). The swings from elation to despair can be very exhausting and test the therapist's trust. Some patients may try to destroy the therapist or themselves rather than face the initial surrender or the enormous task of reparation which follows breakthrough.

Frances Tustin has written about the work of reparation – the capacity to mend – which is crucial to successful therapy with autistic children. The heart of the autistic child is filled with unbearable grief. When the autistic barrier breaks and the heart is laid bare, very special care is needed if it is to mend. In therapy, the place of 'critical hurt' or of 'psychological catastrophe' is unveiled and the child's health and well-being now depend upon the emergence of a new outcome to the 'Gone' experience. In the mending atmosphere of the therapy room, the change which is necessary is dramatically described in the words of an autistic boy: ' "Broken ! Gone! Oh dear! . . . I mend it! I mend it! . . . I fix it! I fix it! Hole gone! Button on! Hole gone! Button on!" ' (Tustin, 1972, p. 19). John was an autistic boy, who started analytic therapy with Frances Tustin at 3½ years of age. He frequently had temper tantrums, in which he would break various objects in the therapy room. In his sessions with Tustin, the 'button' came to stand for the good breast or present, holding mother, who covered over the black hole of absence and the ensuing unbearable grief which John experienced. When John broke up his toys or threw them away, he lost his 'button' which held things together. Then, he was left with the unmitigating pain of the black hole – the 'gone' experience. His first use of the personal pronoun came after he had broken a bus during a tantrum. He said 'I mend it! I mend it!' The theme of mending was repeated in many later sessions. For the autistic child, a broken toy reminds him of the broken lifeline between himself and his mother – a line which he feels is gone forever. With the loss of this life-line, the self (the 'I') is broken.

The 'Gone' experience is re-evoked in adult bereavement. An elderly spouse may die of heartbreak within a few weeks or months of bereavement. We know that young children can also waste away and die of grief. Until recently, some of the autistic children who had been consigned to institutions died. The films of James and Joyce Robertson on the separations between mothers and young children show most poignantly how children seem to dwindle away very rapidly. Some of the post-encephalitic patients described in Sacks' book died overnight from the unbearable grief and disappointment which followed the initial L-Dopa awakening. One woman seemed to die of unrequited love for her doctor (Sacks, 1973, p. 122). Others retreated back into the repetitious world of echolalia and palilalia.

So, at the end of the myth, we come to Narcissus' death. Though bereaved of a mere delusion, his grief is all the more intolerable. His grief is over the insurmountable barrier which lies between himself and his beloved. Death – total annihilation and cut-off – is the one release open to him and from the intolerable pain of separateness: 'I have no quarrel with death, for in death I shall forget my pain: but I could wish that the object of my love might outlive me: as it is, both of us will perish together, when this one life is destroyed' (Ovid, 1955, p. 86). Graves gives a different account of Narcissus' grief which is, perhaps, more consistent with Teiresias' prophecy. He says: 'Grief was destroying him, yet he rejoiced in his torments; knowing at least that his other self would remain true to him, whatever happened' (Graves, 1955, p. 287). Graves's version suggests that Narcissus had some awareness that the self in the mirror was, in Winnicott's terms, a 'false self', an as-if personality, or a self-representation fabricated out of the views and attributions of others. Narcissus' belief in a 'true self' suggests that he realised that self-knowledge involved the destruction of the perfect image and that liberation lay in the separation, the prising-apart, of two images – one self, one other – which had been condensed into one.

Narcissus embraces the image for the last time. His tears disturb the once rippleless pool. The image dims. Although Echo has not forgiven Narcissus, she remains faithful to the end. She grieves with him: 'As often as the unhappy boy sighed "Alas", she took up his sigh, and repeated "Alas!" ' (Ovid, 1955, p. 87). As he gazed into the familiar pool, he uttered his last words 'Ah youth, beloved in vain, farewell' and the spot re-echoed the same words. As the image disintegrates in the rippling water, Narcissus cries 'Where are you fleeing? . . . Let me, by looking, feed my ill-starred love' (p. 86). According to Ovid's account, Narcissus beat himself and his white marble skin turned red tinged with purple. When he saw this in the water, he could bear it no longer.

> As golden wax melts with gentle heat, as morning frosts are thawed by the warmth of the sun, so he was worn and wasted away with love, and slowly consumed by its hidden fire. His fair complexion with its rosy flush faded away, gone was his youthful strength, and all the beauties which lately charmed his eyes. Nothing remained of that body which Echo once had loved. (Ovid, 1955, p. 87)

Just as, earlier, nothing remained of Echo except her voice, so nothing is left of Narcissus' beautiful body. Only a beautiful flower remains: 'He laid down his weary head on the green grass, and death closed his eyes which so admired their owner's beauty' (Ovid, 1955, p. 87). 'His blood soaked the earth, and up sprung the white narcissus flower with its red corollary, from which an unguent balm is now distilled at Chaeronea. . . . This is recommended for affections of the ears (though apt to give headaches), and is a vulnerary, and for the cure of frost-bite' (Graves, 1955, p. 188). When the pyre was being prepared, 'his body was nowhere to be found. Instead of a corpse, they discovered a flower with a circle of white petals around a yellow centre' (Ovid, 1955, p. 87).

The narcissus flower which sprang up on Narcissus' grave is surely a representative of the child of Leiriope's dreams – a beautiful and soothing flower. So the story ends where it began: with the prophecy of Teiresias. 'When the story became known, it brought well-deserved fame to the seer Teiresias. It was told throughout all the cities of Greece, and his reputation was boundless' (Ovid, 1955, p. 87).

In conclusion to Part I, I suggest that in normal development the narcissistic relationship (or attachment) with its characteristics of synchronous interaction, mirroring responsiveness and mutual imitation-games expands outwards into a larger world of other people and new things. The infant does not 'hatch' or learn, through harsh reality, to relate. His predominant attitude towards his mother and his environment is not one of passivity, withdrawal, paranoia or active aggression. He is not primarily negative towards others. Through the security of his first harmonious attachment, he seeks out more of what life seems to offer.

In my interpretation of the myth and presentation of illustrations from the literature and from my own clinical experience, I focus on a particular type of narcissistic fixation – namely, a mirroring or doting symbiosis which resists change. This fixation results from pathologies arising in the area of mother–infant individuation. However, the extensive literature on narcissism suggests a variety of narcissistic pathologies which issue from the early stages of infant–mother relations. Kohut, for instance, has focused on a particular type of narcissistic fixation which results from deprivations in *mirroring responsiveness*. In this type of narcissistic pathology, the person seeks out the missing attachment. Rosenfeld, on the other hand, has concentrated on another type of pathology in which the narcissistic person retreats from an awareness of separateness and dependence and adopts various defensive attitudes, such as hostility and omnipotence.

In chapter 4, I referred to some of the contemporary research on patterns of early mother–infant communication. The complexities of these interactions contribute not only to the richness of the first relationship but also to the distortions which all too easily may occur. The varieties of narcissistic pathology, described in the psychoanalytic literature, reflect the many ways in which communication between a mother and her baby may go wrong. However, the ways in which these pathologies are described do not only represent different fixations in development. They make sense within the specific model of infancy employed by a particular analyst. I have concentrated on that type of narcissistic pathology which results when differentiation between mother and infant is embryonic or partial, thus perpetuating the kind of symbiotic, and synchronous, exchange, which is benign at the earliest stage of the developing partnership between mother and child.

The theoretical implications of the new view of infancy (outlined in chapter 4), which is both constructed through, and at the same time guides, the findings of contemporary research in developmental psychology, are large and, in my view, of relevance to the psychoanalytic view of child development. The relational and interactional model, in which mutuality and interdependence are stressed, is not beset by some of the kinds of logical problems to which the traditional Freudian model of human development falls prey. From an original, intense and affectionate, relationship, such problems as how to relate, how to care about another person, or how to curb one's anti-social instincts and desires, do not arise. In relation to the practice and technique of psychoanalysis, the new theory has a particular advantage, since it allows for transitional phenomena and transcontextual communications which are expressed in the old theory in terms of absolute discontinuities. The importance of some of these transitional schemas, together with their relevance to a theory of development and change, will be outlined in the next part of this book.

TRANSITION

You would not find out
the boundaries of soul, even by
travelling along every path:
so deep a measure does it have.

Heraclitus,
Fragment 235

7
The concept of transitional schemas

Between the two stages of development named after the two great myths of psychoanalysis, Narcissus and Oedipus, I posit a transitional stage – a stage characterised, as you might expect, by the use of transitional objects and the emergence of transitional phenomena. According to my interpretation, the myth of Narcissus and Echo illustrates a relationship of synchrony, undifferentiation and mutual illusion; the *Oedipus Rex* dramatises various conflicts related to individuation, agency, responsibility and knowledge. During the first stage of development, the mystery for both partners is to join in the dance;[1] during the second stage, each partner must solve the problem of disjunction that is part of the riddle of life. Oedipus' task is to clear away the delusions in which he was all too happily enmeshed before he consulted the Oracle. By his answer to the riddle of the sphinx, Oedipus 'becomes a man' who walks on his own two feet. In the tragic myth of Narcissus and Echo, echoing and mirroring synchrony is achieved at the expense of mutuality and dialogue. Oedipus' journey from Corinth to Thebes ends in tragedy because he is implicated in two dramas, adoption and incest, which bring his project to no avail. In the play,[2] Sophocles' use of both themes makes nonsense of the notions of adult intentionality and responsibility which, in the play, the character of Oedipus portrays. Tragedy reaches an excess when the mother, who discarded her offspring on the barren hillside, gives willing entry to his seed, and when the son, whose father practised philocide, commits parricide.

Transition

Winnicott's concept

Let us now turn to an examination of the type of relationships between the infant, his mother, his parents and the outside world which pertain during this transitional stage. In the title of this chapter, I choose to use the term 'schema', because I think it indicates more clearly the use which Winnicott intended for the concepts of the 'transitional object' and 'transitional phenomena'. The object of Winnicott's investigation is not any specific object, but its use. 'It is not the object, of course, that is transitional. The object represents the infant's transition from a state of being merged with the mother to a state of being in relation to the mother as something outside and separate' (Winnicott, 1953, p. 2). Like an attachment which endures after all proximity-seeking behaviour has dwindled, the capacity to use a transitional object remains long after a particular teddy bear has been forgotten. The use of the transitional object marks the development of a sense of separateness and the beginning of the use of symbols. However, *during this stage*, the *specific* object used is as irreplaceable as the child's attachment to a specific figure. The object

> becomes vitally important to the infant for use at the time of going to sleep. . . . The object goes on being important. The parents get to know its value and carry it round when travelling. The mother lets it get dirty and even smelly, knowing that by washing it she introduces a break in continuity in the infant's experience, a break that may destroy the meaning and value of the object to the infant. (Winnicott, 1953, p. 4)

After this stage of development has passed and the transitional object becomes decathected as cultural interests develop, a third or intermediate area of experiencing remains 'as a resting-place for the individual engaged in the perpetual human task of keeping inner and outer reality separate yet interrelated' (p. 2). To this 'third part of the life of a human being' (p. 2) both inner reality and external life contribute.

Winnicott makes at least three claims for his concepts of the transitional object and transitional phenomena:

1 The transitional object has its use at a particular developmental stage. At this stage, the object is of crucial importance.

The stage is linked to the separation–individuation process and is transitional between two specific poles.
2 The child's use of a transitional object creates a third or intermediate area of experience which is neither subjective nor objective and which endures throughout life. This third part of the life of man cannot be challenged as to whether it belongs to inner or shared reality. It constitutes the greater part of the infant's experience and 'throughout life is retained in intense experiencing that belongs to the arts and to religion and to imaginative living, and to creative scientific work' (1953, p. 14).
3 Transitional phenomena exist in this third area of experience. Unlike the chosen teddy bear or doll, transitional phenomena are not concrete but abstract. They span any two poles which they either distinguish or bridge. They are defined entirely by their use. Although Winnicott specified some of these phenomena – dreams, humour, religion, etc. – they acquire the characteristic transitional solely by virtue of their transcontextual use. The third area of human experience is *communicated* through transitional phenomena. Winnicott thus brings to our notice a third type of communication which is not covered by the primary and secondary processes studied in psychoanalysis.

1 *The developmental stage denoted by the emergence of the transitional object*

Most writers on this subject agree that the transitional object plays an important role in the separation–individuation process. However, analysts disagree as to the *dating* and conceptualisation of the *two poles* between which the object is transitional. Hence, we find a complementary variation in the dating, and criteria for the identification, of the transitional object itself. The transitional object marks a development out of the primary state of being and must be seen in the context of the primary relationship. With reference to the positions delineated on the spectrum presented in Part I, the role allotted to the transitional object depends upon the conceptualisation of the infant's primary state. Winnicott's concept reflects a particular view of early mother–infant relations.

Anthony Flew (1978, pp. 485–501), a moral philosopher, suggests that the present response to Winnicott's ideas is to something which is not to be discovered in his original paper on 'Transitional objects and transitional phenomena'. Flew points out that part of the explanation of the impact of this paper must lie in the antecedent concerns and beliefs of those impressed by it. In my view, this does not detract from, but further advances, the importance and relevance of Winnicott's contribution. The impact of this paper is related to strong beliefs about infancy. I agree with the philosopher of science, Laudan, that one 'can only understand a system of ideas when one knows, in detail, the problems to which it was addressed' (1978, p. 176). To do this, we must examine concepts in relation to their traditions and the traditions of their rivals. We are then required to show how 'the introduction of certain conceptual variations improved the overall problem-solving capacity of one or another system which embodies the variation' (p. 183). Winnicott introduced a concept which was valuable just because it met a specific gap or deficit in the psychoanalytic theories of child development and consciousness. The gap is reflected in non-relational concepts or images of infancy such as the amoeba or egg. Hence, the enormous contemporary interest in his work by analysts of many different orientations.[3] The concepts of the transitional object and of transitional phenomena were introduced to deal with a neglected area of individual development and experience. Hitherto, there had been a focus on psychic reality, which is personal and inner, and its relation to external and shared reality (Winnicott, 1971a). We find this focus in Freud's work and in the works of the two pioneers of child psychoanalysis, Anna Freud and Melanie Klein. Winnicott's theory of infancy points to a third area of *'overlap'* between infant and mother and to realities that are both personal and shared. In this section, Winnicott's concepts are examined against the background of Freud's conception of mind and the theories of child development proposed by Anna Freud and Melanie Klein. Precursors of Winnicott's concepts may be discerned in Freud's views on the transformations of narcissism and in his concept of the 'watching agency' as the inheritor of narcissism (1914).

Winnicott is telling us not only that many children form a relationship with a transitional object at a particular developmental stage and that this type of relationship persists throughout life, but that we need to find new concepts through which to describe the earliest infant–mother relationship. In Part I (chapter 4), I discussed Winnicott's conception of infancy; in this section, I reiterate his views, since his concepts of the transitional object and of transitional phenomena make sense in the context of the earlier of the two poles between which the transitional object is transitional – that is, the holding relationship. Winnicott points out that although 'it is generally known that there is almost infinite subtlety in a mother's management of her baby', it has taken a long time for psychoanalytic theory to reach to 'this area of living experience' (Winnicott, 1970, p. 246). The psychoanalyst was always fighting the battle for the individual against those who ascribed troubles to environmental influences. The analyst concentrated both on the conflicts within the psyche, that is on unconscious, primitive phantasy, and on those stages of childhood when relationships could be described in terms of relations between separate, whole persons. However, when analysts turned to the investigation of infancy, when dependence is so great, the environment could no longer be ignored.

Klein's concept of the part-object relationship and Kohut's concept of the self-object are addressed to this level of dependence. However, in Winnicott's view, the term 'internal object' does not do justice to the infant's phantasies at this most primitive level of dependence. Winnicott's point is that the infant's phantasy or representation of the relationship must include his experience of the maternal care and holding which he has received. The infant's feelings of disappointment, rage, annihilation, etc. are not adequately described in terms of subjective reactions to frustrated omnipotence or control over his part-object, the breast. The 'inner' life of the baby (such as it is) develops because of the baby's actual experience of his mother and cannot be written in purely individualistic terms. The phantasy construct must include the holding environment which precedes the separation of inner from outer, the subjective from the objective.

Winnicott compares the transitional object concept with Klein's concept of the 'internal object'. The transitional object is not an internal object which is a mental concept – 'it is a possession. Yet it is not (for the infant) an external object either' (Winnicott, 1953, p. 9). However, the qualities of both types of object depend upon 'the existence and aliveness and behaviour of the external object. Failure of the latter in some essential function indirectly leads to deadness or to a persecutory quality of the internal object' (pp. 9–10). The transitional object becomes 'meaningless' too. In Winnicott's view, the transitional object is neither internal nor external; it lies or is created in the expanding gap between mother and infant. The transitional object heralds the *distinction* between individual mental functioning and shared external reality. It is misleading to state simply that the transitional object is transitional between internal and external reality or between illusion and perception since this can suggest that a boundary *already* exists. It does for the observing adult, but, from the baby's point of view, the transitional object is itself used to create, to discover, and to tolerate the increasingly clear perception of boundaries. In other words, the synchronous 'overlap' disperses into a gap which takes shape as a line or boundary. Initially, the transitional object partakes of both inner and outer reality simply because no border between them has been delineated. The transitional object is the vehicle by which a boundary between two objects is created. The teddy bear signifies the distinction between infant and mother. Logically, this evokes the issue of how we make a distinction, such that a space is severed, so that two parts or spaces are created. But the mark of distinction is not itself one of the two objects which fall on either side of the boundary. Thus, the transitional object is not a *representation* of an internal or an external object. It spans the distance between the early relationship of interactional synchrony between mother and baby and the emerging world of discrete persons and objects. The object is used as a tool of differentiation – both as a comforter to deal with the pain of separation and as an instrument in the child's creation of his own world, including the private world of the mind.

Winnicott also discusses the transitional object as a development out of a primary state of narcissism but refrains from using this language, as it leaves out the idea of dependence which is crucial at the earliest stages. Mahler, employing the primary narcissism hypothesis, observes the use of transitional objects during the third phase of the separation–individuation process – the 'rapprochement' phase. Ambivalent motivation predominates throughout the rapprochement phase as the child oscillates between fears of symbiotic engulfment and helplessness. The transitional object serves as a buffer against these terrors. The rapprochement phase has a duration of about six to twelve months; it begins at about fifteen to eighteen months and culminates from twenty-four months to thirty-six months with the consolidation of individuality and object constancy.

Mahler's dating of the appearance of the transitional object might be considered late by writers holding positions further to the right of my spectrum (see preface to part I), such as positions 3 and 4. An infant's attachment to his vest or fingers at about three months might indicate the use of a transitional object, since the infant, firmly attached to a specific figure, is aware of the separateness and turns to certain objects or movements when he is alone. Winnicott, purposely leaving room for wide variations, suggests that transitional phenomena begin to show at about four to six to twelve months and can include such things as a bundle of wool, the corner of a blanket, a tune or a mannerism. My nephew, Stephen, would pull on his little vest, sometimes bringing it up to his mouth to suck on, when his mother left his immediate vicinity. By five months, he made a characteristic circular hand movement when going to sleep, usually with his left hand. He made this gentle, sensuous movement on the left side of his forehead, on the breast, on his bottle, on his tummy and sometimes moved his mother's right hand with his left so that her hand made the movement in the air.

2 *The third area of experience*

In Winnicott's view of human development, the third area of experience, which is neither inner nor outer, exists from the beginning of life in the mutuality and play overlap between mother and infant; from four to eight to eighteen months onwards, it becomes embodied in the transitional object at the stage when both mother and infant are differentiating themselves out of the primary relationship; the object subsequently dissolves by expansion outwards into a whole spectrum of experience and activities which help bridge and separate inner and outer reality. The third area is, at once, a resting place and a source of creativity and rejuvenation. As in the stage of development when the transitional object first makes its vital appearance, human beings continue to need this area because it is hard to maintain harmony between our inner lives and the worlds outside us. At times, the pull towards projection of mental phenomena onto convenient externals and the countervailing suffusion of the mind by the outside world can be strong. Some patients need to find this resting place in their therapy. A twenty-five-year-old anthropology student, Brenda, with a rich imagination and dream-life, which she employed in hard work in her analysis, silently requested and savoured a few minutes' silence towards the end of some sessions. She simply wanted to rest, looking out of my window at the moving trees and clouds, and it was sometimes important to her that she could leave me and depart from this quiet, tranquil space which she found so refreshing.

Winnicott stresses that the enlargement of our sensibilities and their integration depends upon the *use* to which we put the objects around us. Transitional objects and transitional phenomena may be used, valued or devalued in many different ways. Those children, who adopt a transitional object as an aid through the vicissitudes of a particular developmental stage, treat their teddy bears and dolls very differently. Transitional phenomena, such as dreaming, may be used to provide a potential space between a defensive adhesion to the 'facts' and a dissociated domain of phantasy. The dream throws light on both areas and provides a setting in which both reality and phantasy may be thought about from a new perspective. But a stream of associations or dreams may also be used defensively. An epic dream may be used to dazzle the analyst's mind so that neither the analyst nor the analysand can use the analytic setting. The important thing is not the having of a dream or the elaboration of a rich symbolism but the use of the dream in the dreamer's life. Winnicott describes the change in function of a child's use of a bit of string from a denial of separation to communication (Winnicott, 1953, p. 19).

The analytic setting provides a potential space for this third or intermediate area of experience. Transference phenomena, like the use of the transitional object, demand the tolerance of a paradox which should not be resolved. The area remains unchallenged and, as Winnicott said of the transitional object, the question ' "Did you conceive of this or was it presented to you from without?" . . . is not to be formulated' (1953, p. 12). An appealing, but ultimately counterproductive, route out of the uncomfortable ambiguity would be to declare that all which transpires in an analysis is transferential or, on the other hand, to insist on a confrontational, reality-oriented approach.

3 *Communication through transitional phenomena*

Flew, who provides a general philosophical comment on the collection of essays on Winnicott's work entitled *Between Reality and Fantasy* (1978, p. 485), has pointed out that Winnicott's concept is in danger of over-generalisation. We must specify what are the objects or terms between which the class of transitional phenomena are transitional. Without such specifications, we are in danger of falling into a Heraclitean world of flux. As Flew points out, Winnicott's concept is useful because it is limited. A concept which is too fluid becomes open to misuse. I have suggested that transitional phenomena, which are abstract, cannot be specified in the way that a particular teddy bear may be pointed out. Neither do they appear at a particular developmental stage. They simply cross boundaries. Although their use is similar to the use of the transitional object, their development does not *necessarily* depend upon an attachment to a transitional object. For instance, someone who never had a transitional object may dream or be able to use analysis.

Winnicott is not alone in spotting the conceptual necessity for transitional structures in the theory of the mind and mental development.[4] The anthropologist and cyberneticist, Gregory Bateson, and the psychoanalyst, Wilfred Bion, have also been led by their interest in borderline phenomena and, in particular, schizophrenia to a similar conception. All three are concerned with types of human communication and with the enlargement of sensibility. Their project is to draw some sort of map of the mind and experience which includes all varieties of mental functioning arranged in a spectrum from the most inaccessible (unconscious phenomena) to the most immediate level of awareness. As Flew points out, this project involves a *phenomenological* rather than an ontological classification. These authors delineate a third area of consciousness which is not covered by Freud's original distinction between the primary and secondary processes.

In communication theory, which is the theoretical model used by Bateson, at least three types of human communication are distinguished: *analogical*, *digital* and *paradoxical*. Analogical communication is predominantly non-verbal, kinesic, iconic and concerned with matters of relationship. In earliest infancy, it is the primary mode of communication. Digital communication consists of a number of purely conventional signs which have no simple relation with what they stand for. Verbal language is almost purely digital and serves a different function to analogical communication. It contains devices for naming the relata (or terms of relationship) and for making simple, indicative statements, both positive and negative. Analogical communication is only positive in so far as it has no simple device for statements of negation.

We may compare the distinction between analogical and digital communication with Freud's distinction between primary and secondary processes, a notable feature of the former process being the absence of negation.[5] Paradoxical communication, a third type of communication, may be the most common form of human discourse. It contains overlaps of *both* types of communication and has an essentially 'transcontextual' (Bateson, 1969, p. 272) character. Bateson's concept of the 'transcontextual syndrome' (1969, p. 272), which includes complex communicational structures such as play, humour, art and psychosis, relates to Winnicott's concept of 'transitional phenomena'. A joke is funny, in part, because its meaning derives from both fact and fiction. It crosses contexts. Winnicott points out that the *use* of transitional phenomena involves the *toleration* of paradox. (Winnicott's use of the concept of paradox does not coincide with the strict philosophical usage.)

The view that the tolerance of paradox, ambiguity or anomaly, is central to development has been held by many thinkers. The topic of discussion might be the development of a new science (Kuhn, 1962) or the thinking process of a young child. An approximation of Winnicott's idea is found in Freud's belief that the tolerance of frustration involves the experience of ambivalence. Bion describes a similar situation in terms of the acquisition of 'binocular vision' (1962a, p. 86) in which a person is able to switch from one point of view to another with respect to a particular event or situation. Bion takes the psychological experiment of the ambiguous figure as a model for situations of insight and mental development. There must be a simultaneous awareness of two kinds of perception with respect to the same object. The transitional object acquires meaning through such vision. In analysis, the transference relationship demands the capacity in both analyst and analysand for 'binocular vision'. Where there is one-sided perception, either the analyst is regarded as a receptacle of projections only, or exclusive attention is paid to the realities of the therapist's situation. Change in analysis and development in childhood may occur after a period of wrestling – that is, tolerance of frustration and paradox. Bion uses the term 'catastrophic change' (1965, pp. 8–9) to emphasise the torment involved for some people. Winnicott asks us to accept, tolerate and respect the paradox without one-sided resolution. For Winnicott, the tolerance of paradox may also be fun: play and humour flourish at this interface. Winnicott's point is that there are certain people, often of a compliant nature, who miss out on this area of experience because of a basic anxiety connected to an absence of holding and consequent break in their sense of continuity. Various potentially enjoyable activities, such as games, are pursued from a compulsive basis. They become joyless since their main function is to fill in a gap. The 'false self' or 'as-if' person, many of whom Winnicott studied, has devised a system of ordering his existence which provides the thread or line of his life which is missing. An addiction, such as smoking or gambling, could be sustaining in this way. Such a person might appear quite normal but have no use for dreaming or playing, both of which have a transcontextual, non-linear character. The following sketch of a 'normal', well-functioning teenager is drawn to illustrate this point.

Jean – an illustration

An adolescent girl of fifteen, Jean, had been in analysis with me for one-and-a-half-years. She was pretty, except that one's first observation might have been that she was mousy and plain. Her aim in life was, in fact, to be plain. She must never stick out. She dressed simply in brown and tan tones, she was quietly stylish, neither 'flashy' nor 'baggy'. Everything must fit exactly right on her slim and well-formed body. At the same time, she was scornful of girlfriends who wore tight-fitting jeans. It was silly to be uncomfortable or to stick out (ambiguity). Her elder sister of eighteen dressed like a 'granny', her younger sister of ten like a '*Vogue* model'. Her goal and her complaint were the same; she was 'in between'. She was interested in her hair and knew what it should not look like – namely, like one of her five sisters. There were six girls and two boys in the family. The result was that it was nondescript, neither short nor long, curly nor straight, layered nor bobbed, dark nor light. She liked a tan as well as a pale complexion, but she was lightly tanned winter and summer. Although comfort was important, she regarded a wrinkle in her trousers or extra cloth in her sleeve or a dent in the toe of her shoe as flaws inflicted upon her. She felt wrinkled, sagging and dented. When things didn't fit, she felt irritable in mood and on her skin. Occasionally, she entered my room and said that she was 'allergic'. Her nose and eyes were itchy and inflamed. She had an occasional rash on her back. However, neither condition was serious enough to count as an illness or to merit discussion. Indeed, she stressed that she was a very 'healthy kid'. She was wrapped up in being normal and straightforward. It seemed to me that her rather dull, 'in-between' appearance and personality resulted both from her fear of transitional areas and from her attempt to fix things in their proper place. Overlaps *and* extremes seemed threatening.

Jean was an excellent all-round student. She was good at sports and in her studies. She could not miss out a subject without feeling she was defective or missing. She was liked, though not popular. She did not seek popularity but 'straight A's'. I am stressing her compulsiveness although, in the sometimes constrained atmosphere of our sessions, her sharp intelligence, wit and empathic understanding of others were never faraway. She was addicted to maths because, more than any other subject, points in maths were impressive. Solutions were guaranteed. Geometry, unlike algebra, annoyed her because more than one possible proof of a theorem existed. As she reached higher levels of mathematical reasoning, she became increasingly panic-stricken. Piecemeal learning no longer made sense. She was terrified of getting lost. As is often the case, her teachers failed to give explanations of the basic principles. Any mark short of an 'A' was evidence of stupidity. Anthropology, on the other hand, was a useless and 'stupid' subject. 'People digging around in the dirt for bits of broken bones and stones'. She poured scorn on the value placed on good field notes. 'Can you imagine shelves and shelves of useless field notes nobody will ever read and which will never ever bring in any money?' All investigations had to produce unambiguous results. Anything unclear precipitated a state of confusion.

An obvious connection can be drawn between digging around and note-taking in anthropology and in the psychoanalytic process. Jean's derision of her anthropology class and teacher coincided with her move off the couch after I had taken a ten-day vacation. I interpreted her hostility towards me for taking a holiday, thereby rendering all analytic work useless. She felt like the notes piled up on the shelf unread and unthought of. She agreed to this interpretation but it also seemed that her scorn, in place of previous compliance, marked the onset of more open independence. By leaving the couch and facing me, she was trying out a new stance towards the world from which she could challenge all the authorities whose praise she had previously sought. The couch pinned her down and made her feel small. She wanted to cut loose and to define herself.

After a few furtive reconnoitres, Jean began to use the face-to-face meetings to scan my face and the surrounding room for flaws. One day, she asked for a change of time because of a final exam and indicated the time of day which she preferred. She was unusually strident in her request which was, in part, defensive against her customary acquiescence. After discussion of her anxieties about not fitting in with me and her desire to give me directions, I offered a time which seemed mutually satisfactory. Near the end of the session, she asked me why I had 'fallen apart'. When I asked her what she was referring to, she said, pointing her finger at me, 'You did, you did . . . you got all nervous, you touched your hair, fidgeted in your chair . . . I didn't say anything at the time because I thought you were falling apart.' I was not aware of feeling uncomfortable about meeting her request, but I had hesitated whilst I thought it over. I decided to take up the thoughts and anxious glee which had prompted her to prove my break-up. I felt that any crack in my 'cool' – she had often remarked that I 'never seemed to have moods' – any sign of uncertainty, or hesitancy, let alone anxiety, threatened her own sense of normality. And yet she clearly wanted to poke at my contours, to shatter my cool, to splinter my collectedness not only in order to triumph over me but also to make me (and our relationship) come to life. She only had time for the pursuit of straight A's; she had no time for digging around in the mud or for roaming in the formless space of the analytic setting. In her attacks on me, she was trying to sever the suffocatingly pleasing relationship. And yet any break, or shift, or gap, or resting place in the session was immediately filled in. She would then complain that she was bored. 'You never say anything new, you've just said the same thing over and over again for weeks.'

One of my windows is covered with a Victorian lace curtain behind which is drawn a white blind. There is a slit of about a quarter of an inch between the window frame and the blind when it is not pulled straight. Even though Jean was in the midst of filling me in with the details of her math homework and her chair was swivelled at an angle of about 120° away from the window, she saw someone pass. During the same session, she commented that I had mud on my boots and that my carpet was 'all mushed up'. 'How come you got a new house and a grungy carpet?' The pile of the carpet was not of good-enough quality to spring up and spontaneously erase footprints. I told Jean I felt that, when she stopped for a minute, thoughts rushed in upon her of all the other people in my life who were waiting on the outside to seize her place and trample all over her. I pointed to all the cracks and blemishes through which she spied these dangerous predators. I said that I felt she also feared the gap which was *not* filled up. Then she felt exposed and on the spot, although she was longing to be noticed. It seemed that her complaint about my carpet, about things being mushed up and not clear, covered her anxieties about being at the centre, at the top, about being noticed. I related these observations to her complaints about her younger brothers and sisters who always seemed to be able to get attention, even when being 'totally obnoxious'. She then told me how the au pair girl had to walk through her room to get to her bathroom and how two sets of feet, especially a heavy scuffling set, mushed up her carpet. Not only had her space in the house and in her mother's attention been over-run by noisy, greedy, newborn babies, but even the employees, representative of her elder sister who had left home, squashed her into the ground. Six months away from her sixteenth birthday when (in California) she would be able to drive, she hovered on the border between her future power and triumph and the safety of being in her parents' space, which was already too small and 'boring' for her.

In the sessions, I noticed that when I drew the 'bad object' on to myself through transference interpretations – for instance, that my muddy boots indicated a lack of care and sloppiness – Jean obviously felt tremendous relief. However, this technique sometimes served to mask the alive 'good' mother who saw life in her offspring and welcomed it. In comparison to the 'potential space' of becoming and growing, the bad, persecutory object seemed welcome. The bad, rivalrous object was at least a familiar contender for the tiny space that she might claim to occupy. In fact, her elder sister had been thrown out of the house the week before Jean first consulted me. She had been sent to a boarding school for fairly mild delinquent behaviour in the home. Jean had had the job of packing up her sister's belongings which she had described to me with excruciating pain. Needless to say, she was terrified that the same fate would befall her if any of her challenging feelings were noticed. She could not envisage how she would get free unless someone – she or I – was cut out or dropped. She could not imagine that someone would take pleasure in her growth. In fact, she did not menstruate until she was 16½. Although she was relieved about this, she was also afraid that her comparatively late menarche was a sign of abnormality.

After six months of alternating tension and tedium, in which the atmosphere of the sessions reminded me of a game to win, there were interludes which brought life and play into our communications.[6] These lightened the relentless pursuit of scoring points. One day when Jean was filling me in on the moves of a basketball game, a shadow flitted across the dusty particles illuminated by a beam of sunlight. On previous occasions, she had batted at the specks of dust which drifted towards her eyes. 'Oh,' she exclaimed, 'a butterfly.' She paused and smiled and continued her description of the game, now focusing on how well she had played and how 'it was so much fun'. We both noted and savoured the quiet, light touch of the butterfly's wings. I had thought that she had previously felt allergic to the dust which the sunbeam exposed, but in fact she had 'always loved sunbeams' since she was little. It seemed that by batting at the sunbeam, she wanted to participate in it so as to make its warmth and brightness more tangible.

Jean dreamed very occasionally. After these nights, she woke up 'all tired'. There was no end to the worry and toil of the day before and of the day to come. The dream was like a homework assignment, a production demanding more work; it was also proof that she had not thought of everything, that something was not covered. All day, she flurried from one class to the next, she waited anxiously at the end of the day for a bus which never seemed to come or, when she got a ride home, she would find no one there and no supper on the table. A dream on top of such a typical day was just too much. Jean felt that she would never get enough sleep. It did not matter how many hours she slept. She could not imagine that a dream might offer a resting place. Her parents worried that she slept too much. They would tell her how most normal teenagers had boundless energy. She felt goaded by them for being tired and felt that yet another demand was being placed upon her – not to sleep.

After the visit of the butterfly and further discussions of her fear that any free space felt dangerous since it would be snatched away, Jean dreamed that the fat, Italian maid had taken her favourite blouse and put it first in the refrigerator and then in the oven. Jean had taken to washing her own clothes because the maid did not understand the settings on the washing machine and dryer. Several of her favourite garments had been shrunk, bleached and dyed. However, the substitutes in her dream of the fridge and cooker for the washing machine in daily reality gave this typical daytime event the quality of a dream. The dream could be used as a transitional phenomenon, bridging, yet separating, inner reality from daily life. Since the dream was not a literal representation of life, we were released from 'going over the same old facts'. In the dream, her precious clothes were deposited in the productive cooker-mother, inside whom the hidden babies baked, and then in the preservative refrigerator-mother, whose insides were cold and dead. I saw the cooker and the refrigerator as two representations of growth, of the space of potential. In her search for a secure, 'holding', yet roomy, mother, enabling her to grow and develop, she oscillated between these two models; one alive, but unbearably hot with fertility, the other vacant enough to have room for her, yet cold and preservative. One model was represented by her step-mother, the mother of her younger brothers and sisters, the other by her real mother, with whom her elder sister now lived. Her natural mother was a successful business woman who had left the house to go to work when Jean was a baby. I think that these two models of inner space, represented in the mother's body and in her own maturing body, may have contributed to her late menstruation. One home (her step-mother's) was full of noisy, jostling children, the other (her natural mother's) was peaceful, yet somewhat sterile.

The content of this dream also threw light on Jean's fear of dreaming. In dreams, things appear 'in the wrong place'. 'Silly' things happen. She laughed at herself for putting the clothes in the cooker and refrigerator in the dream. Discussion of her feelings of incompetence and the unreliability of her care-takers led back to sports and to her physical deficiencies which she felt as physical deformities. She could not run fast, swim fast, high jump or do back flips. And yet, as her teacher remarked with puzzlement, she was very springy and had long legs. In fact, she could do all these things very well, but she could not 'take off'. She felt rooted to the ground just as, in the sessions, our minds were weighed down by adhesion to facts. When running, she would tell her legs to run faster. Her inability to take off was linked to its opposite – that to leap was to fall infinitely. The empty space, the air through which she jumped or sprinted, had no boundaries. No one was there to catch and hold her. I think that these fears may also have linked with her inability to leap into higher levels of abstract thinking, particularly when explanations of basic ground principles were lacking.

For the next two sessions, Jean talked of childhood injuries, many of which she had kept to herself for fear of being ridiculed or seeming incompetent. One day, she had whizzed round the pedal of her mother's exercise bicycle until the spokes of the wheels were invisible. She was fascinated by the whirring, line-less circle. Forgetful for a moment, she reached out towards the wheel. As usual, forgetful excitement ended up in torture. She guarded her mangled hand throughout the day until darkness enclosed her in throbbing pain. She could not sleep and eventually got up and told her mother. With the stabbing pain of these recollections, flashes of humour and insight, as well as tears and sadness, passed between us. The dreams, our discussion of what was physically missing, of the gaps or holes in her competence, broke up the one-dimensional normality by which she had tried to forge a sense of self-continuity. I felt that we both began to enjoy the sessions.

The following session, I opened the waiting room door and said 'Good morning'. Jean was reading *Life* magazine. She looked up at me and pointed at the cover and said, 'Look, aren't they sweet, cute little puppies.' She bounced into the room in her tennis shoes and exclaimed, 'What a pretty morning.' She was so glad after the rain. Nevertheless, she had remembered to bring her ski-jacket 'just in case'. In fact, it started to spot with rain at the end of the session. This was a forward-looking session in which, for the first time, she talked of going to college with anticipation, despite her tear-filled eyes. She could look forward because she could look back on the younger children as the cute little puppies, rather than as predatory babies destroying her life-line to the mother.

In presenting the above material to illustrate the importance of transitional phenomena, I have suggested that Jean's adherence to facts and to the achievement of straight A's, her avoidance of non-purposive activities were all related to fears of being lost and forgotten. Any event, like a dream, which appeared to be meaningless, threatened her sense of security. Suspicious of all transitional or transcontextual phenomena, she had a tendency both to make everything the same – to keep things flat – and to partition things so that nothing would cross, overlap or get in a muddle. This was exhausting. Jean had devised a style of living in which she was not particularly noticeable; however, she was constantly upset because someone else (whom she felt was less remarkable) was chosen. She desperately wanted to be noticed. Adolescence challenged the 'in-between' style which had seemed functional during latency. Jean was forced to deal with differentiation, especially sexual differentiation, and with competition. She was afraid to grow up, to become prominent and attractive to men. She saw all change in absolute, all-or-nothing, terms; to grow was to take a terrifying leap into the unknown where she would find no one to pick her up, or hold her, if she should fall. Since she could envisage no bridges to help her cross over, she tried to fill in all gaps with ordinary, normal, 'boring' details. Everything had to make immediate sense. An important shift in the therapy with Jean occurred when she felt able to tolerate, and eventually enjoy, 'nonsense'.[7]

8

The 'fate' of the transitional object

In the previous chapter, I discussed Winnicott's view of the use and misuse of the transitional object. Recently, there has been discussion over the 'fate' of the transitional object. Let us consider three alternatives:

1 The transitional object is held on to and becomes a 'patch'.
2 The transitional object is replaced by an inner representation of the mother and/or her regulatory, soothing functions.
3 The transitional object loses significance because of an expansion of sensibilities and interests beyond the mother-infant relationship.

In this chapter, I present a case in which a transitional object was used as a patch rather than a bridge, thereby losing its transcontextual and playful quality.

A comparison of the views of Donald Winnicott and Marion Tolpin

Marion Tolpin, a child psychoanalyst, has written about the role of the transitional object in the development of a cohesive self (Tolpin, 1971). Using Kohut's concept of 'transmuting internalization', Tolpin takes issue with Winnicott over the 'fate' of the transitional object. In her view, the transitional object loses meaning just because the transitional object does ' "go inside" '; the 'soothing functions of the transitional object' become part of an individual's 'mental structure' and 'precisely because of this the treasured possession is neither missed, mourned, repressed, nor forgotten. It is no longer needed' (p. 320). However, by focusing on the gradual internalisation of the soothing and regulating functions of the transitional object, Tolpin overlooks the transitional or bridging aspect of the transitional object which becomes 'diffused' into the 'intermediate territory' between 'inner psychic reality' and 'the external world' (Winnicott, 1953, p. 5). Also, the play element tends to diminish when the object is viewed solely as a comforter. According to Winnicott, a comforter lacks the quality of a true transitional object. The comforter is a simple substitution for the mother or her functions and is closer to a patch over the hole created by separation.

The 'fate', or transformation, of the transitional object follows, in part, from the view of the primary state of being – that is, from a particular concept of mother–infant attachment. This connection is clearly stated in Tolpin's paper 'On the beginnings of a cohesive self'. Tolpin states: The transitional object *'illustrates the self–object bond'* (Tolpin, 1971, p. 323; my italics) and replaces both the physiological attachment of intra-uterine life and the merger experience of the symbiotic phase. Thus, Tolpin seems to assume the existence of a primary *bond* from the beginning of life. If the transitional object is viewed as an *illustration* of the self–object bond, obviously its destiny is linked to that of the first attachment. According to Tolpin, the transitional object, like the attachment it illustrates, passes away. When attachment is looked at in the stage-specific terms of the intra-uterine link or the symbiotic phase, it becomes redundant as the child passes out of the separation–individuation phase. As Tolpin says, the infant–mother unit lays the foundation for a separate mental organisation and a cohesive self which replaces attachment.

In Bowlby's view, by contrast, attachment is an invariant which continues throughout the different phases of the life-cycle. Although early patterns of attachment *behaviour* may wither away, attachment itself does not cease with differentiation and independence.[1] My observations and views on attachment lead me to agree with Bowlby and Winnicott rather than Tolpin. As a vehicle of discrimination within the affectional bond, the transitional object does not simply lead to the cohesion of the self and pass away thereafter. The transitional nature of any specific transitional object remains as an area of 'overlap' – that is, as a paradoxical, or transcontextual, schema. This view of the fate of the transitional object parallels Bowlby's view of attachment as an invariant schema in the life of all human beings. An object which is used merely to represent the mother (as Tolpin suggests) – i.e. as a mother-substitute – would tend to lose its *transitional* value at that point in the separation–individuation process when the child might begin to tolerate ambiguity and duality. The transitional object which is only a substitute might then become a fetishistic *object* or a patch over the black hole of absence.

However, the subsumption of the transitional object under a structural, or minimally 'spatial' (Wollheim, 1969, p. 219), conception distinguishes it from a 'patch' which is needed to enhance a defective sense of intactness. The transitional object which is used as a patch leads to a fixation on external *objects*, such as we find with addictions and fetishism. In other words, the patch is a concrete embodiment of the *failure* to develop transitional schemas and signifies a structural deficit. In line with this viewpoint, Frances Tustin draws a developmental distinction between the use of an 'autistic object' and a transitional object:

> Broadly speaking, the *autistic object* is an object which is experienced as being totally 'me'. The *transitional object* has an admixture of 'me' and 'not-me', the child being dimly aware of this. Winnicott defined it as 'the child's first not-me possession'. . . . The transitional object is distinguished by the child as being separate from its body, the autistic object is not. The function of the autistic object is to obviate completely any awareness of the 'not-me' because it is felt to be unbearably threatening. It is to close the gap. In the child's use of a transitional object, the 'not-me' is not completely shut out, although awareness of it may be diminished. (Tustin, 1972, pp. 66–7)

Tustin comments that it is not always possible to make distinctions between these two types of object. 'We might say that some transitional objects are more autistic than others' (p. 67). An example of an over-concretised understanding of the transitional object is given by the mother who says she is going off to the store to buy her child a transitional object. She misses the point that the transitional object must be found by the child.

André Green, an eminent French psychoanalyst, discusses the situation studied by Winnicott in which a person has at some time in his early life moved from distress to 'unthinkable anxiety'

(Winnicott, 1970, p. 254). Anxiety of this order renders the transitional object useless. For such an infant 'the only real thing is the gap; that is to say, the death or the absence or the amnesia' (Winnicott, 1953, p. 22). Thus, the 'real thing' becomes the thing that is not there. The non-object is the object. The trauma is a negative trauma (a 'zero message' in the language of communication theory), a trauma that *'did not occur'* or a message which the patient did not receive *'owing to an absence of response on the part of the mother/object'* (Green, 1978, p. 183). In analysis, this negative trauma is exhibited by

> a need to hold on to and to preserve at all costs a bad internal object. It is as if, when the analyst succeeds in reducing the power of the bad object, the subject has no other recourse than to make it reappear, in fact to resurrect it, in its original or in an analogous form, as if the thing most dreaded were the *interval between the loss of the bad object and its replacement by a good object. This interval is experienced as a dead time, which the subject cannot survive. Hence the value for the patient of the negative therapeutic reaction, which ensures that the analyst will never be replaced, since the object which would succeed him might never appear or might only appear too late*. (Green, 1978, p. 184)

The bad object becomes a patch.

Freud introduced the concept of the 'negative therapeutic reaction' to describe the patient's negative reaction to a positive experience with his analyst. Instead of relief and/or gratitude, the patient returns the next day in a state of rage and despair. His expectations, based upon the *familiar*, have been thrown into disarray. In the myth, Narcissus clings to his mirror-image despite his knowledge that it is no other that he sees. According to Teiresias' prophecy, Narcissus is granted a long life on condition that he does not come to know himself. However painful, the familiar situation may nevertheless become the hallmark of safety. As we know, orientation to the familiar is vital to the development and maintenance of well-being and security in the young infant.[2] One of the chief points of difference between the theoretical schema proposed by John Bowlby and many current psychoanalytic formulations is the emphasis which Bowlby places on 'the environmental parameter familiar-strange' (Bowlby, 1973). The attachment to the familiar throws light upon the perseverative nature of the patient's transference of the bad object.

Bowlby, Green and Winnicott are looking at certain analytic phenomena, which have been described traditionally in terms of 'resistance', 'negative therapeutic reaction' and the projection of the bad object. These authors point out that *positive* experiences may be resisted because they are unfamiliar. The bad object is preferred to the unfamiliar, yet potentially fulfilling, object. The patient reacts negatively to effective therapy, to the healing process itself. In these cases, Green suggests that the work of the analyst is aimed at transforming the alternatives of delusion or death into something less extreme 'so that delusion may become playing, and death absence. In this context, absence does not mean loss, but *potential presence*' (Green, 1978, p. 184). In the literature of psychoanalysis, it has been more common to stress the transition from the positive transference of an idealised good object to the negative transference of the bad object. Green brings to our attention the common situation in which it is the *good* object which is feared.

In Jean's case, the potential space was filled over and over again with a bad, predatory yet familiar, object – namely, one of her siblings. She avoided the empty space which she longed to claim for herself. Winnicott presents a session with a woman who preferred the blank which was real to either a comforter or a familiar bad object (Winnicott, 1953, pp. 20–5). She had experienced 'unthinkable anxiety'. In retrospect, it is possible to surmise that the mother of such a person was absent for x minutes or hours too long so that the child was unable to hold on to *any* representation, even of the mother as a bad object. In Bowlby's terms, the child has moved from a state of protest, to despair and to a final state of detachment. A comforter is useless in the face of this reality. Of the rug which she did not use, Winnicott's patient said ' "You know, don't you, that the rug might be very comfortable, but reality is more important than comfort and *no rug* can therefore be more important than *a rug*" ' (Winnicott, 1953, p. 25). She made the point that the transitional object must include the recognition of separation or separateness. It must acknowledge part of reality – in this case, the reality of absence.

These views on the perseveration of the tie to the bad object, or the non-object (absence) which is familiar, clearly affect psychoanalytic technique and interpretation. The analyst working from this perspective keeps an eye open for transitional schema or their absence, and will interpret the projection of the bad object or the complaint that the analysis is dead or boring accordingly.

The analytic setting itself is a member of the class of transitional phenomena. At the same time, it provides the setting, the background of safety, for the emergence of transitional schemas which are required if the intolerable gap between two extremes is to be bridged. As a class which is a member of itself, it is paradoxical. Like all such 'transcontextual syndromes' (Bateson, 1969), psychoanalysis contains the potential for pathogenic double-binds. The analyst himself is a sort of transitional object which must be used maximally by the patient and left behind. Winnicott was particularly vigilant of the stage in the psychoanalytic process when the patient must 'place the analyst outside the area of subjective phenomena' (Winnicott, 1969, p. 87). When this does not happen, there is a danger of self-destruction or that the analysis itself may become 'a way of life'. However, 'we all hope that our patients will finish with us and forget us, and that they will find living itself to be the therapy that makes sense' (p. 87). This is the analyst's 'fate'. When we think of the analyst and his setting as a kind of transitional object, we remind ourselves that the analyst is not only the receptacle of projections of inner phantasies or simply a screen or mirror of psychic reality; he is also a bridge or raft which is used to cross over into an expanded, more clearly differentiated, outer reality.

My patient, Brenda, had a tendency to resist transference interpretations since these threatened her tenuous sense of separateness. Gradually, she began to trust the analytic relationship and to understand that the transference frame could lead to an *expanded* external world. She expressed this shift in a series of dreams in which she was at my house. As I work at home, my house is divided into two parts, each with its separate entrance. In the first three dreams of the series, the dominant theme was her inclusion in, or exclusion from, my private life. In one of the dreams, she was in the home side of my house, hovering about on the edge of one of my dinner parties. In another, she was in my consulting room, but the room was filling up with people from my private life. She described this as 'the seeping-in or draining-out effect' in which she lost all sense of boundary and place.

However, in the fourth dream, she was at a party in my house, and I 'seemed to think it was all fine'. But she 'didn't think it was quite right'. Nevertheless, although she felt this way 'it didn't matter that much it was no big deal – but just that we both felt differently about it'. She 'could see my point of view but still it didn't seem right' to her. She commented that, although this was 'my recurrent dream', there was a difference. The following image came to mind:

> 'You are the pillar or pole and I am on a leash going round – it's not unpleasant – it's a long leash, plenty enough room for me, and also you rotated on your axis too – so it's like two moving poles except that I'm the one going round you. This is how I have thought of coming here – but in this dream, it was different. More as if the leash wasn't there – feeling of relief. I feel relieved that you have an outside place, outside opinions. And that I can choose whether to agree or not. Like in the dream, I could feel that it wasn't right being at your party *and* it was no big deal that we thought differently. I felt I could talk to you about it.'

Brenda went on to relate her relief that I had 'outside opinions' to an 'uncharacteristic comment' I had made in support of her view that people should be wary of divorce lawyers. She was in the process of divorce from her husband, from whom she had been amicably separated for some time. A lawyer friend of hers had advised her to choose her attorney carefully as a lawyer might protract the proceedings. By my 'Mm' of agreement, I had acknowledged not only that I had opinions about external matters, but that she too could make judgments about people which were not simply transferences of analytic phenomena. She made another association to a recent phone call with her mother. Brenda had reluctantly informed her mother that she had left her old job before she had found a new one. Immediately, her mother started to suggest various jobs such as typing and computer programming and added 'Oh, if I were young again, that's what I'd do.' Her mother continued to talk in a self-pitying way about her own job and limited opportunities. Brenda related this incident to exemplify her mother's inability to grant her daughter a separate and difference existence outside her orbit.

When the analyst is unaware of the potential at this stage for map-territory confusions, analysing differentiation in relation only to the transference, the analysis can go on interminably awaiting a convenient external circumstance for its resolution. The analytic relationship recapitulates the pathology of the early narcissistic relationship in its avoidance of the outside world. If the patient's attempts to relate to, and discuss, extra-transferential phenomena pass unrecognised, the analysis may even go well but the 'only drawback is that the analysis never ends' (Winnicott, 1969, p. 87). Winnicott observes that:

> the subject of relating is a much easier exercise for analysts than is the discussion of usage, since relating may be examined as a phenomenon of the subject, and psychoanalysis always likes to be able to eliminate all factors that are environmental, except insofar as the environment can be thought of in terms of projective mechanisms. But in examining usage there is no escape: the analyst must take into account the nature of the object, not as a projection, but as a thing in itself. (Winnicott, 1969, p. 88)

Winnicott's point is that when the subjective object (e.g. of the analyst) has been maximally *used*, the subject wishes to release him from egocentric usage and to acknowledge him as a person in his own right. At this point, projective mechanisms 'assist in the act of *noticing what is there*, but they are not *the reason why the object is there*' (1969, p. 90, italics in original). In Winnicott's opinion, 'this is a departure from theory which tends to a conception of external reality only in terms of the individual's projective mechanisms' (1969, p. 90). In the projection the analyst is destroyed, but in reality, the objectively perceived object survives. *And* the patient is fully cognisant of this ambiguity. He sees the analyst with binocular vision. If destruction takes place, it is the result not of the *impulse* to destroy but of 'the *object's* liability not to survive' – i.e. to retaliate or collapse (1969, p. 91). If the analysand's fear of the destructiveness involved in the dissolution of the transference relationship is not met by resilience, the analysis may fail to reach completion. In the *Oedipus Rex*, no contrast is drawn between what happens and the unconscious motives, such as patricide and incest, we attribute to Oedipus. Dramatic tension is maintained by the overlap between premonition and disclosure. Tension and change in psychoanalysis lie in the overlap between the familiar, transferential relationship and the new and different relationship.

In this book, I suggest that we classify the analytic process as a form of play. Both Bateson and Winnicott have placed psychotherapy within the class of transcontextual (Bateson) and transitional (Winnicott) phenomena. In play, map and territory, the subjective and the objective, 'overlap' (Winnicott) and are 'equated and discriminated' (Bateson, 1955, p. 185). At the stage in the analytic process under discussion, discrimination is crucial. Bateson points out that successful therapy depends upon a change in rules. At the beginning of treatment, the patient thinks and operates in terms of a certain (familiar) set of rules for the making and understanding of messages. So long as these rules obtain, the game is unchanging, and no therapeutic change will occur. To facilitate change, the analyst uses interpretation to remind the patient of the gap between meaning and denotation. The patient comes to the perception of transference itself.

Let us compare the meta-message 'This is transference' with the message 'This is play.' Bateson expands the message 'This is play' as follows: ' "These actions, in which we now engage, do not denote what would be denoted by those actions which these actions denote." The playful nip denotes the bite, but it does not denote what would be denoted by the bite' (Bateson, 1955, p. 180). The bite, which is not playful, denotes aggression. In other words,

> not only does the playful nip not denote what would be denoted by the bite for which it stands, but, in addition, the bite itself is fictional. Not only do the playing animals not quite mean what they are saying but, also, they are usually communicating about something which does not exist. (Bateson, 1955, p. 182)

In the analysis, the message 'This is transference' would expand somewhat as follows: 'These feelings, which we now express, do not denote what would be denoted by those feelings which these feelings denote.' The hateful or envious verbal attack upon the analyst's breast denotes the bite, but it does not denote what would be denoted by the bite – (for instance, actually gobbling up, or scooping out, the breast).

But how is this change of rules communicated? Generally, the communication about a change in rules is not verbalised and may remain unconscious. Bateson observes that change is usually proposed by 'experimental action, but every such experimental action, in which a proposal to change the rules is implicit, is itself a part of the ongoing game' (1955, p. 192). The single action combines different logical types and gives therapy the character, not of a rigid game like canasta, but that of an evolving system of interaction. Without these paradoxes, the evolution of communication would be at an end. 'Life would then be an endless interchange of stylized messages, a game with rigid rules, unrelieved by change or humour' (1955, p. 193). Humour gives the therapist, and the patient, elbow-room. However, in the literature of psychoanalysis, experimental actions are often construed as 'acting out', that is, acting outside the transference or even acting out within the transferential frame. But at the stage of transference dissolution and of healthy differentiation, the *experimental* action must be discriminated from *acting out* which is usually conceived as compulsive and repetitive. Like the mother who sees the child's departure as an escape or a rejection and scoops him up into her arms, the analyst can confine the patient within the closed system of the transference. He misses the point that the experimental action may be the only way in which the patient can break out of the transference and experience a larger or different reality. A patient may take the experimental action of cutting down the number of sessions. The analyst could interpret this action in terms of destructive phantasies against the analyst or analytic process; or he might interpret it as the patient's attempt to destroy the analyst *as a transference figure*. The implications of these two interpretations are very different. In what I have called the differentiating transferences, the analyst must continually remind himself of the distinction between class and class-members. If the analyst makes the second type of interpretation, he acknowledges that he has been used by the analysand and that the latter has no further use for him. The analytic work has been successful insofar as it has delineated and confined the area of projection and thereby enabled an expansion of the patient's sensibilities.

In summary, the analytic process exhibits many of the features of the theory of development proposed in this book. At the beginning of an analysis, characteristics of the narcissistic type of relationship may be observed. The patient seeks out consonance and synchrony. The analyst may pick up on an intensely undifferentiated – 'merger', 'mirror' or 'twinship' (Kohut, 1971) – transference. The patient may resist the analyst's interpretative activity, since interpretation entails at least two levels of discourse and introduces difference, contrast and unfamiliarity which the patient may shun. Thus, despite conscious wishes and claims to the contrary, change in the patient's perceptions may precipitate anger and disappointment. Jean, for instance, found my interpretations unnerving for this reason, although she desperately wanted something new to happen.

During adolescence, the oscillations between the negative and positive transferences, the positions of absolute commitment and total denigration, the projection of both the bad encapsulating and the good encouraging objects, can be alarming and stressful for parents, analysand and analyst alike. The all-or-nothing attitude of the healthy adolescent flies in the face of transitional structures. And yet, perhaps more than at any other time of life, the analyst involved in adolescent processes needs to be used as a bridge between close, familiar family life and the expanding, unknown, outside world. If the analyst is really to be of *use*, all these conflicts must be expressed within the analytic setting, including the transference frame. Like a true transitional object, the analyst is both part of the young person's inner life, i.e. a projection, and has a place outside it. This is the paradox which the analyst must tolerate without resolution. Whereas previously, both analyst and analysand seemed to be at one, they may seem now to be totally at odds. At this point, the negative transference may play a transitional role over and above the projection of bad, internal objects. The negative transference may signify the patient's anxious renunciation of a synchronous, comforting type of relationship and his attempt to reach out and establish himself outside the analyst's orbit. In the transference, the analyst is used as a transitional object to mark an emerging distinction rather than as a convenient container of bad feelings. The analyst must have a capacity to be used maximally without recourse either to collusion, for instance by acting as the ally of the patient against his parents, or by refusal to abdicate control and to acknowledge extra-transferential phenomena. Through denigration, an adolescent may try to separate himself from his earlier closeness to the analyst and to challenge the unchanging, analytic setting. He now seeks out the strange and may 'act out' in order to provoke the unfamiliar situation. He wants to find contrast. Jean's move from the couch can be viewed in this way. The challenge of the oedipal drama is brought into the analysis – but with a difference. The wish to know, to question, to puncture containment and to participate in sexual intercourse are demanded as a right.

During this transitional period, a young person may experience terrifying feelings of fragmentation and loss. As his fixations crumble, including the familiar image of his own identity preserved intact during the period of latency, he feels that he and the world about him are falling to bits. As differentiation proceeds, he feels that all is delusion. He becomes increasingly mistrustful of the analyst's help and despairs that he will ever find anything good in the world again. Since his own identity is in pieces, he has little sense of agency and therefore seems unaware that *he* is dismembering everyone and picking everything apart. The patient hits out at his projection until he sees that it is a projection. However, through this mutually frustrating and often embittered interaction, another type of operation emerges. Through fragmentation and opposition, the patient comes to the perception of difference. The perception of difference is essential to the acquisition of 'binocular vision' and the tolerance of paradox. It is also essential to the placing of the self, and the discovery of the object, in the world *out there*. When the analyst withstands the attacks on the analytic work and his urges to retaliate (Winnicott, 1969), the patient is not destroyed by the realisation of his own contribution to the devastation he experiences around him. Like the well-used teddy bear, the analyst *survives*.[3] New patterns form out of the bits and pieces. Out of 'formlessness' (Winnicott, 1971a, p. 33), 'noise' (Bateson, 1967, p. 410) and 'catastrophic change' (Bion, 1965), a new order of complexity, co-ordination and flexibility is reached. The complex personal identity, which begins to form, is usable as a secure base for exploration of the unknown appropriate to oedipal development, thereby replacing the two-person synchrony of the narcissistic stage.

The 'fate' of the transitional object

Sara – an illustration

I use the following presentation to illustrate a case in which a transitional object was used as a *patch*, with a consequent diminution in inner security and outer exploration. The information about this transitional object was gathered towards the end of the treatment when my patient actually brought her 'found' object to a session and discussed his use whilst he was present in the room with us. At the time of termination, Freddie (the patch), and his successors in the form of various addictions such as smoking, appeared to have no further use to my patient. For the most part, my patient had found living itself to be the answer. Though no longer adolescent, but mature, she herself clearly described the patch-like quality of her original transitional object and subsequent transitional phenomena.

Sara is a thirty-six-year-old woman who has seen me for once-weekly therapy for a year and a half. She is gifted, thoughtful and loving. She has pursued a very successful academic career and brought up two children who are now in their late teens. She enters the room with exuberance and leaves behind a memory of a joyous presence.

In my presentation of our work, I concentrate upon breaks in the course of the therapy. Since in any one session there is a back and forth movement in time, the following schedule of events may help the reader:

First consultation and beginning of once-weekly treatment.	August 1975
Beginning of my pregnancy.	October 1975
The spider incident.	April 1976
Three-month break during the birth of my child.	June–September 1976
Resumption of therapy.	September 1976
Sara's trip to the Far East.	November 1976
Ten-day Christmas break.	December 1976
Selection of four consecutive sessions prior to termination of therapy.	January 1977
End of therapy.	April 1977

August 1975
Sara first contacted me during a summer vacation. She had a four-week break in which she could attend to herself. She described herself as a 'workaholic' who had a 'chronic problem over over-commitment'. She 'supposed' she'd 'had a lot of loss, especially around [her] marriage, but it was a chronic problem not a crisis'. For our first meeting, she wore black. Her appearance was striking. She was dark, tragic and dramatic.

The first six months of therapy focused upon losses and separation. The dominant emotion was grief. There was so much to grieve over and 'there had been so little time'. Sara herself lived in terror of imminent death. For years, she had suffered from a terror of being destroyed from within by a creeping, invisible disease. At our first consultation, Sara told me that she had been ill and that she was awaiting confirmation of a diagnosis of gonorrhoea. This diagnosis was later dropped, but Sara then discovered a lump in her groin. She delayed before seeking medical advice and treatment. When she did, she again found that her worst fears were not supported. As a child, Sara had almost died from appendicitis because her parents found it impossible to take her pains seriously. Their anxious impatience coincided with Sara's wish that physical ailments would magically disappear. In our discussion of Sara's illnesses, it was difficult to maintain a connection between her body and her mind precisely because the mental and physical realms had never been distinguished. As in her childhood, both physical pain and mental anguish were suffered, but were usually unacknowledged. When we talked about Sara's fears of illness, initially a 'phobic' subject, Sara felt so relieved that she would cancel her doctor's appointments because it was 'all in her mind'. I then became party to her neglect of her body. The lack of distinction between body and mind had led to a disconnection.

April 1976: the spider
In this matter of the distinction between body and mind, we were helped by an incident which was experienced as neither reality nor dream. Sara began the session by remarking that she had been feeling 'on the side of life' which meant her own 'interests and enthusiasms'. She was now looking after herself, had gained weight and made an appointment for a biopsy on the lump in her

groin. Like me (I was pregnant), she had put on twenty pounds since the previous fall. The connection between us was obvious. Sara then said that she had something very important to talk about – 'my spider'. She had been making her bed and there, between the sheets, lay a 'huge, fat spider'. She screamed and screamed and ran out of the room. Her teenage daughter thought that 'at least she had found a body in the closet'. A student friend was called in to look for the spider. But it was not to be found. They concluded that the spider had scuttled into the closet because 'it was looking for a place in which to lay eggs'. This was the reason why the spider was fat and had entered her bed.

Sara connected the feelings aroused by the spider's appearance to notions of evil and witchcraft in the seventeenth century. She was pursued by a feeling of an evil person. That very morning when the spider appeared, she had been feeling particularly well and exuberant: 'One should never take anything for granted.' During the two months (May and June 1976) which followed this incident and which preceded my three-month break due to the birth of my child, we traced the connection between the historical sense of evil, the fat, black spider between her sheets, the possibly cancerous lump in her groin, her smoking addiction and the dark, evil, sexual, witch mother whose productive insides were full of babies ready to burst out and take her space (her own bed and the analytic setting). Her younger brother, who was currently enduring the final stages of multiple sclerosis, had been her mother's favourite child. Sara remembered her mother's fat, pregnant body with disgust. When her mother was carrying her younger brother, Sara had accompanied her on long walks.

The unnerving appearance of a particularly black and fat spider in her own bed gave an immediate meaning to the concept of a 'bad internal object', hitherto ensconced in the unknown recesses of her own body. Almost immediately, Sara became much less concerned with setting up 'ideal goals' for the prevention of her smoking – a plan she had set up for the summer in order to deal both with her evil addiction during my absence *and* with my absence itself. She talked about the meaningfulness of my use, several months earlier, of the word 'connect'. Now, perhaps, the bad, hidden, destructive object could be brought out of the cupboard for mutual observation and reflection. As we worked to unravel this evil object, its contours *as object* dispelled. In its place, we observed a loosely woven set of ideas. The spider's legs, like the curling smoke from her cigarette and the image of infinitely replicating cancerous cells, signified the dangerous extension of this evil object. Previously, the furry, scuttling spider's legs illustrated a dangerous and unpredictable train of thought; all connections to the dangerous object had to be severed. Now that this object was out of the closet, it could be used transitionally to connect inside and outside, body and mind, fantasy and reality. The spider incident, real enough, was used as a dream. Our discussion of its symbolism freed Sara from various compulsive, 'worthy' projects which would have helped to patch over the break in treatment.

September 1976: resumption of therapy

Sara returned eagerly to therapy. During my absence, she felt that she had been unable to hold in her mind the kind of 'connections' we had traced between the spider, the force of Evil and my pregnancy. Nevertheless, she had forgone her habitual, patch-like activities. The 'connections' traced in our meetings, which preserved her from mindless action, depended in part upon the regularity of our weekly sessions. Her sense of personal continuity was still maintained by our contact. The sessions held her embryonic sense of self-continuity and maintained a bridge between inner and outer reality.

November 1976: trip to the Far East

After another two months' work on the subject of separation and connection, Sara left for a 'very important journey' to the Far East. The trip was connected to her wish to give birth to herself as a separate person and to set out on an adventure with the security of me at home. The trip was also important because she wanted to find out about the 'faraway' terror and 'murky' areas of her childhood, a year of which she had spent in this region when she was about ten years old. The area was also of current interest to her both academically and politically. The journey was long, taking her far from home and from her one addiction and comforter, marijuana. Marijuana enabled her to make transitions between work and play, daytime and evening, the lecture room and her study, dinnertime discourse and sexual intercourse. In planning her voyage, Sara recalled vividly the long, lonely trail home from school when she was eight. I imagined a dark waif trudging across an empty plain towards food and shelter but no solace. In wintertime, the plain was white with snow. She felt bleak. As she left the school grounds, Sara was the target of ice-hard snowballs. These memories reflected her childhood feelings about attachment and exploration. She lived in an affectionless world, where emotional absence was experienced as a hard blow and presence was cold as ice.

On our first session after the trip, Sara gave me a beautiful etching of a man on the water's edge filling two buckets yoked across his shoulder. One was full, the other was filling, and the man was lifting it out of the water. The trip had been a great success. She had missed me, and she had re-established an old friendship and she had not missed smoking one bit. It was clear to me that something was on her mind. She seemed anxious about expressing her success. Together with the presents, I surmised that she was thinking of stopping our sessions and that she was wondering whether I would let her go – whether she was full enough. If she were the full one, then surely she had emptied me. She had no right to a life of her own. Near the end of the session, she told me just this with considerable trepidation. We discussed the urgency she felt to stop therapy quickly and abruptly. After further work, we made a tentative date for several months ahead. Our work continued and Sara used the sessions maximally.

January 1977 – April 1977: termination phase

SESSION 1

I select four sessions from the termination phase of the therapy during which Sara's transitional object made its appearance. Sara returned in a sober mood from Christmas vacation. The trip was behind her and she was back at work. As she was on a sabbatical, work was now located in her study – a space she had previously been unable to enter without at least a cigarette and often a joint. But now she was not smoking. She was uncertain about her capacity to write the book which had been commissioned. It presented a challenge since the project, which was a textbook, was both limited and potentially lucrative. She was considering going up north for the weekend to meet up with a man whom she endowed with great intelligence and creative power. Towards the close of the session, she pondered over the thought that she might just not go. Why not remain at work on her book which was just beginning to involve and excite her? We talked about her need to find a bridge into her use of her own creative power and her own study. Hitherto, this bridge had been provided by the joint, which dissolved her compulsive 'workaholism', and by various successful, somewhat 'narcissistic' men.

SESSION 2

The next session, Sara greeted me in the waiting room with 'Freddie'. Freddie was her original teddy bear who had been 'lost' – that is, unfound – in a drawer. Freddie was bald, mangy and barely a teddy bear. Sara felt there was something ghoulish and creepy about him. For a long time she had been unable to look at him even though he intrigued her. He repelled and fascinated her. I too found his appearance compelling yet unattractive. We agreed that he certainly had been used. We laughed. Sara said that she had been unable to look at him because, until now, she could not think about the time when he was important. She described how much she had liked to stroke his fur and she thought that this had masturbatory significance. But the pain to which Freddie's tortuous appearance bore witness was connected to the fact that he had been used '*too* much'. With that, Sara put him down on the couch and covered him with her coat. Freddie's dramatic entry into our session evoked a flood of painful memories about her deprivation, loneliness and her mother's unpredictability. At the end of the session, Sara put on her coat and took Freddie home under her arm.

SESSION 3

The following session, Sara told me that she had been thinking about 'transitional objects' (a term which we had not actually used in our discussions) and had decided that people had over-glamorised them. She could not share the general opinion that they were so wonderful. Freddie had been used as a patch to cover over the black hole of affectionless abandonment, though, physically, her mother had not been absent. Not much wonder Freddie was so unappealing. Freddie 'hadn't really helped'. However, in the present, Sara was enjoying her work on her book more and more. Freddie was back in the drawer and she had not started smoking. For most of the session, Sara thought about her family and, in particular, her relationship with her mother and her mother's relationship with her grandmother. Each suffered from emotional deprivation and lack of mothering, yet each had been denied the pleasurable growth of independence. Sara's grandmother had lived with them when she was a child and, indeed, Sara had shared her grandmother's bed. Sara's mother resented her own mother (Sara's grandmother), and Sara and her grandmother had formed an alliance against her mother. Each found the other overbearing. At the end of the session, Sara remarked that her mother 'had fought for her own space but she could not live in it'.

SESSION 4

Sara greeted me with the news that she had had a most satisfying weekend. She had started work on her house and on the kitchen, in particular. She even had made two trips to the hardware store and had arranged for the framing of the prints she had brought back from the Far East. She had never spent time on her own home before. At last, she was discovering a resting place in her own living quarters. She had both fought for, and taken possession of, her own space. Her family, however, were in a state of 'high drama'. Her father had been ill and, in his absence in hospital, her mother had had a face-lift. She talked about her mother's denial of time and of history and she related this to her mother's 'unpredictability' during her childhood. Her mother was prone to take 'dramatic steps because she lives through symbols'. Sara's sense of history and of the importance of the linkage between events could be seen as extensions of an early resolve to build predictability in a universe of discrete, unconnected, happenings. Freddie hadn't really helped to build predictability. This morning, Sara had looked at herself in the mirror and said, 'Well, good morning'. She was pleased and untroubled by the image she saw. She made no conscious connection to her mother's face-lift but, when I did, she agreed that it was a great relief to look in the mirror and see her own face which, moreover, bore the marks of her mother's *daughter*. No longer identified with her mother, she did not have to deny her history. During one of our last sessions, Sara remarked that a fundamental part of the therapeutic process for her had been the usefulness of 'the space metaphor' or 'how to live in my own space'.

I use these fragments to illustrate the thesis that a tenacious attachment to a transitional object used as a patch can fill up the space in which transitional, mental phenomena might ordinarily develop. As a *transitional* object, Freddie had become meaningless. He did not facilitate communication between Sara and her absent mother. The play element was supplanted by Freddie's defensive function as a denial of separation. He thus came to represent a *fixation* rather than a bridge in development. Potentially pleasurable activities, such as pot-smoking or original work, were spoiled because they could not patch over a primary failure in the holding-environment in which Sara grew up. Whereas Jean, my adolescent patient, had tried to forge a sense of continuity through the pursuit of ordinariness, Sara took dramatic steps to sever connections which were potentially disruptive.

Transitional schemas have a double function: both to distinguish, and to bridge, two elements which may have been confused or severed. In both uses, the transitional schema *connects*. When everything is the same, no connection is required.

9
The watching agency and its products

Freud and transitional phenomena

In this chapter, I examine Freud's account of the stage of development which falls between primary narcissism and the oedipus complex. Although Freud did not use the concepts of the transitional object and transitional phenomena, his understanding of 'the watching agency' and its products can be compared with Winnicott's work in this area. Though there is some overlap in their accounts of specific transitional phenomena, their views on the developmental significance of these phenomena differ radically.

Freud said that primary narcissism is transformed, via repression, into conscience or the watching agency. The watching agency is both a transformation of the primitive, narcissistic ego and, at the same time, it contributes to the foundation of the mature ego. Contemporary Freudian writers have developed Freud's ideas and have linked some of the products of the watching agency described by Freud, such as memory, dreaming and the sense of time, to the emergence of transitional phenomena. The development and function of the watching agency, for instance, links closely with Tolpin's account of the child's internalisation of the mother's regulatory, care-taking and soothing functions. The watching agency could be viewed as the mental structure which renders the child's attachment to his transitional object redundant.

Freud made an important connection between the development of the watching agency and speech. The character of the watching agency is a revealing indicator of the child's feelings towards his care-taker; that character is revealed most obviously through speech. Although Freud and many contemporary Freudians differ from Winnicott in their conceptualisation of the primary state of being – i.e. the first of the two poles between which the transitional object is transitional – most writers, including Winnicott, observe that the development of speech is linked to separation and individuation. Bower and Winnicott point out that the beginning of language use marks the end of infancy, since an infant is, literally, someone who does not talk. Bower says 'The normal duration of infancy, in this strict sense, is about eighteen months. . . . By the end of infancy the baby is sociable and cooperative. He has learned what is necessary for language, possibly the most important of all human skills. He can walk on his own two feet' (Bower, 1977, p. 1). The child's use of the 'I', usually considerably later than eighteen months, is perhaps the most dramatic evidence of a sense of personal identity and agency. The first person pronoun shows that the child has integrated the 'me' part of the me/not-me distinction, the second person pronoun 'you', the third person pronoun 'he' or 'she', and the proper name. The 'I' is, thus, the product of social interaction and, in the self-referring 'I', we witness the utterance of both watcher and watched. In normal circumstances, these are well synchronised.

Freud says that the evolution of the watching agency, which marks the end of narcissism, has its own products. These products are mental functions. Many psychoanalysts have followed Freud in the assumption that various cognitive skills, such as speech and memory, are the products of preceding intrapsychic processes. Originally, the infant is said to have 'protothoughts' (Bion, 1962a, p. 84; Tustin, 1972) from which thoughts proper are later formulated. In support of their views, these analysts point to various pathologies, such as autism and paranoia, which are connected to phantasies and experiences which impede the development of these mental functions. For instance, they might refer to the sexual meaning or oral phantasy which accompanies acts of speech. Or they might discuss the destructive phantasies which erode the very capacity to think.[1]

But, it seems to me that, although 'inner reality' or certain pathological family relationships may *interfere* with the development of a child's mental capacities, it does not follow that these cognitive processes are the *products* of specific phantasies or relationships. Many developmental psychologists and child ethologists regard the environment and the child's early experiences as the necessary facilitators, rather than the originating causes, of cognitive skills. For instance, problems over separation and individuation might lead to various communicational disorders such as a refusal to speak or a confusion over the use of pronouns, but it does not follow that speech development is a *result* of the separation–individuation process.

Freud lists the following products of the watching agency:

A The ego-ideal
B Speculative systems
C Memory
D The sense of time
E Dreams
F Self-regard.

A *The ego-ideal and paranoia*

Freud asks (1914) What transformations does this state (of infantile narcissism) undergo? Does it all pass over into object-cathexes? No. Some of it is subject to repression. Freud's point is that the narcissistic attachment to the self is not simply transformed into attachments to others. The ego ideal is set up by the watching agency, so that the infantile narcissism is now displaced from the infantile ego on to the ego-ideal; like the infantile ego, the ego-ideal deems itself the possessor of all perfections. The reason Freud gives for this displacement, and the consequent withholding of love from others, is that 'man has here again shown himself incapable of giving up a satisfaction he had once enjoyed' (Freud, 1914, p. 94). Throughout life, man seeks to restore the blissful or withdrawn state of primary unrelated narcissism.

However, even in Freud's estimation, the ego-ideal is not only the inheritor of the infantile ego which deems itself the proud possessor of all perfections. It is also formed out of the *relationship* which has developed between the child and his parents. In particular, it is a representation of parental criticism which, as we might expect, is generally conveyed by the voice.

> For what prompted the subject to form an ego ideal, on whose behalf his conscience acts as watchman, arose from the critical influence of his parents (conveyed to him by the medium of the voice), to whom were added, as time went on, those who trained and taught him and the innumerable and indefinable host of all the other people in his environment – his fellow-men – and public opinion. (Freud, 1914, p. 96)

Thus, the repression of narcissism comes about because the desires of the individual come into conflict with cultural and ethical ideas. These ideas are introjected by the individual so that he sets up an ideal in himself by which he measures his ego. Narcissistic gratification may still be achieved from the ego-ideal 'on whose behalf his conscience acts as watchman' (p. 96), constantly watching and measuring the actual ego by the ideal.

Freud says that these origins of the ego-ideal and of conscience are revealed in the delusions of being watched of the paranoic.

> Patients of this sort complain that all their thoughts are known and their actions watched and supervised; they are informed of the functioning of this agency by voices which characteristically speak to them in the third person ('Now she's thinking of that again', 'Now he's going out'). This complaint is justified; it describes the truth. A power of this kind, watching, discovering and criticizing all our intentions, does really exist. Indeed, it exists in every one of us in normal life.
>
> Delusions of being watched present this power in a regressive form, thus revealing its genesis and the reason why the patient is in revolt against it. . . . The voices, as well as the undefined multitude, are brought into the foreground again by the disease, and so the evolution of conscience is reproduced regressively. But the revolt against this 'censoring agency' arises out of the subject's desire . . . to liberate himself from all these influences, beginning with the parental one. . . . His conscience then confronts him in a regressive form as a hostile influence from without. (1914, pp. 95–6)

Thus, Freud concludes, the lament of the paranoic shows also that at the bottom the self-criticism of conscience is identical to, and based upon, self-observation.

If we place Freud's observations in the context of the separation–individuation process and the development of speech, it would seem that the typical laments of the paranoic reveal an intermediate position between early narcissistic synchrony and the oedipal sense of identity and agency. In normal circumstances, the sense of personal identity is a product of multiple attributions, but the use of the 'I' usually demonstrates the child's co-ordination and ownership of the qualities observed by others. However, when there is a mismatch between the child's own perceptions of his actions and emotions and the observations and attributions of others, an emerging sense of identity might be felt as a diminution of power rather than as an achievement. In consequence, the child might diffuse or fragment the 'I' over his environment in order to rid himself of a false or burdensome sense of identity. All the statements of the paranoic are made in the third person. The voices echo what the paranoic has heard – 'now he is doing this', etc. Unlike Echo, who waited to hear Narcissus' words, the paranoic's voices are 'in his head'. This suggests a partial internalisation of the voices of others (which, therefore, do not have to be heard immediately before they are reproduced), but, nevertheless, a defect in co-ordination and owning of them. The paranoic has collected various attributes to form a common referent, 'He'. The paranoic may go on to identify these 'he's' by giving them a proper name – God, for instance. If language development marks the end of infancy, it could be said that the paranoic's use of language leaves him in an infantilised position in relation to his care-takers. The paranoic's complaint is that he is not a free agent.

Even in the best of circumstances, the infant's participation in his natural social environment incurs a diminution in the range of his communicational potential. Hopefully, the pay-off of friendship and participation in the social community makes the loss worthwhile.[2] However, one may wish to withdraw one's membership of a club when the social rituals or obligations demanded outweigh the gains of belonging. The balance between eager engagement and aversion, prompted by the intrusion of too many unfamiliar communicational cues, is delicate and an individual matter for each child. My nephew, Stephen, tried out new gestures such as head-shaking, waving, saying 'Tss, Tss' (indicating hullo) on each new visitor to his house. Each responded, or did not respond, to these approaches in individual ways, which intrigued and delighted Stephen. He would subsequently incorporate some of the idiosyncrasies in people's responses into his routine, which he would then try out on the next visitor. Two male friends, who fixed Stephen with prolonged eye-to-eye gazes with no other accompanying gestures of greeting, precipitated, at first, silent turning away and finally loud protest and turning to mother.

Sally, at the age of thirteen months, was extremely precocious and charming. She already spoke well and was quick and keen to learn. However, when her brother was born when she was fourteen months, she retreated into a private language. Her parents struggled to understand Sally's language which, later, became her little brother's first language. Although she was classified as 'autistic' at the local child guidance clinic in England, her language was not totally excluding of others, but it was her invention. Her special language was adopted into the family communicational system. When her brother went to nursery school at three years of age, he quickly began to speak ordinary English which he re-introduced into the household. Until he did so, Sally's speech therapy classes had been useless. Soon after her brother went to school, Sally returned to a normal primary school and began to function very well, being above average in most of her classes. When I saw Sally again when she was eleven, she had become very interested in acting and ballet. She hoped to enter a school for drama and ballet. She could impersonate and take on identities as a duck takes to water. In retrospect, one might surmise that she suffered from a precocious sense of differentiation in some areas. Her mental and verbal development at one year seemed to outstrip her position in the process of separation–individuation from her mother. Both Mahler and Tustin have commented upon the unevenness of development which can affect both normal and autistic children. In her book on the separation–individuation process (Mahler *et al.*, 1975), Mahler describes some of the difficulties which may beset a child who is unusually precocious in his or her motor development. A child may accomplish physical independence from mother by crawling or climbing before he or she is able to tolerate such autonomy emotionally. Tustin describes children who have a precocious sense of differentiation but lack a sense of containment. Differentiated from mother and yet incomplete in themselves, they may use autistic processes in order to produce a pseudo-sense of self-sufficiency.

The achievement of certain 'milestones', such as head-raising, sitting-up, crawling, walking, talking, toilet-training, etc., may count for little when a child is not ready for the mental, emotional and relational changes set in train by these events. The position and character of the watching agency or internal regulator in the child's mind is reflected in these achievements. One late walker saved his first perfect steps until the day when both his parents were out. His nanny remarked that it was as if he were saying 'See, I can do it perfectly when I want to and when no one is watching me.'

Winnicott (1953) subsumed the young infant's use of sounds under the class of transitional phenomena.[3] Although many analysts agree that vocalisation becomes increasingly specific and differentiated as the child separates himself from his surroundings, there is disagreement over the communicational value placed on pre-verbal vocalisation or 'babbling'. These differences reflect the author's conceptualisation of the first of the two poles between which the phenomenon of babbling is transitional. Is babbling to be understood in a relational context or does it, as Freud implied, have autistic/narcissistic value only for the infant?

In the volume *Between Fantasy and Reality* (1978), early vocalisation is discussed by several psychoanalysts. Although respectful of Winnicott's concepts, these authors view infant speech and its transitional value from a classical Freudian perspective. I shall contrast the view of one contributor, Martin Weich, with the communicational view proposed by Bower. In Weich's view, the infant uses intonation and gesture during the pre-linguistic stages to express himself, his wishes, demands, etc., which are more or less undifferentiated. Weich divides early language development into five stages:

babbling by the fourth month;
lallation by six to twelve months;
echolalia by nine months;
one word utterances by twelve to eighteen months;
two word utterances by seventeen to twenty-two months (Weich, 1978, pp. 414–15).

Like Ekstein and Greenson (two eminent analysts in the USA, both contributors to the same volume on transitional phenomena), Weich views thought and language as a parallel development to that of object-relations – i.e. a development from primary autism, to fusion, to increasing differentiation out of the symbiotic sac. During the auto-erotic stage, sounds have a simple 'tension-reducing function' (p. 417). The sounds function as a 'pacifier'. Lallation, which precedes the echolalic stage, refers to the 'imitation of the infant's accidentally produced sounds'. At about nine months of age, the child becomes narcissistically attached to his sounds and 'indulges in a form of self-echoing'. Only after the child 'cathects his mother's soothing voice' – i.e. relates to objects – does he imitate her sounds and words (p. 417). He then reaches the stage of the one word utterance. According to Weich, transitional language maturation occurs at around sixteen to eighteen months and is transitional between one and two word utterances. Whereas one word utterances are like names with a global reference, two-word utterances may be carried around by a child like a companion or teddy bear. In Weich's view, the idiosyncratic significance of the word is evidence of early internalisation. The word is used as an object or a proto-symbol. Progress in the development of one word utterances is marked by an increase in the variety of forms, variation of intonations, differentiation of attitudes and the adoption of vocal patterns resembling the adult situation.

Even apart from my theoretical bias and the considerable evidence of developmental psychology, my limited observations of young infants lead me to believe that primitive speech is often communicational and that Weich's dating of object-related speech development is too late. Stephen babbled by the third month and, at four months, would put himself to sleep by a sort of singing or crooning. He had learned this from his mother who often sang him to sleep. By seven-and-one-half-months, he was repeating sounds, at first echoed from others, to himself – a mixture of lallalia and echolalia. Although these sounds seemed comforting and interesting in themselves, Stephen clearly enjoyed making them *to* other people, especially his mother. He said ba-ba-ba and da-da-da, when exploring his environment with excitement and particularly when he found an object of interest. He would pat it and repeat these two sounds, frequently turning round to communicate his discoveries. He had first learned the ba-ba-ba/da-da-da sound when he was in his father's arms on a car trip. To amuse him, his father had made the ba-ba-ba sound whilst Stephen was lying facing him at a distance of about eight inches. Stephen was delighted and it turned into a game. On return home, Stephen scampered round the house, patting familiar and favourite objects in accompaniment to the ba-ba-ba sound and looking up at his parents as if to tell them how great it was to be home. Stephen repeated a sound to himself, which was not initially accidentally produced, and, moreover, the sound communicated his excitement to those around him. At eight months, he repeated the word na-na-na to communicate 'No' and all states of dissatisfaction such as tiredness, discomfort and annoyance.

In Part I, I alluded to the research of Condon and Sander in which the newborn's capacity to participate in any language community is demonstrated. Most psychologists, however, who have studied the noise-making aspects of language have completely ignored the fundamental desire to communicate which goes hand-in-hand with attachment. The quantity of the baby's vocalisations increase significantly when the partner enters into communication.[4] Although the baby's language is private, in the sense that he uses a different system of coding to that of adult language, it nevertheless serves the same function, namely, to communicate. In analogical communication, the baby imitates the rhythms and patterns of the language he hears. In digital or verbal communication, the child is able to discriminate the on-off occurrences of words out of the surrounding 'noise'. These words stand for the actions he formerly imitated.[5] To continue to respond only synchronously and sensually to the variety around him might make the infant an unviable member of his community.

Bower (1977) divides vocal productions into two phases. During the first half-year, the babbling baby is prepared to participate in all possible linguistic communities. By the second half of the first year, this repertoire has narrowed down to the sounds reproduced by the adults around him. This loss, however, is not regrettable. Restriction serves an important function, because our information-handling capacities are limited. I suggest that *some* of the psychoanalytic work on autism, for example, makes good sense when viewed from a communicational model and that autistic features may appear when the normal restriction in general responsiveness fails. In some cases, the autistic child might continue to respond indiscriminately and variously to a range of information which is *too wide* for participation in a normal language community. Donald Meltzer, a Kleinian psychoanalyst who has worked with autistic children in England, has described the sensitivity and 'nakedness' of these remarkable children.[6] (Meltzer *et al.*, 1975). In his experience, the autistic withdrawal is preceded by an unusual intensity of sensuality and perceptiveness. I use the psychoanalytic research of a group of Kleinian child analysts working in Britain (Meltzer *et al.*, 1975) to suggest that, in autistic processes and behaviour, we witness an arrest in the development of attachment and communication at a stage best described in terms of Bower's 'interactional synchrony' or Balint's 'intense relatedness'. Of course, there are many other analytic, and non-analytic, theories of autism which are totally at variance with the communicational model. However, these authors concentrate upon the understanding of the communicational or relational value of autistic patterns of relationship. From this research it seems that the children described are not fixated in a need-orientated, auto-erotic stage of development. The autistic child's intolerance of separate self-object relationships is not evidence of a non-attached, primitive state, but of a 'possession of the maternal object' constitutive of 'a primitive form of love which is both tender and highly sensual'. However, the 'surface, skin-to-skin intimacy they seek tends to be insatiable and to resent, and resist, the impact of time' (Meltzer *et al.*, 1975, p. 10).

Our understanding of this necessary restriction in the range of the newborn's communicational potential is greatly enhanced if we turn to the cybernetic model. In cybernetic terms, we are talking about *restraints* rather than the *positive* selection of clues. The 'selection' of a stimulus is to be understood in negative terms and in relation to the total number of alternatives available. The restriction in the range of sounds enables the infant to pay more attention to the sound sequences which make up the words of a particular language. The ease with which the baby 'detects' a particular stimulus or makes a response depends on the number of other stimuli which have been knocked out as much as on the characteristics of the particular stimulus. In contrast, learning theory and psychoanalytic theory define the selection of a piece of information in positive terms. Both tend to view the process of development as cumulative only and never restrictive.

B *Introspection*

Introspection is another product of the watching agency. The

> activity of the mind which has taken over the function of conscience has also placed itself at the service of internal research, which furnishes philosophy with the material for its intellectual operations. This may have some bearing on the characteristic tendency of paranoics to construct speculative systems. (Freud, 1914, p. 96)

Freud's view raises the question as to whether *all* introspection rests on a paranoid foundation or even upon self-observation. Every child hears himself addressed, and talked about, by others before he understands fully the content of the conversation. However, these voices and looks need not be judgmental in a *negative* sense. The watching agency might also have a cautionary function in relation to the unknown and the unfamiliar, since the growth of knowledge proceeds with a certain measure of care and circumspection. From earliest infancy, curiosity and anxiety go hand in hand. As the child steps forth on his own, the parent naturally feels anxious, but the parent's increased watchfulness may be matched by a belief in the child's growing competence. We can imagine that, in Victorian times, introspection might have led a young child mainly to encounter the voices of a persecutory and strict internal watcher. Victorian children were to be seen and not heard. Independent exploration and thought were not encouraged. A parent sometimes talks about his or her child in front of him as if the child could not hear. The child may interrupt to correct the story according to his version. However, the child of strict parents cannot intercede in the face of misattributions.

In analysis, the introspective capacities of the analyst and analysand are called forth. There is a danger that this valuable activity may be used in a paranoid or defensive way. Each partner may pre-empt the comments and realisations of the other. The analysand may tell a dream, interspersed with associations and interpretations, so as to get in there first. He may justifiably fear the analyst's invasiveness and insistence on his interpretations. A well-meaning analyst may pre-empt the patient's self-understanding by his perspicacious, yet prematurely voiced, insights. Winnicott was concerned with this tendency amongst analysts.[7] He was particularly attuned to those patients 'in a certain classification category' who manifested compliance, the complementary defence to resistance. With patients in this category, the analyst must be prepared to wait; in particular, he must wait for the patient to find *the questions*.

Brenda, the twenty-five-year-old anthropology student (see chapter 7, p. 148) whom I saw in three times a week therapy, would seem to fit into this category. She was noted amongst her friends for her excellent memory and insight. In therapy, she was so articulate and emotionally available that understanding was almost too easy. Her accessibility gave the impression of 'a mental apparatus naked to the wind' (Meltzer *et al.*, 1975). She was eager to communicate and to understand, particularly as she suffered from catastrophic depressions; during these episodes, she would cut up her clothes, an activity which gave her a brief sense of power and direction. (There were many other meanings to this destructive act.) Gradually, after a year or so, she became suspicious over our ease of communication. This was exactly where her problem lay – her permeability to the communications of others, coupled with her own intense desire to communicate herself. She had always been lonely, although she had never had enough time alone. Basically, I felt that Brenda had a gentle, open and passionate disposition, she was eager about the world and what it had to offer. However, these admirable characteristics seemed to have been exploited by an extremely possessive, isolated and envious mother. Brenda told me that she literally felt that when she breathed, she breathed for her mother. To think of another was to breathe for them. Since she had been so frequently misunderstood, she bathed with pleasure in our mutual understanding, which was by no means the result of compliance and collusion. But it was also threatening, because she had to find her own mind. To think the same way was to be inextricably entangled. It was very important for me to hold back, even when my comments simply reiterated her own insights.

Transference interpretations were also tricky. They indicated that there was another point of view which she had not thought of. Moreover, it seemed to her that everything and everybody in her outside life was a reflection of me. It took some time for Brenda to express thoughts of this kind, as, initially, she had been very adept in connecting her comments about other people to myself. One day, before I was going to take a vacation, Brenda was extremely angry with a boyfriend, John, who had let her down on the previous Friday night by going out with someone else. I related her feelings to my holiday. At first, she reacted with silence and changed the subject. I interpreted her difficulty in connecting her feelings about John to myself, and she responded with a self-accusation: 'It always astonishes me that, every time, I miss the most obvious connections between what I say about outside things and what goes on in here. . . . I just can't understand how I miss something so obvious.' Her angry reprisal against herself could be seen as a confirmation of my interpretation, particularly since she could not afford to be angry with a person whom she was about to lose. However, I had the feeling that the more important reaction to my interpretation was that I was taking away the small world which existed outside my orbit. In fact, she immediately went on to talk about how she had no one to go and see after she left me. She said this in a rather petulant, yet placating, way. I said that I thought she felt she had to confirm my interpretation by telling me that she had no friends. She replied somewhat tentatively that, although she was anxious about my departure, this time she felt that she did have quite a lot of things in her life to do and, moreover, that she was 'even quite excited' to see how she would do on her own. Irrespective of the validity of the content of the transference interpretation, the making of it on her last session threatened to divest her of her own life away from me. It was important that I should recognise her feelings of anger and anxiety about my holiday and that I should not undermine her tentative anticipation of a few days on her own.

Freud linked the practice of introspection and the construction of speculative systems to paranoia and to obsessional doubt. Brenda had developed an interesting way of dealing with her emotional permeability and lack of self-continuity. She applied a compulsive doubt to every thought which crossed her mind. She could come up with a host of alternatives to any construction. In her *methodical* application of doubt, she obtained a curious sense of security. I was reminded of Descartes's Second Meditation when he says: 'Perhaps the only thing which is true is that nothing is certain. . . . How do I know that there is not something which I have not mentioned which is certain? . . . Am not I nonexistent? . . . But there is some deceiver, supremely powerful, supremely intelligent, who purposely always deceives me . . .' (Descartes, 1961, pp. 66–75). When Brenda suspended her doubt for a minute, she felt that she had fallen into collusive agreement, only to find out that she had been 'duped' again. If she applied the doubt, upon which her sense of existence depended, she ended up in a state of mistrust and despair, since everything had to be undermined; no resolution was possible from within the self-referring system which she had constructed. She held on tenaciously to doubt as her security and her only possession. To trust was to be fooled. She was frequently 'duped' because the security and certainty she sought in vain was total and absolute – the absolute dependence to which the infant has a right but which no analyst can promise. In conclusion, I suggest that introspection, speculation and doubt *can* be used in order to protect a vulnerable and permeable self. In this sense, these mental capacities may have a paranoid, watchful foundation. In the consulting room, it might seem, as it did to Freud, that this is their sole origin and use.

C, D *Memory and the sense of time*

Freud adds in a footnote to the paragraph on internal research 'merely by way of suggestion, that the developing and strengthening of this observing agency might contain within it the subsequent genesis of (subjective) memory and the time-factor, the latter of which has no application to unconscious processes' (Freud, 1914, p. 96).

René Spitz is a child psychologist and psychoanalyst who is particularly well-known for his research on separation and stranger anxiety. As a young man, Spitz left Budapest, where he had been studying with Ferenczi, and moved to Vienna to begin analysis with Freud. In his late forties, he began four decades of research into the earliest psychical development of infants and children. He was a pioneer in the direct observation and photography of infants and their interactions with their mothers. In their work on transitional phenomena, Spitz and his colleague

David Metcalf (1978) have linked the development of transitional objects to the development of memory, 'libidinal object-constancy' (i.e. the conception of the mother-figure as a constant object), the capacity for symbolisation and the inception of dreaming. They relate the development of memory to Spitz's first two 'psychic organisers': the smiling response at three months and stranger anxiety at six to eight months. These two responses indicate the achievement of two critical stages in the development of psychic organisation. Memory is a pre-requisite for the development of libidinal object-constancy. The child must remember the object which is absent to perception. Following Fraiberg, another Freudian child analyst, Metcalf and Spitz distinguish 'recognition memory' – memory in the presence of object stimuli – and 'evocative memory' – memory in the absence of a need for the object or the presence of the object (1978, p. 101). The appearance of stranger anxiety (at six to eight months) is evidence for recognition memory, although the smiling response of the three-month-old is also a recognition. But 'recognition proper' involves the recognition of the object's specific, unique attributes. According to Metcalf and Spitz, the recognition of the smiling response is related to need-satisfaction rather than to patterns of attachment and social interaction. These writers place the development of memory and also of transitional objects within traditional Freudian theory. For instance, they postulate that smiling at three months demonstrates that the percept of ' "privileged Gestalt" is recognised as the *signal* for need gratification' (p. 101). The stranger response, on the other hand, demonstrates that smiling no longer takes place as a function of a need or as the provider of relief from unpleasure, but that the infant now responds to a unique individual and recognises the percept of the libidinal object as the object of complex, dynamic exchanges and relations. Stranger anxiety 'indicates that the approaching person is a nonobject' (p. 101).

Although the attachment theorists clearly dispute these views on the nature of the stimulus of the smiling and stranger responses, they would agree that the development of attachment parallels an increased discrimination of the main attachment figure and a narrowing of the range of earlier social responses to a focus on one or two immediate figures. Metcalf and Spitz consider that stranger anxiety is a response to the infant's recognition that the approaching stranger is a 'nonobject' who does not correspond to the infant's *needs* at the moment. From the attachment point of view, stranger anxiety is not a mark of the memory of a need-gratifying object but rather demonstrates that the infant is unable, as yet, to communicate with a person who does not use the same language as his primary partner.[8] In the view of Metcalf and Spitz, transitional objects and transitional phenomena appear between the development of recognition memory (six to eight months) and evocative memory (towards the end of the second year). The transitional object serves as a 'quasi-evocative stimulus' which evokes the 'total affect-gestalt, "mother", with the unique meaning of security' (p. 102). The child endows one inanimate thing with an essential attribute of the libidinal object, security.

The capacity to remember, forgive and forget depends upon an expectable environment and, in infancy, a reliable maternal figure. Habits cannot grow in an unpredictable setting. Both Sara and Brenda used their memory to create a mental sense of security and continuity in an environment which was composed of discrete and haphazard emotions – their mothers' moods. In neurosis, perhaps, memory is *used* as if it were a product of a paranoid, watching agency. However, the use of memory as a substitution for habit, built on an environment which is predictable, can become very uneconomical. Moreover, the motivation to record out of revenge is taxing and may prevent memory from being used in a creative or exploratory way. 'I'm going to remember this till I die, she's never ever going to do this to me again.' Brenda was noted amongst her friends for an excellent memory of past events. She could put her memory to good use in her anthropological studies, as she did in her analysis. She was relieved to discover in our early meetings that I too had a good memory. Soon after the beginning of therapy, she was surprised to discover that she had forgotten what had gone on in the previous session. She had 'forgotten to remember'. Of course, she was also anxious about my memory – as I sometimes was about hers – and it became a matter of urgency to distinguish those times when my memory of her lent vitality to her existence and when it became constricting. If she and I remembered each other constantly, she could have no life to herself away from me. Nevertheless, the thought of my forgetting her threatened her with annihilation. On one session, after I had had a cold, Brenda came in with a very bad cold. She expressed relief that I had been sick, which she clearly felt as giving her licence to be sick herself. Her mother had always regarded Brenda's illnesses as an attack upon herself and Brenda was rarely sick. She talked about how she felt that she could never have been sick before, either because I was not sick or because she might infect my children, or because the sessions were so desperately important. My cold assured her that I was human and not invulnerable. Whilst we discussed this matter, she reminded me that I had been sick with a cold once before and said, 'I'm sure I could remember exactly when this was if I put my mind to it. But I don't think I will.' Laugh. 'What a relief. That's the sort of thing I used to do all the time.' She paused, 'Still, it could be fun to do it once in a while, just to see if I could still do it.'

A good memory is also assisted by constancy of *physical* surroundings. An infant is usually more insecure in a strange environment. A baby-sitter with whom an infant has been secure and exploratory, may be surprised when, on entry into a strange house, the infant breaks down into tears. Usually, emotional dependability and constancy will make up for physical unfamiliarity but there are limits. Two ten-year-old boys, Dennis and Timothy, whom I saw in therapy, had both lost their homes in the second year of life. Their parents had divorced and, in each case, the children had remained with the mother. Each child had a step-father and a number of care-takers. Both Dennis and Timothy had moved house every year until they were four and seven respectively, after which they were sent to boarding school. Neither could remember much of these early years except a jumble of images of houses in disrepair and of packing and travelling. There were no places to which their experiences could be attached. In the therapy, I myself found it difficult to picture them at any age, as I could not quite visualise where to place them.

In classical and medieval times, memory was developed as an art. Some of the techniques for the cultivation of this art seem relevant both to the development of memory and to its use in the practice of psychoanalysis. The classical memory system was made up of places (*loci*) and images (*formae, notae, simulacra*). The material remembered depended upon the number and order of the *loci*. Frances Yates (1966), an eminent scholar of the Renaissance, describes how when the loci ' "have been arranged in order, the result will be that, reminded by the images, we can repeat orally what we have committed to the *loci*, proceeding in either direction from any *locus* we please" ' (Yates, 1966, p. 22). Therefore the 'formation of the *loci* is of the greatest importance, for the same set of *loci* can be used again and again for remembering different material' (p. 23). Images fade and are effaced, but the *loci* remain in the memory and can be used again. A *locus* is a place such as a house, a corner, an arch. Memory *loci* are best formed in deserted and solitary places because crowds of passing people tend to weaken the impressions. These *loci* should not be too much alike; the spaces should not be of similar type, nor should they be too large, because this makes the images placed on them too vague, nor too small since this makes an arrangement of images too crowded. Many people continue to set their dreams about contemporary issues in the house of their childhood.

The rules for the memory of words differed from the memory of images. Memory of words was thought to be much more difficult. Since words required a vast number of *loci*, an image had to be found which would be shorthand for several words and which had high associative potency. A friend of mine, Sigrid, had grown up in Norway in a situation which seemed to conform to the conditions required for the memory of images. In her early life, people and things rarely changed their places. She told me how she would never forget the excitement she felt on the two or three occasions when her bed was moved during her childhood. She could scarcely wait for the day to be over so she could experience the room from the new viewpoint. The schedules of her closest companions were dictated by the seasons. Her house was surrounded by old trees and by fields. She knew all their colours and the order of the budding and falling of the leaves of each tree. Like all the other children in the district, she had tasks to do such as hoeing, sowing, fruit-picking, forestry, etc. Most of these activities followed the seasonal rhythm, the seasons being sometimes good and sometimes bad. After these tasks were accomplished, she had long stretches of time with little distraction. There was no television, radio or electric light. During winter nights, which began at 2 p.m., she would read and join in the village entertainments. Like the external conditions, the strict atmosphere in which she was brought up was conducive to a good memory. One reason she gave for entering therapy was that she felt overwhelmed by the reams of memories which filled up her mind. She wanted to be liberated from a compulsion to record. She began to allow herself to sleep deeply, to forget dreams and every word which the analyst spoke.

Dreams of different periods of my life often take place in *loci* from my early childhood – stairs, doorways, corners, wood-clearings, etc. I wake up with these *loci* fresh in my mind. I know the time of day and the time of year, the light and shade are all clear and yet I could not tell you what the dream was about. The *loci* are bright; the images are dim or absent. In the classically trained memory, the space between the *loci* was measured and the lighting also noted. On falling asleep one night, the *loci,* which formed a constant backcloth to my dream life, unfolded in a seemingly perfect order. I saw each room, its overall colour and lighting, its wallpaper, curtains, carpet, coverings, its dark corners and open spaces and its smell. During my analytic training, I found the recording of *loci* particularly useful when presenting sessions with young children. Since play and non-verbal behaviour predominated, my headings referred to different spots in the room – couch, window-ledge, sink, changes of light, etc. – instead of topics.

Freud noted that sequence is crucial to the development of memory. The sense of sequential time depends upon order in the environment and emotional reliability.

Young children in therapy can learn to tell the time very quickly. A two-and-one-half-year-old child I saw learned within three months to decipher the unrelenting clock-face which punctuated his time with me. A therapist might concentrate on the paranoid and controlling motivation behind this learning. The watch is sometimes interpreted as a symbol of the father who tells mummy 'That's enough' and who marks out the lines of the relationship. The watch-face is sometimes thought to symbolise the breast, whereas the hands symbolise the hard, Daddy-nipple, which is the precursor of the penis. The penis has its own demands upon the mother. This focus on the symbolism of the watch can analyse out the child's experience of time itself. The child wants to share the therapist's sense of time, *partly* as an attempt to deal with separation, but also because he wants to know what is going on and to know about things, such as time, which are so important to other people.

E *Dreams*

Freud also related the critical watching faculty to dreams. During transitional states between waking and sleeping, we can directly observe the translation of thoughts into visual images. Indeed, Freud says, 'we frequently have a representation, not of a thought-content, but of the actual state (willingness, fatigue, etc.) of the person who is struggling against sleep' (Freud, 1914, p. 97). The end of a dream or some section of the dream content may signify the dreamer's own perception of his sleeping and waking. Thus, not only does self-observation continue during sleep but it plays a part in dream-formation. Dream-formation takes place under the sway of a censorship which distorts the dream thoughts. The censor not only distorts the content of thoughts, but also their form, since it translates thoughts and bodily sensations into visual images.

As in cases of paranoia, Freud proposed that the dreamer's delusion of being watched contributes to the dream content thoughts, such as ' "now he is too sleepy to think, . . . now he is waking up" ' (p. 98). Freud assigned to the watching agency many functions in the transformation of the dream:

1 The presence of the critical watching agency is evidenced in the dreamer's *observation* of the translation of thoughts into visual images during a state between sleeping and waking. Here, the watcher plays a passive role of bare attention to the translation.
2 Self-observation also plays an *active* part in the translation and, therefore, in the process of dream-formation itself. Thus, the watching agency does not merely attend to the translation but is itself the *translator* into visual imagery.
3 The watching agency plays a part in the *content* of these dream-formations so that what is translated is not a thought-content but the actual state of mind (readiness, fatigue, etc.) of the person who is struggling with sleep.
4 The dreamer's self-observation may also form part of the content of the dream. The end of a dream may signify the dreamer's *perception* of his own sleeping and waking. Dreams of this kind are sometimes called lucid dreams.

5 The watching agency also *distorts* the dream content through its *censorship*. It edits as it translates.

Whereas Freud emphasised the critical and paranoid aspects of the watching agency, contemporary exponents of Freudian theory stress the *caring*, benign functions of the watcher. Spitz, like Tolpin, discusses the role of the transitional object in the internalisation process of the mother's soothing and regulatory functions. Metcalf and Spitz, using Freud's drive theory, describe how, when going to sleep, the ego which is 'a recently and as yet not firmly established caretaker of the child, relinquishes its executive control of the drives' (Metcalf and Spitz, 1978, p. 103). These drives, now controlled, become threatening. 'A delicate balance of regulatory switching must take place which can easily miscarry' (p. 103). These miscarriages may be manifested in infantile sleep panic and perhaps by 'sudden infant death'. According to Metcalf and Spitz, the problem-solving gratification, which is involved in the child's ability to use the transitional object in the service of his becoming the caretaker of his own security, is linked with 'narcissistic gratification'. These authors postulate 'an equivalence between the transitional objects of waking reality and the representational dream in the sleep state' (p. 105). Transitional objects are endowed with a significant part of the 'need-gratifying object's recognition cathexis' (p. 105). Thus, 'the transitional object becomes a constituent of the building memory structure, which represents the total gestalt of need-gratifying tension-reduction' (p. 105). At this point in development, the transitional object is a representation or substitute. However, following Winnicott, Metcalf and Spitz assert that the further development of the transitional object leads in two very different and dialectical directions. Whereas the establishment of evocative memory proper involves the *relinquishment* of the transitional object, the *retention* of the transitional object leads, by way of change of function, to the highest levels of imaginative objectification.

F *Self-regard*

In the final section on the products of the watching agency, Freud discusses self-regard. Like the ego-ideal, self-regard has an intimate connection with narcissistic love. The aim and satisfaction of a narcissistic object-choice is to be loved: to be loved raises the self-regarding feelings which are lowered when love is withdrawn.

In my view, self-regard reflects the early relationship between the self and the other. More than any of the other products of the watching agency, self-regard reproduces the most primitive attachment. It is in a person's regard of himself that all the words uttered in the third person, the projections and attributions of other, come to rest. Winnicott said that the infant's first mirror is the mother's face. What does he or she see reflected there? What if one was to look in the mirror and see nothing, one patient of Winnicott's asked.[9] In some cases, we might say that self-regard does not exist – or rather, it exists as a blank, an emptiness. The regard of others must be sufficiently coherent, predictable and consistent for the self to be there for reflection. Frances Tustin observes that the mothers of some autistic children have suffered a severe and prolonged depression after the birth of the child. One can imagine that the handling by these mothers of their babies was stereotyped and lifeless. When these babies looked up into their mother's faces, they did not see a lively, mobile expression. If they were energetic babies, their liveliness was not reflected back to them. In these cases, a terrifying discrepancy comes to exist between how the baby feels and what he sees. In the primitive relationship of interactional synchrony when the I is not yet differentiated, this discord has devastating effects because of the intensity of the relationship to the object. Winnicott has described the child who learns to read his mother's face like the weather (Winnicott, 1967, p. 113). The child may become peculiarly perceptive. When such a child looks at himself in the mirror, he may scrutinise his own face like a weather-forecaster. He will calculate how he looks from the outside. A child with a depressed mother may grow up to be both watchful and caring of his mother.

When in a state of fragmentation and dissolution, Brenda spent hours looking at herself in the mirror. She turned her features this way and that to find herself. From one angle, she looked like her father, from another like her mother. She also described to me her difficulty in listening to music and in reading a book. These activities screened out the backcloth which she felt must be her constant foreground – namely, the emotional field of her mother's moods. To forget for an instant was to not know what was going on around her. When listening to music, she also had to try and hear the sounds which the music drowned out. To hear was to overhear. Even on a beautiful walk in the countryside, the pleasure in a tree meant that her brief focus had screened out a possible impingement on the edges of her visual field.

A forty-five-year-old man, who was successful in many fields, experienced acute disintegration when he was not in front-to-front, physical contact with a woman at least once a day. At one time, he had to make love with a woman at least three times a day, two or three times. Only then, did he have any regard for himself. His two wives, who became involved in the feminist movement, regarded him as the archetypal, male chauvinist pig. In fact, his situation was quite the opposite. He needed frontal contact in order to exist. As his second wife withdrew, he was barely able to function. In the beginning of our work together, he sat opposite me, disarmingly observant of my moods and gestures; sometimes he would bring his chair up closer to me. At weekends, he could barely think or move. After he renounced all hope of sexual contact, he would follow his wife around the house until he could force her into face-to-face, visual contact with him. She felt pursued and trapped and would spurn him as 'a little boy' who needed Mummy. She would scold him, telling him that she was not there to 'meet his needs'. If they went out to do something together, for instance for dinner or to a drawing class, he found the situation intolerable as he had to sit side-by-side with her. He described all their activities together as 'parallel play'. He was reproducing in his marriages and in the therapy a painfully close early relationship with his mother in which she never let him out of her sight. He had grown up incapable of breaking out of the spell of her orbit. Every trophy that he won was for her. Often, I found it difficult to think in the sessions, as I felt that we were pressed up against each other mindlessly. Although it is not unusual for me to see therapy patients face to face, I often wished that he would use the couch. He had had five years of analysis and had found the contact distant and intellectual, because he had never seen the analyst's face. It felt to me that he could not take advantage of the privacy and spaciousness of the analytic setting because, as a young boy, he could not turn his back on his mother and play in the security of her presence.

The painful situation of this man reminded me of my observations of my nephew, Stephen. Like my patient, Stephen was a very affectionate baby who loved to be held and who actively cuddled the three people with whom he was most familiar. He would seize on their faces and cover them with drooly 'kisses'. At about nine months, he would love for a while and then turn away outwards to get on with whatever it was that caught his attention. Rather than rejecting them, he was primarily turning *towards* and *outwards*. But, in order to do this, he had to turn *away* from them. He would also get very excited if the other person got down on the floor beside him and looked at the toy or object with him. But a common situation was to find him seated very squarely on the ground with his back to his mother and a couple of feet in front of her. Every few minutes, he would glance over his shoulder and return to his current preoccupation. This was the sort of togetherness for which my patient longed. Instead, he would find himself compulsively pursuing his fleeing partner, or, at best, sitting beside her staring ahead disconnectedly at something in which he could feel no interest.

For another type of patient, the couch can play an opposite role. One performer I saw in three times a week therapy gave up the couch because of the feelings of isolation, emptiness and non-responsiveness aroused. She became quite phobic about the white wall which faced her, which she saw as the precipitating cause of an almost unbearable depressive episode. The white wall mirrored back to her a blank. On the session before she abandoned the couch, she entered my room wearing a gold crash helmet which she kept on throughout the session. A year or so later, however, during which time she had both sat opposite me and lain down on a sofa I had in my room, she returned to the couch. Now she experienced it as most relaxing and as a source of creativity. During the previous year, she had begun to use her considerable musical talents, not as a product for the enjoyment of an audience, but as the source from which she wrote her own songs and lyrics. The wall opposite the couch became a space of potential, a space of imagining, where it once appeared as an absence, a blank, an ungiving presence or command for performance. In my experience, a notable characteristic of a Narcissus or an Echo is an inability to turn his or her back on another person and to get on with his or her own preoccupations, without feeling that the other has thereby been obliterated.

Freud pointed out that self-regard is raised when love is returned. When object love is not returned the satisfaction of love is impossible. However, the return of object-libido to the ego and its transformation into narcissism re-establishes 'a happy love once more . . .' (Freud, 1914, p. 100). Freud concludes his account of self-regard with a statement with which I am in complete agreement – a statement, moreover, which is consistent with the attachment view of the growth of love. Although the return of object-libido and its transformation into narcissism represents the original happy love, 'on the other hand, it is also true that a real happy love corresponds to the primal condition in which object-libido and ego-libido cannot be distinguished' (p. 100). In other words, the return of the love of another represents the original affectional bond between the individual infant and his mother.

In this chapter, I have tried to present the classical Freudian approach to the development of transitional objects and transitional phenomena. I have tried to demonstrate that the primary narcissism hypothesis leads to a radically different view of child development to that of the attachment or interactional models. Transitional objects and phenomena become the indicators of the development of a bond or object-relation and of a loosening of narcissistic relationships based on need-gratification and drive-reduction. From the primary narcissism hypothesis, we do not look at cognitive skills either as primary or as maturing in the context of a primary mother–infant attachment and communicational system. Memory or the sense of time, for instance, are not viewed as communicational skills. Following Freud, many of the authors discussed in this chapter (such as Spitz) *describe* non-oral, social interactions suggestive of a primary affectional bond but, in the conceptualisation of these observations, they resort to the theory of non-relational primary narcissism.

Part II

OEDIPUS

We shall not cease from exploration
And the end of all our exploring
Will be to arrive where we started
And know the place for the first time.
Through the unknown, remembered gate
When the last of earth left to discover
Is that which was the beginning;

T. S. Eliot,
Four Quartets

10
The Theban legend: *Oedipus the King*

> Men of Thebes: look upon Oedipus.
>
> This is the king who solved the famous riddle
> And towered up, most powerful of men.
> No mortal eyes but looked on him with envy,
> Yet in the end ruin swept over him.
>
> Let every man in mankind's frailty
> Consider his last day; and let none
> Presume on his good fortune until he find
> Life, at his death, a memory without pain. (Sophocles)

In some versions of this much interpreted myth, we are told that, even before Oedipus was born, his life was clouded with the presage of disaster for Apollo's oracle had nothing but ill to foretell of him. Laius, who was grieved by his prolonged childlessness, secretly consulted the Delphic oracle which informed him that this seeming misfortune was a blessing, because any child born to Jocasta would become his murderer. In Aeschylus' play, Laius is told, 'Do not beget a child; for if you do, that child will kill you.' Laius

> therefore put Jocaste away, though without offering any reason for his decision, which caused her such vexation that, having made him drunk, she inveigled him into her arms again as soon as night fell. When, nine months later, Jocaste was brought to bed of a son, Laius snatched him from the nurse's arms, pierced his feet with a nail and, binding them together, exposed him on Mount Cithaeron. (Graves, 1955, vol. 2, p. 9)

Oedipus' conception arises out of deception: Laius consults the oracle about his childless marriage *in secret* and is told that this state of affairs is a blessing; he banishes Jocasta as a precautionary measure without sharing any of the vital information given by the oracle; Jocasta, resentful and misunderstanding of this injustice, inveigles Laius into the drunken intercourse out of which Oedipus, the future pollution of Thebes, is conceived. Thus, through secrecy and unexplained preventative measures, the blessing of their marriage is turned into a misfortune. So far, the moral of the play is more about defences than wishes and, as Freud noted, the defences precipitate the very dangers they are supposed to avert.

'Yet the Fates had ruled that this boy should reach a green old age. A Corinthian shepherd found him, named him Oedipus because his feet were deformed by the nail-wound, and brought him to Corinth, where King Polybus was reigning at the time' (Graves, 1955, p. 9). We are told that the infant was snatched from his nurse's arms and that his legs were pierced and bound together so that no chance remained that he might find his way back home.

> One day, taunted by a Corinthian youth with not in the least resembling his supposed parents, Oedipus went to ask the Delphic Oracle what future lay in store for him. 'Away from the shrine, wretch!' the Pythoness cried in disgust. 'You will kill your father and marry your mother.'
>
> Since Oedipus loved Polybus and Periboea, and shrank from bringing disaster upon them, he at once decided against returning to Corinth. But in the narrow defile between Delphi and Daulis he happened to meet Laius, who ordered him roughly to step off the road and make way for his betters; Laius, it should be explained, was in a chariot and Oedipus on foot. Oedipus retorted that he acknowledged no betters except the gods and his own parents.
>
> 'So much the worse for you!' cried Laius, and ordered his charioteer Polyphontes to drive on.
>
> One of the wheels bruised Oedipus' feet and, transported by rage, he killed Polyphontes with his spear. Then, flinging Laius on the road entangled in the reins, and whipping up the team, he made them drag him to death. It was left to the King of Plataeae to bury both corpses. (Graves, 1955, p. 10)

Oedipus panics at the horrifying words of the oracle. He leaves Corinth in order to spare his parents the enactment of the prophecy. From the Freudian viewpoint, Oedipus' flight is defensive against the primitive and universal *wish* to commit parricide and incest. In civilised society, Freud observed, prohibitions against such crimes go unsaid, but this is not evidence that we no longer harbour such wishes. The conscience of mankind which now appears as an inherited mental force, was acquired in connection with the Oedipus complex. However, from Sophocles' text, it would seem that Oedipus does everything in his power to avert these two crimes. On his journey to Thebes, he informs Laius that he is servant to the law of both the gods and his parents.

Laius was on his way to ask the oracle how he might rid Thebes of the Sphinx. The Sphinx had been sent to Thebes by Hera as a punishment and she settled on Mount Phicium, close to the city, and asked every Theban wayfarer a riddle taught her by the Three Muses. Those who could not solve the riddle she throttled and devoured on the spot.

> Oedipus, approaching Thebes fresh from the murder of Laius, guessed the answer . . . The mortified Sphinx leaped from Mount Phicium and dashed herself to pieces in the valley below. At this the grateful Thebans acclaimed Oedipus King, and he married Jocaste, unaware that she was his mother. (Graves, 1955, p. 10)

Oedipus' answer sets the stage for his entry into Thebes, no vagrant, or incestuous intruder but a man of supreme strength and insight. In the Prologue to Sophocles' play (transl. Fitts and Fitzgerald, 1951), the Priest of Zeus acclaims Oedipus 'the noblest of men', 'the man surest in mortal ways and wisest in the ways of God'. The city turns to him again, as their saviour from the Sphinx, to rid them of the plague. The law-abiding Oedipus sends Creon, Jocasta's brother, to Delphi to learn 'what act or pledge of mine may save the city'.

Apollo's word is that if, by exile or death, 'blood for blood', they rid the city of the defilement of Laius' murderer, then all will turn out well. Oedipus asks what is known about Laius' murder, since he never saw him, and why it was that the killers were not hunted down. The reply is that 'the riddling Sphinx's song made us deaf to all mysteries but her own'.

Again, Oedipus stands out as the seeker of truth at all costs: 'Then once more I must bring what is dark to light.'

> You shall see how I stand by you, as I should, . . .
> Until now I was a stranger to this tale,
> As I had been a stranger to the crime.

He pronounces the penalty for any man who conceals the murderer and decrees that he be driven from every house.

> I pray that that man's life be consumed in evil and wretchedness
> And as for me, this curse applies no less
> If it should turn out that the culprit is my guest here,
> Sharing my hearth . . ..

Sophocles portrays Oedipus as a man of utter loyalty and dedication to the house of Kadmos. Oedipus has no thought of using his new position of power to spare himself. Neither does he use his status as a foreigner to absolve himself of responsibility. He acts as if he were both the son of Laius and the brother of Laius' children 'if Laius had had luck in fatherhood'. Sophocles engages and intrigues the audience by the range of imagination and phantasy, the levels of consciousness, revealed by Oedipus' words and deeds. Was Oedipus a man of great sensibility who had the breadth of imagination to fantasise himself to be Laius' heir or did he unconsciously know that he was? Interpreters have woven this dramatic thread into a moral and legalistic debate (Dodds, 1973, pp. 64–77). From the moral point of view, the play appears to be about the justice of the gods and about the rightful attribution of blame to wayward mortals who upset the natural and social order of things. These interpreters emphasise Oedipus' intentions. Freud too examines the play from this vantage point although, under the novel concept of *unconscious motivation*, moral condemnation gives way. Freud's perspective added another dimension to previous simplistic disputes as to whether an action was freely willed, and thus subject to moral injunction, or determined by fate. Freudian intentionality implied that there were actions which, though not intended (consciously), nevertheless were compulsive enactments of inner latent *wishes*. The new discipline of psychoanalysis demonstrated that such compulsions could become conscious. Thus, although condemnation is inappropriate, the implication remains that Oedipus did know unconsciously what he was doing. The as-if references, which Oedipus makes to his relationship with Laius, Jocaste and their children, would seem to suggest pre-conscious knowledge. However, *within Sophocles' play* the audience are given no hint that Oedipus' pledge to the loyal Thebans of services, as devoted as those of a loyal son, is intended to indicate unconscious knowledge.

A different interpretation is prompted if we include the information that Oedipus was an adopted child. The adopted child lives in an as-if world. A sense of belonging can be a guiding force in his life. Like Oedipus, the child eagerly assumes the part of natural son or daughter. He pledges himself to loyalty or exile. For such a child, there is no easy transition between feelings of inclusion and exclusion. The child may try to cross a line which is uncrossable. Some children come to accept this fate. Others always feel outside and are drawn into an endless search for the real parent to whom they once belonged. The Victorian child belonged neither in the nursery nor in the drawing-room. In the nursery, the child enjoyed a relationship with one parent-figure. But this figure also belonged in another house from which the child was excluded. The nurse looked happy on her days off. The child was then left behind with those to whom he rightfully belonged, but for whom he was a nuisance.

As a last expedient, Creon and the Chorus suggest that they call in Teiresias, the blind seer. As in the myth of Narcissus, we are told that Teiresias was unsighted as a punishment for seeing the unacceptable – in this case because he had inadvertently seen Athene bathing. Once more Teiresias must pronounce an unacceptable truth:

> How dreadful knowledge of the truth can be
> When there's no help in truth! I have known it all,
> but made myself forget. I should not have come.

Teiresias does everything he can to withhold his knowledge. But Oedipus begs in God's name and on behalf of all. Teiresias tells them 'You are all ignorant' and vows

No; I will never tell you what I know.
Now it is my misery; then, it would be yours.

Oedipus is enraged and insults Teiresias, blaming him for the crime. He will have the truth at all costs. Eventually Teiresias is shamed' into telling Oedipus that he is the murderer. Oedipus responds that all Teiresias' words are worthless mouthing. 'You sightless, witless, senseless, mad old man.' He accuses Creon of a wish to destroy him, because he brought in the 'prophet fraud'. He disparages Teiresias' 'mystic mummery' which did nothing to rid the Theban people of the Sphinx; he, on the other hand, 'the simple man who knows nothing' thought it out for himself. Teiresias responds,

Listen to me. You mock my blindness, do you?
But I say that you, with both your eyes, are blind:
You cannot see the wretchedness of your life,
Nor in whose house you live, no, nor with whom.
Who are your father and mother? Can you tell me?
You do not even know the blind wrongs
That you have done them, on earth and in the world below.
But the double lash of your parents' curse will whip you
Upon your precious eyes.

When Teiresias refers to the 'wrongs' and wretchedness caused by Oedipus, he does not make a moral accusation. Thereafter, he touches the weakest point in Oedipus' tale of success. Oedipus scoffs at Teiresias' foolery and Teiresias replies, 'A fool? Your parents thought me sane enough.' Oedipus falters: 'My parents again? – Wait: who were my parents?' 'This day will give you a father, and break your heart,' he is told. The desperate Oedipus rages, 'Your infantile riddles! Your damned abracadabra!' Teiresias retorts, 'You were a great man once at solving riddles.' 'Mock me with that if you like', says Oedipus. 'you will find it true.' 'It was true enough', Teiresias affirms, 'it brought about your ruin.' He leaves, warning the Thebans that the damned man, the murderer of Laius, is in Thebes.

To your mind he is foreign-born,
But it will soon be shown that he is a Theban,
A revelation that will fail to please.

There is no escape for Oedipus. Flight will not avail him, the man of courage and insight, 'for the world's heart calls him desolate'. At this point in the play, the Chorus casts doubt on Teiresias' words:

> No man can judge that rough unknown or trust in second sight,
> For wisdom changes hands among the wise.

In the following scene, Creon is presented as the man who speaks on the basis of facts. In his frenzied and panic-stricken search for the truth, Oedipus makes wilder accusations and judgments. Creon's prudence and straightforward argument increase Oedipus' suspicions of Creon's duplicity. They quarrel. Jocasta enters to try and solve the fight. She intercedes successfully on the behalf of the just and loyal Creon. Oedipus lets Creon go, convinced that he is to die at Creon's hand.

Jocasta talks assuringly to her distraught husband. But her revelations, designed to ease Oedipus' suspicions and bewilderment, only trigger off new puzzles and jog his memory. Her 'proof' of Oedipus' innocence is to show that soothsayers, and even the oracle itself, can be wrong. She tells Oedipus that Laius was told by the oracle that he would meet his death at the hands of his own son. But, Laius was killed by marauding strangers where three highways met. Moreover, even before his child was three days old, Laius pierced his ankles and left him to die on a lonely mountainside. Oedipus wonders:

> How strange a shadowy memory crossed my mind,
> Just now while you were speaking; it chilled my heart.

He questions Jocasta about the crossroads and about where and when it happened. She tells him that the news reached them not long before Oedipus came 'and proved the right to your succession here'. 'Ah', he reflects, 'what net has God been weaving for me?' He asks how Laius looked, how he was escorted, and who told her how it happened. Jocasta tells him of the servant who, when he came back at last to Thebes and found Oedipus enthroned in the place of the dead king, came to her and begged to be sent away to the frontier district where only the shepherds go – as far away from the city as she would send him.

Again, Sophocles brings to our attention the flight from sights so unbearable that to share them would precipitate total destruction. Now, the shepherd is recalled. Oedipus muses whether he may be accused by his own ignorant edict. Perhaps he has taken too much upon himself without enquiry. He has 'reached a pitch of wild foreboding'.

Oedipus tells his story to Jocasta. He tells of the circumstances which led to his departure from Corinth, of his wandering further and further away 'to a land where I should never see the evil sung by the Oracle', of his meeting at the crossroads of the three highways and his murder of the charioteers and their master.

> Now if that stranger and Laius were – kin,
> Where is a man more miserable than I?
> . . . Am I all evil, then?

Oedipus' last hope is that the shepherd will say that Laius was killed by several marauders and not singlehandedly. Jocasta assures him that, even if this detail of the story is altered, the shepherd will not be able to show that Laius' death fulfilled the Oracle because her child, who was destined to kill him, had already died.

Now the Chorus declares its loyalty to the oracle's obscurities: how can 'the world's core' be discredited and the Delphic vision be blind? The laws are 'of the pure universe'; throughout the generations, heaven has been 'their bright nurse'.

> Never of mortal kind were they begot,
> Nor are they slaves of memory, lost in sleep:
> Their father is greater than time, and ages not.

Once more, we, identified with Oedipus, are offered a reprieve. A messenger comes from Corinth with news which appears to prove the unreliability of the oracle. Polybus is dead and the people of the Isthmus proclaim Oedipus their King. Jocasta rejoices. This is the man whom Oedipus fled in dread of destroying – but he died by another fate. Oedipus questions the messenger and is assured that Polybus died simply of old age. For a moment, Oedipus is able to dismiss the 'empty words' of the oracle. 'And yet – must I not fear my mother's bed?' Jocasta comforts him,

Have no more fear of sleeping with your mother:
How many men, in dreams, have lain with their mothers!
No reasonable man is troubled by such things.

Jocasta's good sense is sadly inappropriate to the reality of the situation. He and we, the readers of the play, know that Jocasta's wise words are true. But the knowledge that we all dream of such things does not alter the fact that Oedipus' mother still lives. Moreover, the oracle's words do not refer to dream wish-fulfilments. The messenger asks Oedipus who is the woman that he fears. Oedipus repeats the oracle's dreadful saying and tells him the reason why he has kept clear of Corinth all these years, 'though it would have been sweet to see my parents again'. The messenger questions whether these really are the reasons that Oedipus did not go home. He reassures Oedipus that all his fears are groundless. But why, ask Oedipus, 'they are my parents surely?' The messenger tells him 'Polybus was not your father. . . . Long ago he had you from my hands, as a gift.' 'Then,' asks Oedipus, 'how could he love me so, if I was not his?' The messenger replies that Polybus had no children and 'his heart turned to you'.

The messenger tells the tale of his discovery of the abandoned infant. He came upon him in the crooked pass of Kithairion. Like any adopted child, Oedipus puzzles 'What of you? Did you buy me? Did you find me by chance?' He asks the messenger what he was doing at Kithairion. He was tending his flocks. 'A wandering shepherd?', Oedipus queries. Yes, 'but your saviour, son, that day'. The messenger describes how he untied Oedipus' ankles and himself named him Oedipus. Oedipus asks whether his mother or father had tied his feet and left him on the hillside. The messenger tells him that it was another shepherd, 'one of Laius' people'. Upset again, Oedipus must find this shepherd for whom they have already sent in order to verify the circumstances of Laius' murder. They advise Oedipus to ask Jocasta. In vain, she blocks his questions and advises him to forget it all. But now that the clues to his true origin are almost assembled, Oedipus will not desist. Jocasta fails to dissuade him. 'The truth must be made known.' Jocasta leaves, uttering her last words:

Ah, miserable!
That is the only word I have for you now.

Oedipus, still ignorant, thinks that she has left because she is ashamed to reveal his possible low origin. But he is 'a child of Luck'. He

> cannot be dishonoured.
> Luck is my mother; the passing months, my brothers,
> Have seen me rich and poor.
> If this is so, How could I wish that I were someone else?
> How could I not be glad to know my birth?

Luck is the mother of an adopted child.

The old shepherd, servant of Laius, arrives with the messenger from Corinth. They reminisce about the time they spent three whole seasons on Kithairion together each going home in the autumn, one to Polybus' household, the other to Laius' kingdom. The messenger asks the shepherd whether he remembers the baby boy he once gave to him, who is now King Oedipus. 'Damn you, hold your tongue!', snaps the shepherd. Oedipus, overhearing, threatens him until he admits that the baby he gave away was, indeed, a child from Laius' palace. Oedipus asks if he was a slave child or a child of his own line? The shepherd, 'on the brink of dreadful speech', tells Oedipus, on the brink 'of dreadful hearing', that it was Laius' child and advises Oedipus to ask his wife for more information. Oedipus rushes into the palace to find Jocasta.

The Chorus laments the fate of Oedipus, whose 'splendour is all fallen' and whose 'mind was a strong bow'.

> True King, giver of laws,
> Majestic Oedipus!
> No prince in Thebes had ever such renown,
> No prince won such grace of power.

No doubt is cast on Oedipus' integrity, his allegiance to the law. He had 'grace of power', not wilful omnipotence. Oedipus, the doer of unlawful actions, has fallen through no fault of his own.

> And now of all men ever known
> Most pitiful is this man's story:
> . . . . All understood too late
> . . . But all eyes fail before time's eye,
> All *actions* come to justice there.

> Though never willed, though far down the deep past,
> Your bed, your dread sirings,
> Are brought to book at last. (my italics)

A messenger announces Jocasta's death. *Now the place shelters evil* – 'evil not done unconsciously, but willed . . . The greatest griefs are those we cause ourselves'. The Queen is dead at her own hand. Oedipus bursts through the twin doors into her room. When he sees her hanging, he rips the golden brooches from her gown and plunges them down into his eyeballs, striking at his eyes many times and crying:

> No more,
> No more shall you look on the misery about me,
> The horrors of my own doing! Too long you have known
> The faces of those whom I should never have seen,
> Too long been blind to those for whom I was searching!
> From this hour, go in darkness.

Oedipus calls for someone to lead him to the gates so that all the children of Kadmos may look upon Laius' murderer. Self-exiled, he will leave Thebes, a sight 'dreadful indeed for men to see'. A punishment, heavier than any mortal can bear, has befallen him. Worse still, the Chorus exclaims, 'What god drove you . . . to rake black night across your eyes'. Even though Apollo brought his sick, sick fate upon him, the 'blinding hand was his own'. But, Oedipus tells us, how could he bear to see 'when all my sight was horror everywhere?' Oedipus curses his saviour, the man who unbound him and brought him from death to such a life. 'More primal than sin itself, this fell to me.' And yet he has sinned so vilely against his parents that he could not make his peace by strangling his own life. All he can do is blank out the sights about which he, though guiltless, can do nothing.

> Thrice miserable! – Oedipus, noblest of all the line
> Of Kadmos, have condemned myself to enjoy
> These things no more,
> . . . If I could have stifled my hearing at its source,
> I would have done it and made all this body
> A tight cell of misery, blank to light and sound:
> So I should have been safe in a dark agony
> Beyond all recollection.

He enumerates the misfortunes of his life: Kithairion who sheltered him so that the world was shown his 'execrable birth'. Polybus and Corinth,

> city that I believed
> The ancient seat of my ancestors: how fair
> I seemed, your child! And all the while this evil
> was cancerous within me!
> For I am sick
> in my daily life, sick in my origin.

The three roads where he drank his father's blood, his own blood, spilled by his own hand. His marriage:

> The net
> of incest, mingling fathers, brothers, sons,
> With brides, wives mothers: the last evil
> That can be known by men: No tongue can say
> How evil.

Again Oedipus asks to be led out and concealed.

> You need not fear to touch me
> *Of all men, I alone can bear this guilt*. (my italics)

He curses and regrets in the full knowledge that, in the objective order, his personal emotions are of no importance. No forgiveness can alter his actions and redeem the House of Labdakos. Suicide will not bring peace. He must live on senselessly 'a tight cell of misery . . . safe in a dark agony beyond all recollection.'

Creon takes possession of the situation. He has no thought of revenge for the personal wrongs which Oedipus has done him. He neither mocks nor reproaches. He asks Oedipus to remove his presence, which is a 'pollution' to man's dignity, from the family house. Oedipus begs him to drive him out to a place where no human voice will ever greet him. But Creon insists that they must wait to listen to the god. 'Although the Oracle has said that the parricide should be destroyed, it is not clear what must be done.' Oedipus asks to go to Kithairion, to the tomb appointed by his parents. And yet he knows that death will never come to him, 'through sickness or in any natural way'. He has been preserved 'for some unthinkable fate'. He asks for his children so that he may lay his hands on them – the hands which have brought his 'once clear eyes to this way of seeing'. He tells them how he had neither sight nor knowledge then, their 'father by the woman who was the source of his own life!' All the tragedies and wonders of life are wrought by men's ways of seeing; though their eyes are clear, they do not see. He weeps for his children. For when they come to marriage, who will dare risk the bane which lies on them? There is no evil wanting to a child whose father killed his father, sowed the womb of her who bore him, and then engendered the child at the fount of his own existence! Incest and sterility end up as one and the same. Incest's offspring must 'wither away' their lives 'in sterile dreaming'.

All await the words of the oracle. Creon, the obedient servant of the Law, will not 'speak beyond knowledge'. Unlike Laius and Oedipus, he is reluctant to pronounce banishment as the solution for social ills. Laius banished Jocasta. They banished their child. Oedipus exiled himself from Corinth. In the play, he has threatened to banish Teiresias, Creon, the shepherd, the messenger, Jocasta and, finally, himself. In the drama, there is little about intrusion and provocation and much about banishment and denial. Creon stands for the acceptance of fact and order just as Oedipus stands for truth and justice. But, at this point in the play, Oedipus is beside himself with grief, rage and remorse. The unswerving Creon will not give in to these indulgences. A man may act freely but he may not take life, whether he acts in ignorance or in despair. Man must live according to the oracle – or according to the reality principle. Oedipus too acknowledges the futility of suicide – even at the house of death, he could not bear the sight of his father.

The play ends with Creon's rebuke to Oedipus for his last refusal to obey him and leave behind his children.

> Think no longer
> That you are in command here, but rather think
> How, when you were, you served your own destruction.

Oedipus bows to Creon's authority.

'Time eases all things.'

11
The riddle of life

> 'What being, with only one voice, has sometimes two feet, sometimes three, sometimes four, and is weakest when it has the most?'
>
> 'Man, because he crawls on all fours as an infant, stands firmly on his two feet in his youth, and leans upon a staff in his old age.'

I have linked the Oedipal phase with the age of enquiry and exploration which begins when the child is able to crawl and which is well underway when the child takes his first steps. This stage progresses with the child's pronouncement of the 'I' and the concomitant development of language, and his use of identity as a secure base for exploration. It culminates with the comprehension of the 'reality principle', which I associate with the capacity to relate to an order of things outside the area of subjective control and wishes. Transitional schemas assist in the differentiation of the personal from the consensual. In my interpretation, the riddle offers an invitation to leave behind the world of concrete action (characterised by analogical communication) and to enter a new domain of information and knowledge (characterised by paradoxical and digital communication). The riddle is a *word*-puzzle. In Sophocles' play, we are told that Oedipus' downfall is brought about by 'blind deeds'. Actions are taken because of a lack of understanding. The acquisition of language allows the child to participate in an interpersonal world of ideas. The child and his parents are freed from communication through action. The relationship becomes less intense and immediate. Words may wound or soothe but they do not physically strike or stroke.[1]

Myths, like humour, dreams, play, riddles belong to the class of 'transcontextual syndromes'. They survive over time and are usable by different cultures and disciplines. Their flexibility contributes to their invariance. Freud used the oedipal legend to point out that the oedipal situation befalls every man. And yet Sophocles' play is about an adopted child whose origins are shrouded in multiple levels of deception. Perhaps, the *Oedipus Rex* is a better example of a particular, rather than a universal, situation. Disaster follows from unilateral *actions* taken at the expense of the communication of information. Horrors occur which are of Oedipus' doing, and yet he has been preserved 'for some unthinkable fate' and caught in a net woven by the gods and by his predecessors. 'More primal than sin itself, this fell to me', he comments. In the play, Oedipus' search for self-knowledge ends in tragedy. Consistent with my interpretation of the Narcissus myth, I emphasise that a tragic outcome of the stages named after the two myths is neither necessary nor universal. I use both myths to illustrate a particular type of relationship between the child, the family and the outside world; tragedy may ensue when these relationships go wrong, but it is not the necessary outcome of either the first intense, two-person, attachment, or oedipal development *per se*. In my view, there is nothing fateful, tragic or condemning about the Oedipus complex, provided that the challenge of the riddle is not immersed in deception or generative of social pollution.

The *Oedipus Rex* conveys the tremendous complexity with which the child at this stage must wrestle. The individual meets the outside world of hard facts. He cannot wrestle with a partner who dances in unison. After the synchronous interaction and mirroring of the narcissistic stage, the individual struggles with objects *and projections* which do not fit. In order to see beyond the mirror and deal in the world outside, the familiar, two-person relationship must be placed in a wider context. In Winnicott's words, the object must be placed outside the area of omnipotent control; it goes without saying that this is only achieved when the subject himself is placed outside the projections or control of the object. Oedipus' fate is that he cannot extricate himself from the web of family relationships in which he finds himself entangled.

In consequence, the theme of the play is not only personal or unconscious guilt but the wider responsibility for the *objective* order of things which lies outside Oedipus' control. At the end of the play, Oedipus assumes the responsibility for a sequence of disasters in which his own actions have played but a small part. The onus of those deeds enacted blindly and by others is greater than the burden of his own mistakes. Oedipus' comprehension of the larger system of patterns into which he was born does not indicate abdication of responsibility or projection of blame, but his acceptance that his powers are limited. Short of suicide, which he acknowledges would create further disasters, his self-imposed, blind exile, finally approved by the oracle, is the most he can do for himself, the house of Kadmos and Thebes.

The *Oedipus Rex*, like the myth of Narcissus, begins with a question and answer which seem at first to be nonsensical. In the Narcissus myth, Leiriope, the mother of the infant Narcissus, consults Teiresias about her son's future. In the *Oedipus Rex*, the curious young man leaves home to seek out the oracle for himself. Between the riddle and its solution lurk the twin dangers of incest and chastity. The chaste man will not ask the question; he conforms. The incestuous man will not accept the answer; he is a social menace. There are many tales which touch on this theme. The stories of the Buddha and the Prodigal Son, like the *Oedipus Rex*, are about a young man who turns his back on his home. The son leaves a raging or saddened father, vowing that he will never return. The Buddha did not return to his princedom. The Prodigal Son was welcomed back to the original fold, an ending which has comforted the heart of many Christians. Oedipus returned unwittingly to his country of origin. Peer Gynt, who abandoned his mother on a rooftop to enter the Kingdom of the Trolls, returned to his Solveig.

In all these tales, the point is made that the fold is not enough. However 'good', mother is not the world. A symbiotic or narcissistic child need not ask questions. Externality does not exist. Such a child remains contained within the maternal space. Perhaps, mother has produced everything in anticipation, thereby eliminating the child's formulation of a request.

The search for novelty, complexity and riddles, for participation in an intellectual world, for the delineation of the area of personal responsibility and projection – these issues revolve around the child's *independent approach to the world*. Independence is a matter much written about, but fraught with ambiguity both in experience and in literature. It has as much to do with approach as with departure. A parent may try to curb the child's moves away and outwards because unwittingly he or she equates turning away with rejection. In his lectures on attachment and loss given at the Tavistock Clinic, John Bowlby warned us that we could not talk about a child turning away from (his mother) unless we said what he turned towards. Psychoanalytic theory, particularly Kleinian theory, has tended to focus on the rejecting-attacking aspect of the child's movement away from the mother or breast. The larger world outside is viewed as a symbol of the mother's body (see chapter 2). Of course, a child who has built up a backlog of resentment against the mother may be dominated by revenge when he turns towards father or his toys or friends. However, we must picture both sides of this coin. One side faces the familiar, the other the unknown. The individual is poised, more or less precariously, between. The parent or therapist must tolerate this edge. Late-latency children, on the threshold of adolescence when oedipal matters flourish again, give us the opportunity to watch the oscillation between the excitement of excluding teenage friendships and the renunciation of the mother's special comforts such as tucking up and hot drinks at bedtime. One thirteen-year-old boy, the youngest of a large family, would appear in the living room door in his pyjamas every night to tell his mother that he was ready for her to go upstairs after him and say good-night. He gave up this habit quite happily on return from a trip abroad with a friend.

The riddle (a transcontextual phenomenon) signifies the emerging interface between two worlds. When the limits of *my* world coincide with the limits of *the* world, so that the world as I experience it is deemed to be equivalent to the world outside me, the only way out may be to ask nonsense questions or to do something absurd. Fairy tales, the Troll world, may serve this function. They turn the familiar, shared world upside down. For, it seems, to know everything leads to corruption, just as to know nothing results in sterility. To the pre-verbal child, words are riddles just as, to the adult, the child's babbling may seem to be empty nonsense. There is no way for the child to make sense of words without leaving the familiar dance and entering into a new level of exchange. Words cannot be manipulated, seen, smelt, etc. Similarly, the parent of the newborn must recross a boundary into an often forgotten kingdom.

Freud related the riddle of the sphinx to the 'first grand problem of life – where do babies come from?'[2] This is perhaps the one question – the question of origin which is the focus of Sophocles' drama – which has only one answer: my mother and father had intercourse together. From this inter-penetrating couple I was excluded and upon it the fruitful conception of myself intruded. One and only one mother and father, vagina and penis, begot me. In this sense, the solution of the question involves a limit, because its answer cannot be experienced. I cannot get *in between*; the union is forbidden to me. The most I can possibly do is to usurp one member of the couple, an action which would dissolve the very link I seek. That I killed my father, that I, a female, achieved intercourse with my father – these solutions are not the answers to the original question. They lead only to the two cardinal sins of civilised society: incest and parricide.

In Freud's account of the *origin* of scientific curiosity, the child, engaged in the first grand problem of life, is concerned with a dyad, mother and father, and a third, the baby, whose arrival poses the problem. The scientist also investigates relationships between dyads. His problem is how to investigate the hidden link without thereby changing, or destroying, it – without committing incest with one of its elements. A truly successful discovery of the external world would exclude the investigator. But, as Heisenberg demonstrated, this is impossible. The investigator cannot enquire without changing the field of enquiry (to some extent), without intruding upon a relation which excludes him; just as one penis can fit one vagina at any one time, and another presence makes a jealous, incestuous third. Thus, neither the first nor the final problem can be solved by personal observation: the first because the enquirer (child) is outside that which he needs to be inside, the last because he (the scientist) is inside that which he needs to be outside.

Incest and chastity: the two poles by which knowledge is *limited*. But a thirst for knowledge does not necessarily precipitate corruption and an acceptance of its limitations need not induce sterility. Tragedy occurs whenever the balance is lost between these two extremes. In between, and when unfettered by collusion and wilful deception, knowledge of the world and the self may flourish. The tragedies of Narcissus and Oedipus are that the one cannot come to know himself and dies in youth, whilst the other dies in a senseless old age because he would know every lie about himself. Freud's view of the origins of research has left a legacy to the psychoanalytic world which I call the tragic vision of knowledge.

Freud not only linked epistemological curiosity with sexual curiosity,[3] he also believed that all children assumed the universality of the penis. This assumption reinforced the vision that the search for knowledge is painful and frustrating. The child's sexual theories are the product of his psychosexual constitution, in particular the penis. (In women, the penis has its analogue in the clitoris – 'a small penis. . . . But when she gets bigger it'll grow all right' as Little Hans tells us.) Freud says that the child's interest is instigated by excitations in his penis and the threat of castration which later terrorises him is proportionate to the value set upon that organ and is quite extraordinarily deep and persistent. Freud's assumption that children believe that everyone has a penis led to his statement that the child's enquiries and, indeed, all future research resting upon this foundation was bound to come to grief;[4] the child cannot connect a hole, circle, or open space with his mother's body. Freud continues, 'the lack of success of his intellectual efforts makes it easier for him to reject and forget them. This brooding and doubting, however, becomes the prototype of all later intellectual work directed towards the solution of problems, and the first failure has a crippling effect on the child's whole future' (p. 219). If we assume Freud's premises – first, that intellectual curiosity is founded on sexual excitation and, second, that all children assume that the penis is universal – early intellectual exploration is bound to fail and, indeed, would tend to have a crippling effect on the child's intellectual development. Both these premises have been challenged by ethologists, developmental psychologists and contemporary Freudian analysts.

Nevertheless, Freud observed two common attitudes towards curiosity and knowledge, frequently illustrated in relation to sexuality and encountered during adolescence, in particular. In adolescence, incest and chastity reverberate in acts of delinquency or drug excesses, on the one hand, and phobia or purity, sometimes anorexia, on the other hand. I suggest that there is a connection between the violence which Freud associated with curiosity and the withholding, or misconstruing, of information.

A phobia of school, that is, a refusal to leave home, erupted in Doreen's family when, at age eleven, she entered a huge, comprehensive school in London. The family was close-knit and could not foster a difficult entry into the vast, impersonal, glass-house of the comprehensive. Doreen had always been a 'Mummyish' girl. She asked few questions. She habitually said 'Yes'. She displayed no sexual curiosity. Nevertheless, her curiosity was intense and sharp. Five years after she started treatment with me, she explained her first year of silence to me; she was consumed with curiosity about me, where I lived, whether I was married, what I did at weekends, etc. My withholding of this information wounded her and, in retaliation, she decided to tell me nothing. My interpretations along these lines at the time were met with further silence and an expression of blankness. Her curiosity had to be guarded at all times because, unconsciously, she knew it was her most valued possession. Curiosity was linked to autonomy and, therefore, to *having a world away from mother*. It was turned into suspicion, secretive probing and a disarming watchfulness.

During her first year back at a grammar school, she made up for the two years absence and, moreover, was top or near the top of her class in most subjects. On Saturday mornings, she developed a liking for a large and excellent public library near my house. I do not know whether she actually read any of the books there, but she loved to walk about the library, catching sight of titles – simply being in the house of knowledge. People were reading, studying, passing their Saturdays. In the library on Saturday she could experience the other side of her school phobia – her love of learning, her enjoyment of intelligence, all that was inhibited during the week. Her mother found this 'habit' very strange, particularly since Doreen did not *need* to find a specific book. As this was a training analysis, the case was supervised. My supervisor interpreted Doreen's behaviour in relation to the weekend and, therefore, to my absence and involvement in my own home. The library represented my house and my private life. This interpretation, though possibly quite valid, emphasised the intrusive, spying quality of Doreen's researches and, moreover, tied her actions to me. I choose not to make this interpretation and, soon afterwards, Doreen changed her Saturday excursion and brought the Saturday attitude towards learning into her school life and, eventually, into her therapy.

It was fascinating to learn later that, when Doreen first went to kindergarten, her mother took a job in a sweet shop on the corner; when Doreen went to infant school, her mother took a job in the local Woolworths. In other words, it was her mother who followed her to school. Every break-time, Doreen went to visit her mother. Doreen's phobia was related to a fear of leaving her mother alone at home without her.

Christopher started treatment with me when he was ten-and-a-half. He was the eldest of four boys of an English, lower-middle-class family. The parents were kind and well-meaning. The onus of bringing up the four boys fell on the mother, as the father was an anxious and indecisive man. When I first met Christopher, he was beautiful to look at, the epitome of pre-pubescence, with thick, wavy, brown hair, curly eyelashes and a pink and white, spotless complexion. He was an excellent student, was liked, but had few friends. Early on in the therapy, he developed a burning interest in evolution. He had a phobia of roots (of trees), which involved a partial phobia of going outdoors and into his own back garden. To begin with, he played with toy animals and repeatedly fenced them in according to various classifications. As time passed, the fences stayed in the toy box, the animals got mixed up with each other, the domestic with the wild, the males with the females. The roots which had filled him with terror and disgust connected up with his intense curiosity about how things began and, of course, with the enigmatic arrival of his three younger brothers. His mother told the caseworker that, a couple of months before the birth of her fourth son, Christopher had asked her about her fat (i.e. pregnant) stomach. She was astonished. She did not think he would have noticed. Christopher looked everywhere for signs of how things began – the roots of things – but he wasn't supposed to notice. With the diminishing of the roots phobia and his budding interest in evolution and our discussions in his therapy, Christopher himself began to evolve into a teenager. He began to relate to me as a partner in the adventure of self-discovery. He and his girlfriend spent their weekends on a river bank, collecting 'ancient' stones and unusual wild plants for their botany class.

A similarity between the adventurous Oedipus and the phobic Little Hans can be seen in the deceit with which their respective attempts to gain knowledge are enmeshed. Little Hans is an oedipal child who, though phobic, is full of curiosity. His logic of enquiry is rigorous. To his questions about birth, naturally aroused by his mother's pregnancy and the birth of his sister at home, his father responds with the stork story. To his questions about genital organs, his mother insists that women and little girls also have 'widdlers' – despite the evidence of his own eyes. To his concern with his penis, his father responds with tales of castration. But Little Hans remains unsatisfied. Like Oedipus, he will have the truth. Again and again he asks the same questions. He has to choose between his parents' words and his own powers of intelligence and observation. To believe them, he must misperceive. He becomes increasingly obsessed with 'widdlers', '*lumpf*', penises, storks, etc. Freud remarked that 'the child receives either evasive answers or a rebuke for his curiosity, or he is dismissed with the mythologically significant piece of information which, in German countries, runs "The stork brings the babies; it fetches them out of the water"' (Freud, 1908, p. 213). He concludes that he would have given Little Hans the information he wanted and 'put an end to his stream of questions' (Freud, 1909, p. 145).

In contrast to the over-protectiveness and warmth of the school-phobic family, the delinquent seems driven to question everything. He is too provocative. No answer or prohibition deters him. Punishments, expulsions, court orders, probation, supervision orders are too lax. If anything, they spur him on. Two children, a boy and a girl, whom I saw in weekly therapy, had turned delinquent in early adolescence. They were both unusually bright and extremely humorous, an asset which was sometimes hard to handle when one was the object of their jokes. A phobic relationship tends to preclude humour. The parents of these two children were also bright, unusual and successful. But, they were peculiarly secretive both about their own sexual relationships and about the circumstances surrounding the births of their children. Sharon's mother had had two husbands and various lovers. She could provide the curious Sharon with scant information about her father, a travelling salesman, who had left home during the first two years of Sharon's life.

Robert was an adopted child of an American family living in London. His adoptive parents presented the well-composed and united front of successful managing director and director's wife. The family troubles began, they said, when Robert's father was transferred from Korea to London. Robert was then aged nine. From that moment, Robert pined for everything in the American estate in Korea – his friends, the language, the food. He hated London where he rapidly became isolated and disliked. He refused to associate with anyone who spoke with an Oxford accent and spoke a mixture of American and Cockney. Robert began stealing from his father's pockets and from the 'locked' drawer of his desk. I put the word locked in quotes because I was always struck by the ease with which Robert opened everything. Later on in the therapy, mother would report the break-in to the locked space and then, by the way, add the qualification that father must have absentmindedly forgotten to turn the key. Since the parents were well-off and all too willingly bought Robert whatever he wanted, they found his stealing puzzling. They were afraid to invite guests for dinner because Robert would appear in his dirtiest leather and denim outfits and talk loudly in his bizarre accent. If the parents went out to meet their friends, they would return to find that the house had been ransacked. Robert went through his father's pockets and his mother's underwear drawer. Finally, he got into their bed and ruffled up the sheets. Following upon this episode, he 'found' the key to the safe in his father's desk in which his adoption papers were kept. He discovered that he was of New York, Italian origin. He locked himself out of his flat and went up to the flat of a neighbour who was a woman of his mother's age. She was out. He slashed her front door with a knife. Affronted by his anti-social behaviour, particularly as Robert was fond of this neighbour, Robert's father resorted to beating.

Initially, I worked with the mother of the family whilst a psychiatrist worked with Robert. Father was usually too busy to come. Soon Robert could not be contained in the therapy room and the team decided to see all the members of the family together. This was hard to insist upon, as father was frequently called away for business trips, meetings and lunches. In the family meetings, Robert's adoption was discussed reluctantly, but openly, for the first time. I was reading through the case history in preparation for a presentation at a family therapy conference when I was struck by the obvious affinity between Robert and the legend of Oedipus. Again, deception had much to do with the current family crisis. In the family meetings, when mother and Robert sat side by side on the couch whilst father sat alone facing them, the co-therapist and I were amazed by the likeness between Robert and his mother. In fact, physical likeness had played a dominant part in the selection of Robert and his mother had taken pains to find out about the appearance of Robert's parents. Father had not been present at the adoption, for which his mother had flown back from the Far East to Canada accompanied by her sister.

In the myth, Oedipus is teased because of a lack of resemblance. In Robert's case, the resemblance was so deceptive that he forced his misfit upon his parents through his speech and dress. His initial reaction to the news of his adoption was to question his parents about his size and appearance, and to compare himself with his sister (who was also adopted and behaved exemplarily). What would they each grow up like? The parents found these questions 'touching'. Robert's acceptance by the American School in London provided a temporary palliative to his 'homesickness'. But soon his feelings of alienation and outcastness returned and he behaved in a disorderly enough fashion to be expelled. On the basis of his school reports, he was placed in a State school in a poor neighbourhood where he soon became the target of taunts about his accent and dress. He began to dress more shoddily and he refused to wash, so as to display comradely grime-lines. But he was not accepted into any of the gangs. He began to steal vehicles. First, he stole four mopeds. Then he drove his parents' car through red traffic lights. He was sent to a permissive, country boarding school with children of diverse nationalities and backgrounds. Again, the school failed to contain him. He was hell bent on getting on the other side of the law. He was convinced that, in borstal, his sense of belonging would return.

Robert reasoned as follows: If they are not my parents, why should I obey them? Why should I adopt their manners, clothes, habits, mealtimes, etc.? They have nothing to do with me. It's not my fault that they chose to be my parents. Let them suffer. For Robert, he and his parents were on a par. Lacking a blood-relationship, their connection was utterly contingent. If his parents went out to dinner, saying that they would be home by midnight and returned later, so could Robert. If they carried $100 in their pockets, so could he. English law did not pertain to him. Any leniency extended towards him was a manifestation of the weakness and stupidity of authority and a verification of his own cunning and power. After his adoption had become public knowledge, Robert found the ensuing sympathy and understanding ridiculous.

Robert's father felt extremely hurt and resentful about Robert's grudges against him. These feelings were in proportion to the envy he felt of Robert's situation. He would have done anything to have been adopted out of his family and to have been given the wonderful opportunities which he, through struggle and hard work, was able to offer his adopted son. Robert's father epitomised the 'self-made' man, who owed nothing of his success to his birth. As far as he was concerned, he might as well have been parentless. Robert's mother described a newborn baby as 'a bloody mess'. She had been afraid that she might produce a deformed monster. It was unclear whether the marriage had ever been consummated, and their sexual relationship was never discussed. The adoption procedure gave mother the freedom to choose her baby just as a little girl might go to a shop to buy a doll. Robert's rage and dissatisfaction were equally incomprehensible to her; after all, she did not need to rescue him, she chose him out of all the others. But, why should the 'lucky' one rejoice? Robert felt no gratitude towards them; after all, he had done nothing to be selected. He wanted to tear down the false solidity which surrounded him and to break into the hidden space of his mother's womb. Freud described the violent feelings which accompanied the child's first researches and the frustrations entailed by his inability to postulate the existence of the mother's vagina. Little Hans had 'premonitory sensations' which he expressed in his desire to 'coax' with his mother. It seems to me that the *urgent wish* to know about sexuality and about one's own origins may be instigated by oedipal feelings of exclusion and possessiveness, but that the *violent enactment* of these wishes may be precipitated by deception.

In his study of the *Oedipus Complex,* Freud constructed 'an average legend' of the hero and a 'family romance' which encompassed the child's fantasies of adoption. Freud took up Otto Rank's theory of 'The Myth of the Birth of the Hero' and constructed the average legend to bring into prominence the essential features of all such stories. He arrived at 'the following picture': (Freud, 1939, pp. 10–11).

> 1 The hero is the child of the *most aristocratic* parents; usually the son of a King.
> 2 His conception is preceded by difficulties, such as abstinence or prolonged barrenness or his parents having to have intercourse in secret owing to external prohibitions or obstacles. During the pregnancy, or even earlier, there is a prophecy (in the form of a dream or oracle) cautioning against his birth, usually threatening danger to his father.
> 3 As a result of this, the new-born child is condemned to death or to *exposure*, usually by the orders of *his father or of someone representing him*; as a rule he is given over to the *water* in a *casket*.
> 4 He is afterwards rescued by animals or by *humble people* (such as shepherds) and is suckled by a *female animal* or by a *humble woman*.
> 5 After he has grown up, he rediscovers his aristocratic parents after highly variegated experiences, *takes his revenge on his father*, on the one hand, and is *acknowledged* on the other and achieves greatness and fame.

Freud listed some historical figures to whom the myth of the birth of the hero applies: Sargon of Agade, Moses, Cyrus, Romulus, Oedipus, Karma, Paris, Telephos, Perseus, Heracles, Gilgamesh, Amphion and Zethos. The average legend contained the 'essential substance' of the Oedipus complex, the discovery of which would give to psychoanalysis a claim 'to be included among the precious new acquisitions of mankind'. That the Greek hero killed his father and took his mother to wife 'unwittingly, since he did not know them as parents, is a deviation from the analytic facts which we can easily understand and, which, indeed, we shall recognise as inevitable' (Freud, 1940, p. 187).

Otto Rank, a contemporary of Freud best known for his 'birth-trauma' theory of the origins of psychopathology, took the myth to be 'a symbolic representation of birth in spite of the father's evil intention' (Freud, 1939, p. 12). In Rank's interpretation, the casket represents the womb and the water the amniotic fluid. The intra-uterine relationship is also represented in countless dreams by pulling out of, or rescuing from, the water. Freud's interpretation, by contrast, underplays both the father's intentions and the womb symbolism. In fact, 'the source of the whole poetic fiction is what is known as a child's "family romance," in which the son reacts to a change in his emotional relation to the parents and in particular to his father' (p. 12). Every child entertains a family romance in which he belongs to two families. In fact, these are one and the same and only are differentiated chronologically. To begin with, the child enormously over-values his parents, in particular his father. They are represented in fairy stories as kings and queens. Later, under the influence of rivalry and disappointment encountered in real life, the child begins to detach himself and to criticise and devalue his parents who are then represented as humble. Thus the two families in the myth – the aristocratic one and the humble one – are both reflections of the child's own family as they appeared to him in successive periods of his life. Freud thought that 'these explanations make the widespread and uniform nature of myths of the birth of heroes fully intelligible' (Freud, 1939, p. 12).

Freud claimed that the riddle of another hero, Hamlet – 'whereupon the general lack of understanding on the part of the literary world showed how ready is the mass of mankind to hold fast to its infantile repressions' (Freud, 1940, p. 192) – could be solved by reference to the Oedipus complex. Freud brought to our notice the important insight that these literary projections conform to the *fantasies* and *unconscious wishes* of a child who grows up in a stable family situation, such as that of Little Hans. In Freud's day, the motives of the father were beyond question. Few would dare ask, or even consider the reasons, why a father would absent himself frequently from home or why his children should be excluded from the family circle and left to the care of others from a lower class. We may compare the Victorian nanny with the Carthaginian shepherd who rescued Oedipus from Kithairion. These considerations do not obscure the obvious fact that *any* child may oscillate, during his search for independence, between the aggrandisement and denigration of his parents. Because of his inability to tolerate his ambivalent feelings, the child might split the two sets of feelings into a fantasy of two families.

My difference with Freud is not to deny a universal unconscious motivation but to emphasise the leap between wish and enactment. The *Oedipus Rex* is about 'blind *actions*' as well, perhaps, as unconscious wishes. It spells out the disaster which occurs when the objective order of things is polluted. It tells us of horrors in relation to which individual guilt is useless, indulgent and beside the point. Freud declared unequivocally that the Greek legend translated the Oedipus complex 'from the world of a child's phantasy into pretended reality' (Freud, 1940, p. 189). My point is that, in the case of adopted children and the majority of Victorian middle-class children, no sharp boundary may be drawn between the child's fantasy and reality life – for the adopted child, the family romance is the true story. Freud's over-riding aim was to focus our attention on man's inner life; in pursuit of this goal, he dissolved the objective into the symbolic order. Since Freud, psychoanalysis has concerned itself with the hidden and latent wish rather than the manifest fact. Freud tended to interpret any criticism of his views as evidence of neurotic censorship. The most obvious reminders of the Oedipus complex 'are overlooked by a strange intellectual blindness' such as when people insist upon the difference between the analytic construction and the events of the play. 'What is overlooked in this is that a distortion of this kind is inevitable if an attempt is made at a poetic handling of the material, and that there is no introduction of extraneous material but only a skillful employment of the factors presented by the theme' (Freud, 1940, p. 191). Oedipus' ignorance is a 'legitimate representation of the unconscious state into which, for adults, the whole experience has fallen; and the coercive power of the oracle, which makes or should make the hero innocent, is a recognition of the inevitability of the fate which has condemned every son to live through the Oedipus complex' (Freud, 1940, p. 192). But, as the classical scholar E. R. Dodds points out, the play is not only about the blindness of man, it is also a play about human greatness. 'Oedipus is great because he accepts the responsibility for *all* his acts, including those which are objectively most horrible, though subjectively innocent' (Dodds, 1973, p. 76). Oedipus' responsibility is not for his unconscious wishes, but for blind acts.

Two psychoanalysts, Luis Feder (1974) and Herbert Wieder (1977), have studied the phantasies of adopted children and have looked at the Oedipus myth in this context. Both challenge the popular psychoanalytic view that family romance phantasies are similar in form and function for adopted and blood-kin children. Feder makes the point that the manifest account of the Oedipus myth is the clinical reality of an adopted child and outlines the clinical sequence of the adoption trauma in the following way:

1 ambivalent, conflictual, preconceptive coupling;
2 unwanted pregnancy;
3 somatisation, abortion (phantasied or attempted);
4 traumatic birth resulting from attitudes of a 'rejecting, filicidal, foeticidal mother' and leading to subsequent abandonment;
5 an adoption agent 'romance';
6 adoption by adoptive parents whose profound motivations are unknown but are manifested in
7 pre-adoptive idealisation followed by a
8 post-idyllic period, marked by conflict and possible rejection of the child with infanticidal wishes;
9 appearance of an 'adopted child pathology' – narcissistic personality, psychotic episodes, delinquency, homosexuality, suicide, incest, homicide, patricide or matricide.

Feder bases his thesis on 200 cases studied over a decade at the Texas Institute of Child Psychiatry. For ten years, Feder has researched from a psychoanalytic point of view preconceptive ambivalence, abortion and filicide in order to demonstrate the 'clinical reality' of the unwantedness of adopted children. In his curiosity about his origins and his investigation of the problem of where babies come from, the rejected child wants to find out about the sexual circumstances of his conception and how much he was wanted. The family romance phantasy is a manifestation of the child's unconscious perception that he *was rejected*. Feder emphasises Freud's observation that in every phantasy there is 'a fragment of historical truth' (Freud, 1937, p. 267); for the adopted child, however, the fragment is almost the whole truth. The Oedipus myth tells us of the ambivalent, preconceptive conflict between Jocasta and Laius. For Oedipus, the portion of not being wanted is total. Feder thinks that the adoption trauma, as outlined above, is destined to become a 'marker' in the area of unconscious perception. The unconscious perception of this trauma may be compounded by the unconscious phantasies of the adoptive parents. The 'sterile parents' may expect the 'perfect product' (Feder, 1974, p. 492) and, when disappointed, they may wish or threaten to return the child to the foster home or agency. These phantasies lead to extremely vengeful, destructive and incestuous behaviour so that the children from such beginnings form a large part of the population of clinics, reformatories, penitentiaries and suicides.

In analysis, Feder observes a frequent connection between the representation in the transference of the adoption trauma and negative therapeutic reactions. Both Oedipus and my patient, Robert, flee from their adoptive parents when their bastardy is revealed. The ambivalent, patricidally or matricidally destructive, *yet grateful*, patient will flee from his parental surrogate analyst in order to save him. Through flight, the patient also tries to avoid the painful truth that he was not wanted. At the end of Sophocles' play, Oedipus flees from the sight of the crime and, perhaps, from the realisation that the woman he loved and married had cast him out to die on a barren hillside. His final exile from Thebes is self-imposed.

Wieder (1977) observes that, for most blood-kin children, family romance phantasies are consoling. The typical phantasy reduces anxiety and guilt connected with denigration and incestuous wishes towards the parents and, at the same time, restores the wish for loving parents who never disappointed their child. Nevertheless, normal children react with alarm when they hear of actual adoption or kidnapping. In the analysis of adopted children who were told of their adoption under the age of three years, Wieder encountered the phantasy of having been abandoned to die or of having been ' "gotten rid of" ' by low-class shameful parents until ' "found" ' by a ' "saviour" ' mother who reinfused the child with life. One patient, in analysis with Wieder, enacted this phantasy by always taking ' "a second chance" ' on any undertaking, such as an exam or an analysis (p. 192). The first chance would fail but the second chance would bring about a successful rescue. The ' "second chance" ' phantasy was also instigated by incestuous dangers. Whereas, in blood-kin children, the family romance can relieve incest phantasies, in adopted children, anxiety and guilt are not diminished, since the absence of a biological blood tie to the mother is a threat. As Wieder's seventeen-year-old male patient said, ' "Any girl could be my [biological] mother or a sister" ' (p. 192).

A twenty-seven-year-old male, analysed by Wieder, lived in an environment which was divided into two worlds. One was the ' "real world" ' of his adoptive home where he was loved but which he rejected. The other was ' "the underworld" ' which was a bad, delinquent world where people were ' "rough and bad, stealing, attacking and doing sexual things" ' (pp. 193–5). Like my patient, Robert, Wieder's analysand was drawn to this underworld, partly in order to obtain aggressive and sexual relief. He feared closeness to his adoptive mother and sister because of the possibility of incest. His extreme dependence on his saviours, and his terror of their rejection if he displeased them, forced him into an attitude of hostile rejection. In all the cases analysed by Wieder, the biological mother was represented as sexual and sadistic, whereas the adopted mother was asexual and ethical. The family romance phantasy was a source of terror, rather than comfort, since any thoughts of other parents, even when idealised, evoked phantasies of abandonment, rejection and debasement. The adoption phantasy is the *fait accompli* underlying the adopted child's distress. His wish is to deny adoption, to establish a blood tie to the adoptive parents, and thereby erase the humiliation implied by adoption.

For the adopted child, knowledge and the phantasies associated with knowing, are fraught with the twin dangers of incest and sterility. No blood-tie bans the sterile parents from incestuous relations; no relationship in the world outside the family is free of the threat of incest.

12
Knowledge and the tragic vision

Freud and Wilfred Bion

In the next two chapters, I review two approaches to the origins and growth of knowledge. The first I refer to as the tragic vision, through which knowledge and pain are deemed inseparable. In the second, knowledge is connected to 'a holy curiosity' which does not arise in a dominant context of pain. In the final chapter of the book, I relate these two views of the origins of knowledge to attitudes, such as despair and optimism, towards the *limit* of man's knowledge. I suggest that our feelings about limitation are grounded not only in our ideas and phantasies about the origins of knowledge (for instance, that it is forbidden), but in our most primitive notions of externality. And, again, our formulations relate to our respective conceptions of infancy and infant-mother relationships. Does the boundary inside/outside represent an exclusion or castration which cuts us off from what lies on the other side? Or does it represent a potential space, offering an infinite expansion to our limited sensibilities? To one person, the realisation that his or her mind is but a tiny part in a larger whole brings feelings of relief and comfort, whereas, to another, this realisation is experienced as a humiliation or a castration.

From within the tragic vision, knowledge *originates* in the context of absence, *increases* in a context of pain and deprivation and *terminates* in despair or renunciation over limitation. Like attachment, knowing is regarded as a secondary development to more primary needs and wishes; their frustration or gratification precipitates the search for knowledge. This tragic vision permeates Freud's work on the development and vicissitudes of thinking. The plight of Oedipus or of an adopted child brings this tragedy home to us. The tragic vision reaches one of its more extreme statements in the psychoanalytic writings of W. R. Bion. The central and defining characteristic of the tragic vision is the *all-or-nothing* category of thought. A person with this vision lives in a world of extremes. This category pervades the thinking processes of many analysands and contributes to unrealistic feelings of both grandiosity and impotence. In the context of psychiatric or analytic treatment, this type of thinking is usually regarded as pathological; however, it also pervades the psychoanalytic theory of thinking and knowing.

It may seem curious that the main thesis of this chapter is devoted to the work of one analyst, Wilfred Bion, who is best known within the Kleinian group in England and on the West Coast of America, rather than to a fuller exposition of Freud's original views. Freud's discharge theory of thinking, together with his frustration and mastery (of anxiety) models of the origins of curiosity and knowing, form the foundation of Bion's theory. However, in addition to his debt to Freud, Bion has articulated in much greater detail than Freud, or, perhaps, any other analyst, a theory of the development of mental functioning from infancy to maturity. Bion's work is an extreme version of Freud's views and a fuller statement of the tragic vision, in which truth is seen as absolute and knowledge and pain are inextricably entwined.

In his book 'The Hidden God', Lucien Goldmann (1964) examines the *Pensées* of Pascal as a work of the tragic vision. Briefly, Pascal's vision may be expressed in the statement that man's relation to truth, to God, is that of a 'wager': man may wager that God exists, but he may never know him. Man's knowledge is a source of suffering, as valuable or worthless as any wager. In a similar vein, Bion describes the tragic situation of all human knowledge when compared to the 'absolute truth' (1970, p. 26). Human knowledge is limited and relative. Since knowledge *originates* out of absence, there is a primary connection between knowledge and pain. But the wish for true knowledge can never be satisfied or completed. Thus, truth is a permanent *source* of pain. Bion defines the 'K-link' (knowledge link) as 'a painful . . . feeling' which can be discerned in the question, 'How can x know anything?' (1962a, p. 48).

The all-or-nothing quality of tragic thought expresses a need for a totality, a union of elements inconceivable to reason and which may be felt or intuited through faith – by a 'wager of the heart' (Pascal). Lucien Goldmann has said that the category of 'all or nothing', fundamental to tragic thought, prevents man both from giving up the quest for absolute value and from falling into the illusion that this quest might succeed. Man must search for a synthesis of antagonistic elements – pure goodness, absolute truth, real justice on all and every plane – but this synthesis can never be achieved on earth and can only come from God. In this world of absolutes, relativity has no place. For Pascal, the middle way between two extremes was a paltry substitute for perfect synthesis: 'One does not show one's greatness by being at one extreme, but by touching them both at the same time, and by filling up all the space between' (Pascal, fragment 353 in Goldmann, 1964, p. 184). But it is impossible to fill up the space between two extremes. The two poles persistently refuse each other. A person caught in this paradox may drive himself to madness because he acts as though synthesis were possible within the terms of the paradox. Like Pascal, man can neither tolerate the paradox and give up the search for its resolution through synthesis, nor can he step outside its frame. In the Tibetan tradition, a less tragic philosophy, direct awareness of reality, the 'as it is', is conceptualised as 'not this'. 'Not this' is the maximum statement of completeness which man may make.

Statements which begin with 'All', 'Everything' or 'The One' imply that the limits of man's mind and of the cosmos coincide. Strictly speaking, man, the part, should not make such statements. Like Kant's concept of the 'noumenon', or the cybernetic concept of restraints, the negative definition, 'not this', has a *regulative* use.

The tragic vision of man's knowledge coexists with the belief in an absolute, transcendental truth. Bion formulates the notion of absolute truth as 'a thought without a thinker', which could be considered as a contained which has not found a container (1970, p. 117). Absolute truth is that which is not contained in the mind of man. The absolute view of truth leads inescapably to the miserable conclusion that all thoughts, once formulated (by man), are false when compared with the so-called true fact which they formulate. Compared to the original truth, all formulated thoughts contain a 'restriction' and are 'parasitic' (1970, pp.

97–105). Nevertheless, Bion's view of knowledge implies, tantalisingly, that man *could* be in a position to compare his inferior transformations with the real, ultimate truth.

The philosopher of science, Laudan (1977) points out that the justification for scientific research in terms of man's quest for *truth* has worn thin. Science does not produce theories which are either true or probable. 'By recognising that solving an intellectual problem is every bit as fundamental a requirement of life as food and drink, we can drop the dangerous pretense that science is legitimate only insofar as it contributes to our material well-being or to our store of perennial truths' (Laudan, 1977, p. 225). However, the possible falsity of scientific theories and research traditions does not render science either irrational or non-progressive. Science may still be an intellectually significant enterprise even if every theory is false. Laudan's point is that we have no way of knowing whether science is true or probable, or even that it is getting closer to the truth. Such aims are 'utopian'. 'To set them up as goals for scientific enquiry may be noble and edifying to those who delight in the frustration of aspiring to that which they can never (know themselves to) attain' (p. 127).

Let us consider how the all-or-nothing category of tragic thought applies to the psychoanalytic theory of knowledge and thinking. I suggest that this category is reflected in formulations, first, of the primary state of being – such as primary absolute narcissism, primary fusion, blissful illusionment, mother-infant union (the first position on my spectrum) – and, second, of the development and experience of separateness and separation – such as persecutory anxiety, traumatic anxiety, castration. From within the all-or-nothing category, transitional objects or schemas between the primary state and the development of separate self-object relating are impossible. The boundary between these two stages is absolute. Narcissism and object-relating are two positions which persistently refuse one another. There is no third area of experience, no resting place from the opposing forces leading to self-preservation, on the one hand, and socialisation on the other. Throughout life, a person seeks to reinstate the lost state of primary narcissism and to avoid reality. Similarly, in Kleinian theory, a person oscillates between the paranoid-schizoid and depressive positions; his hold on the depressive position is tenuous even in maturity. Between these two positions, there is no transitional area or overlap.

Psychoanalytic theory connects the origins of thinking with absence and frustration. Absence creates the prototypical situation in which the infant first experiences intolerable frustration and pain. According to Freud, the impetus to thought comes from excessive accretions of stimuli. Thinking is a new kind of activity which is more acceptable than direct discharge through behavioural action. In 'Formulations on the two principles of mental functioning' (1911), Freud outlined his view of the *evacuative* origin of thought. Thought provides a means whereby motor discharge is stopped or postponed. Thinking relieves the increase of tension produced by delaying the discharge, a delay necessitated by the renunciation of the pleasure principle for the reality principle. Thus, the thought processes are grounded on biological processes, since excessive accretions of stimuli find discharge in the working over of the mind.[1]

Bion relates the development of the most primitive thought to the *feeding* relationship. (Bion, 1962a, pp. 1–105). The earliest communication is the taking in of milk, warmth and love, equated with the incorporation of a good breast. However, although the baby has an 'innate preconception' of the breast, he is not aware of the need *for a good breast*. He simply experiences an unsatisfied need. He does not orientate towards a good object. He is enclosed in his own needs. The primitive thoughts or 'proto-thoughts' (1962a) are *bad* objects of which the baby seeks to rid himself. Both the need and the object of the need are a source of bad feelings. Since all needed objects are necessarily bad 'tantalising' objects, this need is equated with a bad breast. The infant tries to get rid of this bad (internal) object by projection of his pain into the mother. The mother modulates this projection of unbearable need and feeds back the baby the milk and warmth which is then equated with a good breast. Thus, the experience of the good object is secondary to the satisfaction of a need which is experienced as a bad object.

According to Bion, the infant's preconception (of the breast) 'mates' (1963) with a realisation (the experience of the real breast) which gives birth to a conception. But a conception is not the same thing as a thought. Thought is not the result of a *positive* experience of linking or union. When preconception does not mate with realisation, a different combination of preconception and *frustration* arises. Bion calls this combination a 'negative realisation' (1962b, p. 307). Only a negative realisation gives place to the appearance of a thought. However, when the intolerance of the negative realisation is too great, the baby evacuates the experience under the conception of a bad breast present. This is the most primitive thought (or 'proto-thought'). At this point, the infant's mind functions like a muscle which discharges 'beta-elements'. 'Beta-elements' are too concrete to give rise to proper thoughts. If, however, the infant is endowed with an inborn tolerance of frustration, the no-breast (which is different from the bad breast) becomes a thought proper and the apparatus for thinking develops. The innate capacity to tolerate frustration is facilitated by the mother's capacity for reverie and her ability to act as a container of all bad, projected experiences. Through her capacity, the infant is relieved and is then able to introject an *emotional* experience of the mother. This is the non-sensual aspect of the mother's love which Bion describes in terms of 'alpha-function'. Unlike the raw beta-element or proto-thought which is simply expelled, the *non-sensual* 'alpha-element' is transformed into thought. The combination of preconception with frustration, which is experienced as a negative realisation, leads, when it can be tolerated, to the first thought of the absence of the object. Frustration is then experienced not as something to be discharged but as 'a problem to be solved' (1959, pp. 312–13). For something to be *thought about*, it must be absent to perception.

The above psychoanalytic account of the origins of thought might be described as the feeding or digestive model of knowledge and thinking. Thinking is modelled upon quasi-biological processes of ingestion and evacuation, in which thoughts only arise when satisfaction is *absent*. Only when a need is unmet is the infant impelled, and able, to think about the object of that need. To my mind, this model has unfortunate consequences. For although thoughts are not sensual, in that they cannot be smelt or seen, it does not follow that they must originate in a *context* devoid of sensuality and human contact. This assumption follows from a confusion between a context and what takes place within it. In my view, the feeding model contributes to the tragic vision of human knowledge: the knower oscillates between hunger and satisfaction, neither of which extremes is acceptable. Is a hunger or thirst for knowledge really like the sensation of hunger or of thirst? Is the satisfaction of knowing something anything like the satisfaction of a full stomach or an assuaged thirst?

Bion's 'container-contained' model of the relation between mother and child connects both the feeding and evacuative theories of knowledge. Clearly, the theory of the evacuative origins of thinking requires an end-point for the evacuated substances – namely, a container. According to Bion, the container-contained model expresses a dynamic relationship between something which is projected, the contained (♂), and the object which contains it, the container (♀). The relation of container to contained speaks for itself and it is scarcely necessary to point out that, in this model, there is no place for transitional structures. Winnicott's concept of the 'overlap' calls for statements containing the prepositions 'to' and 'fro'. The container-contained model invokes statements which require the prepositions 'in' and 'out'. The feeding, in-out, model of communication contributes to a rigid demarcation between inside and outside, internal and external, introjection and projection.

The corollary to Freud's theory of the origins of thinking as a response to frustration and absence is that knowledge evolves in a state of isolation, deprivation and introspection. In Bion's view, these are the conditions to which the psychoanalytic setting should approximate. Since deprivation is painful, so is knowledge. The analysand does not want to know. Only suffering will lead to true knowledge. Thus, the human being's capacity to tolerate truth is fragile and the tendency towards evasive action – evacuation – is great. Moreover, since the search for knowledge is unsatisfiable, any alleviation of the pain inherent in knowledge is temporary. Bion says that the 'K-link' expresses a search for meaning which is never satisfied or completed. Just as there are an infinite number of potential facts, so there are an infinite number of potential meaning schemes. But why should this realisation of possibility be a source of pain?

I agree with Bion that the K-link is as basic as love (L-link) and hate (H-link) and that the legend of Oedipus is primarily a story about knowing (Bion, 1968, pp. 45–9). On this interpretation, the *Oedipus Rex* is a drama about the relation of the individual to the group with respect to self knowledge. Bion relates the tragic outcome of Oedipus' unswerving commitment to the discovery of the truth of his origins to an intolerance of pain, particularly of fear of the unknown. This intolerance precipitates defensive actions which further obscure the original state of affairs and render futile Oedipus' endeavour. However, the intolerance is not Oedipus'; he rarely wavers from his quest. The intolerance belongs to Laius and Jocasta. Bion contends that the K-link is as fundamental as the L- and H-links more commonly studied by psychoanalysts. However, in my view, Bion fails to distinguish the K-link from the matrix of the L- and H-links – namely, the painful or satisfactory relation of the infant to the breast.

The tragic vision of knowledge omits the other side of curiosity – the 'mystery' of reality of which one may 'comprehend a little . . . each day' (Einstein, in Clark, 1973). The feeding model describes an all-or-nothing attitude to knowledge, suffused with possessiveness. The hungry or greedy infant seeks no less than total incorporation. In this model, an attitude of comprehension little by little has no place. Aspiration to a complete knowledge – the swallowing-the-breast-whole model – is necessarily frustrating and invites a transcendental attitude. By attending to the exciting aspect of curiosity, I do not deny that the search for knowledge engenders feelings which range from intolerable frustration, to doubt, to a tolerance of paradox which is always uneasy. Nor do I doubt that frustration, and its mastery, contribute to problem-solving. But we may also draw comfort from the understanding that the world of which we are a part is larger than our conceptions of it. Indeed, the wonder of eternity and of life is that we will never know it.

As well as the all-or-nothing quality of tragic thought which, as we see, characterises both *pathology* and the psychoanalytic theory of *normal* development, we find another, somewhat similar, contradiction in the psychoanalytic account of the development of thinking. Despite its heavy use of a concrete spatial conception of the mind, the psychoanalytic theory of the development of thinking implies that the adult's conception of mind is one very little tinged with spatiality. Cognitive development has been described variously in terms of a leap from 'concrete operations' to 'formal operations' (Piaget), from 'primary' to 'secondary' process thinking (Freud), and from the evacuation and incorporation of 'beta-elements' to a full development of 'alpha function' and the capacity to think intuitively and mathematically (Bion). In this respect, the psychoanalytic theory of thinking coincides with the view of modern communication theory that the leap from iconic to digital communication – from the territory to its map – is essential to mental functioning. It follows that the man who regards a thought as a thing, or a bit of tangible stuff which can be localised, is operating on an erroneous epistemology. Upon this epistemology, the psychotic constructs his world. Despite differences in their respective views on the aetiology of psychosis, Freudian and Kleinian psychoanalysts and communication theorists agree that the psychotic person is enclosed by a type of 'concrete' thinking. He chews up the menu instead of the entrée it denotes, as if unaware of the difference between map and territory.

Recently, psychoanalytic theory has itself been criticised because of its use of concrete thinking and, in particular, its tendency towards anthropomorphism in metapsychological constructions (see Schafer, 1976). When a psychoanalyst talks of 'internal objects', 'incorporation', 'projection', 'identification', 'superegos', etc., he falls prey to the very thinking which he recognises in his patients as germane to their problems. At the centre of this issue lies the spatial conception of mind which leads to the conception of an idea or a thought as a thing localised in the mind.

The British philosopher, Richard Wollheim (1969) has described our ordinary conception of mind as one 'tinged with spatiality'. The mind is a sort of place within which thoughts reside. As Wollheim points out, this still leaves the question open as to whether we ever employ a concept of mind without the colouring of spatiality. Can we talk of the mind and its processes without employing spatial metaphors such as a container and contained? Schafer's action theory of mind (Schafer, 1976) attempts to answer this question in the affirmative. Wollheim relates the notion of a conception 'more or less tinged with spatiality' to psychotic organisation. Psychotic processes are saturated with spatiality. The word cat provokes a scratch from which the person flinches. But this fully spatial conception of mind and thinking also underlies the ordinary conception and, ultimately, inhibits intellectual activity. In this view, psychotics are like children in their thing-like conception of ideas.

Wollheim elucidates an important elaboration by Bion of Freud's theory of the development of thought: namely, that in order for thinking to emerge, the stimuli to be worked over must first be subsumed by the mind under some corporeal conception. Without this subsumption, the stimulus could not be experienced as a fit object for the processes of introjection and projection in which thinking originates. According to Wollheim, our situation is not merely that we are at home in our body, but that 'we are at home in our mind somewhat as in a body' (Wollheim, 1969, p. 219). This, Wollheim says, is the mind's image of itself.

Let us consider whether the 'stimuli' of absence, from which the thinking process is said to originate, may be subsumed under a corporeal conception. Is the conception of absence a conception heavily tinged with spatiality? Or is it, perhaps, a minimally spatial conception upon which we subsequently project a (present) object which, because of the pain connected with absence, appears as a bad object? (You will note that this is not a question about which conception bears closest resemblance to reality. The choice does not lie in the comparison of observable minutiae.) Bion, O'Shaugnessy (1964) and others postulate that the experience of absence is subsumed by the infant under the conception of an object – a bad object. Thus, even if we assume that the infant experiences a primary *bond* rather than a part-object, we would say that the *absence* of this link – the experience of 'gone' – is subsumed under the conception of a thing which is present. This is the logic of Bion's account of the infant's experience of loss as the presence of a bad breast. Absence is subsumed under the corporeal conception of the 'bad breast present'. Absence is a nasty thing like a prick or a blow. Absence is conceived as a representation of something present to the senses.

Green and Winnicott, on the other hand, have suggested that the bad object present may be a *secondary* elaboration of a more primary conception of an absence or blank. It is a defence against absence, for at least the persecutory object is *there*. An absence of response, experienced as a gap stretching to infinity, may be more catastrophic than a constant persecutory presence. These two different constructions of what absence means to the infant relate to the infant's conception of *presence* and to the theory of the primary state of being. For Winnicott, the primary experience is of the holding relationship. Absence of holding, then, is experienced as 'falling infinitely'. For Bion, on the other hand, the primary relationship is to a part-object, the mother's breast, and the absence of the 'good', loving, fulfilling breast is experienced as the 'bad', tearing, hateful breast.

We may conceive of the experience of 'gone' either as a black hole of infinite extension into which we might fall forever or as a looming, dark presence. The debate as to how far back in development we push the Oedipus complex relates to absence. In Kleinian theory, the infant of six months of age has reached the Oedipus complex. This is manifested in the phantasies he constructs about his mother's absence. The conception of the 'gone' experience as a looming, dark presence is a corporeal conception which may be allotted the role of the precursor of the Oedipus complex. In this construction, the gap is transformed into a black presence which is later expressed as that horrid, greedy, hard father-penis who takes mother away from me. The alternative conceptions of absence as a black hole of infinite extension or as a dark presence may relate to experiences of falling infinitely or of intrusion. Perhaps, the 'gone' experience has this double-edged quality for the infant and is felt as a falling from within *and* as a persecutory intrusion from without. If absence is experienced as an intrusion, this would suggest a more corporeal conception. Bion's representation of absence as the 'bad breast present' is a more corporeal conception than Winnicott's metaphor of 'falling infinitely'.

I suggest that the problem of how absence is conceived by the infant relates to the old Platonic riddle of non-being. Non-being must in some sense be, otherwise what is it that there is not? How do we talk about something which has no reference? In terms of infant cognitive development, how does the infant conceive of something which is not there – namely, his mother or her breast? If he has no idea of object-constancy, no evocative memory, no idea that something which is absent still exists and will return, what does he think? Can he even think at all? What does this term 'bad object present' mean? Do the infant's feelings of overwhelming pain and torture have an outline? In communication theory, there are 'zero-messages' (such as the letter which you did not write). An absence of response may *evoke* anger and disappointment. The 'zero-message' of absence can provoke protest, rage or despair without being subsumed under the conception of a bad object present. The question is can the infant experience an absence of response, a non-being, or must he experience all bad feelings as the presence of some*thing* bad? Does the infant construct the presence of a bad object out of the difference he perceives between presence and absence?

The psychologist, von Glaserfeld (1977) observes that the feeding model conjures up an erroneous image of information as something which travels by radio waves from one person to another. However, all that travels is a signal – not meaning or pieces of knowledge. If all goes well, the signal 'tells the receiver out of what and how he can put together or *reconstruct* the meaning or knowledge the sender wants him to have.' Communicational signals have often been called 'selectional instructions'. If the signal is to have communicational meaning, it must convey some rule for selection. Is the infant of a few days or weeks of age capable of constructing meaning out of an infinite number of differences or contrasts? Or does he see everything, every change or difference, in terms of feeding, of a good present, or bad absent, breast? The construction of meaning out of a mass of communicational signals is a very different action to that of feeding. The related infant, orientated towards communication, is engaged in the search for meaning, for pattern and predictability from the moment that he is born. Slowly he builds up a picture out of the infinite number of signals or differences which are triggered by his own sensory and cognitive apparatus.

In the works of Bion and Winnicott, two philosophers have a special significance: Kant and Heraclitus. The 'thing-in-itself' and the 'paradox', for which Kant and Heraclitus are renowned, are terms which appear frequently in the writings of Bion and Winnicott. The Kantian 'thing-in-itself' is seminal to Bion's conceptualisation of the non-sensual, abstract 'object' which we call a thought. In Winnicott's work, the tolerance of paradox seems to hold a similar position in relation to the development of varieties of mental functioning.

According to Kant, the primary act of aesthetic judgment is the *selection* of a fact. Bion describes this act in Poincaré's terms as the discovery of the 'selected fact' (1963, p. 39); a selected fact is an emotion or idea which gives coherence to what is dispersed. The selected fact is the name of an emotional experience of discovery. But Kant's primary act of aesthetic judgment does not imply that there are 'facts' in nature. There is an infinite number of *potential* facts just as there is an infinite number of possible truths. As

Bateson says (1970, p. 453), there is an infinite number of differences in a piece of chalk, but only a few of these make a difference. The selection of a fact relates to the selection of a difference out of an infinite number of differences around and within the piece of chalk.

According to Kant, the 'things-in-themselves' or 'noumena' may not be known through the senses. They are not synonymous with raw sense impressions. The concept of the noumenon has no *positive* definition. Its importance is entirely derived from its *negative* use. Kant's account of the *regulative* use of Pure Reason and of the concept of the noumenon is essentially equivalent to the cybernetic view of explanation in terms of '*restraints*'.

In the *Critique of Pure Reason* (1963), Kant says that the employment of Pure Reason is 'humiliating' since 'it achieves nothing in its pure employment'. Its 'greatest and perhaps . . . sole use . . . is therefore only negative.' It 'serves not as an organon for the extension but as a discipline for the limitation of pure reason, and, instead of discovering truth, has only the modest merit of guarding against error.' Similarly, the noumenon is also 'a merely *limiting* concept, the function of which is to curb the pretensions of sensibility; and it is therefore only of negative employment. At the same time it is no arbitrary invention; it is bound up with the limitation of sensibility, though it cannot affirm anything positive beyond the field of sensibility' (p. 272). Pure Reason has neither an empirical nor a transcendental employment. The 'remaining things' which lie outside the domain of 'sensible knowledge' are 'entitled noumena, in order to show that this knowledge cannot extend its domain over everything which the understanding thinks. But . . . the domain that lies out beyond the sphere of appearances is for us empty. That is to say, we have an understanding which *problematically* extends further, but we have no intuition, indeed not even the concept of a possible intuition, through which the objects outside the field of sensibility can be given' (p. 272).

In my view, Bion does not note the two-faced quality of the noumenon. He misunderstands its regulative and problematical use and, thereby, employs the concept transcendentally. The noumenon indicates nothing, nor may it be perceived through intuition. Bion, however, gives the 'thing-in-itself' a transcendental use in relation to the ineffable, psychoanalytic object (by which he means the process of psychoanalysis). There is an 'as-if' quality to Bion's use of the 'things-in-themselves' which leads ultimately to the tragic vision of knowledge. It is as if man could reach the ineffable truth, if and only if he could use pure alpha function. Kant's philosophy, by contrast, is not tragic but practical. Kant wanted to oppose dogmatism by insisting that all knowledge be grounded in experience and purified of arbitrary speculation. The use of Pure Reason was to combat illusions and dogmas. Kant did not lament that man has a problematical understanding of a domain which he cannot understand nor that his own reasoning powers have a limiting and regulative use.

Bion blurs Kant's distinction between *a priori* and sensible knowledge when he proposes equivalences between the 'things-in-themselves' and the 'beta-elements' – that is, the raw, pure, discrete sense-impressions. Because both are ultimately unknowable, Bion states an incorrect equivalence. The chief characteristic of the 'beta-element' is its corporeality and concreteness. It is 'undigested' – that is, unworked over by mental functions. Inadvertently, Bion subsumes the noumenon under a corporeal conception. An elision occurs in his theory of thinking between the transcendental 'thing-in-itself' and the psychotic 'beta-element'. In my view, this confusion arises because of Bion's misunderstanding of the *problematical* use of the concept of the noumenon. He fills up a concept which is 'empty' (Kant) and gives it a *positive* employment.

When questions of knowledge are framed in terms of perception, it follows easily but nevertheless illogically that a kind of non-perceptual, non-sensible and, therefore, transcendental knowledge is possible. The transcendental object is 'known' by some sort of non-sensible intuition. But, in Kant's words, this 'special mode of intuition, namely, the intellectual, . . . is not that which we possess, and of which we cannot comprehend even the possibility' (Kant, 1963, p. 268). Bion uses the concept of the noumenon as if it refers to an object which is knowable when we step outside the world of phenomena – a world which includes our own conceptual schemes. However, the difference between statements about the internal and external worlds is a difference in coding or conception and not in perception or modes of perception such as 'intuition' (a sort of intellectual vision) and sense-experience.

The constructivist model of knowledge – namely, that there are alternative conceptions or constructions of potential facts – is not open to Bion. Bion's order of knowledge is as follows: first, there is an initial fact (0) which is unknown; second, a process of transformation; third, an end product of this process. His grid is intended as a guide to the passage through different orders of abstraction, starting from the most primitive sense experience in which 'O' appears as an unanalysable beta-element (A) to the most abstract level of the algebraic calculus (H). Despite Bion's respect for Kant's philosophy, there is an assumption throughout his work that the reliability of all knowledge has to do with the truth or falsity of our representations of reality. Even when our perceptions are deemed to bear no resemblance to the 'things-in-themselves', there remains an assumption of a causal relation between the transcendent reality and our meagre experience of it. But, in order to answer the question, 'Does the horse resemble the real horse that causes my perception?', I would have to compare my perception with the real horse which I cannot. Such questions assume that I can draw a distinction between the way I conceive of an object and the object of my conception outside my conception of it. The theory also assumes that the *act* of conception may be distinguished from the object conceived. Of course, such distinctions are to some extent possible, otherwise the theory of projection would flounder. Nevertheless, these distinctions cannot be drawn in an absolute way and always entail comparisons with alternative conceptions rather than with an unchangeable external reality.

I suggest that Bion's philosophy is a work of the tragic vision because of a refusal to accept the limitation of man's knowledge. This is suggested by his expression of limitation as a 'restriction' and, finally, as a 'lie'. Bion misses Kant's point that the function of the regulative principle, expressed through the concept of the 'noumenon', is to curb man's pretensions to knowledge and his tendency towards dogma and illusion. The transcendentalist does not deal squarely with limitation. As soon as we think *positively* of the 'noumenon', we fall into the very attitudes which it was introduced to curb. In particular, we fall prey to the all-or-nothing category of thought. The transcendentalist attributes omnipotence and omniscience to the absent God, the ineffable truth or the good breast. The absence through which knowledge originates is that of a need-satisfying *object*, epitomised by the breast. Thus, Bion regards the unknown 'noumenon' as if it were a bad breast present – that is, a paingiving, frustrating object. The unknown is conceived as an absent 'thing', analogous to the bad breast present, rather than as an empty, and regulative, concept.

Bion's philosophy has unfortunate practical implications. The personal humility, which Bion projects in his declarations of his belief that man may know nothing, nevertheless may foster a belief in his audience that somewhere, 'hidden', there is a truth which we could find if only we would stop talking and, therefore, lying. It is but a short step to the notion that beyond the man, the mere manifestation, lurks the god, the bearer of truth in the ineffable interpretation. When Bion discusses analytic interpretation, he talks as if a pure experience is possible which it is the purpose of interpretation to effect. There is a transformation *in* O in which the patient 'becomes' the reality which was represented by the transformation *of* O. The psychoanalyst assumes the existence of an 'object' which manifests itself through the associations, gestures and emotions of the patient. Thus, psychoanalysis should delimit its study to the non-sensorial quality of psychic reality, or unconscious phantasy, and to the possibility of 'growing', 'decreasing', 'being' and 'becoming' (1970).

In Kant's philosophy, the regulative use of Pure Reason prevents man from enacting the illusion that he may either know or become the 'noumenon' or 'thing-in-itself'. Bion, on the other hand, believes that the analyst may apprehend the 'psychoanalytic object' through 'intuition'. For Bion, the positive exercise of Pure Reason becomes a practical possibility. He suggests a method for the encouragement of pure intuition – 'no memory, no desire and no understanding' (1970). The exercise of intuition may be felt by the analyst and the patient as the experience of deprivation (through the resistance to gratify desires), isolation (from a sense of responsibility which cannot be delegated) and loneliness (related to introspection). When this attitude is reached, it may be said in truth that the patient's associations and the analyst's interpretations are ineffable.

From within the tragic vision, Oedipus appears a fit candidate for the tragic hero. The hero's search for truth leads to greater and greater suffering and finally to a blinding and a castration of his sense faculties. However, the absolute truth which Oedipus pursues is not a transcendental truth, but the precise details of his own origins – a limited knowledge of the facts surrounding his birth. His ruin is brought about by his refusal to rest content with partial truths and with lies.

The tragic hero captivated Freud's imagination. In Western literature, the hero sets out on a journey to a forbidden kingdom or spiritual realm which lies beyond civilised society. In Ibsen's play *Peer Gynt*, Peer, the dreamer, enters the fantastic surreal kingdom of the Trolls. He meets the Great Boyg, the counterpart of the Sphinx, and has intercourse with the Troll King's daughter. Georg Groddeck (1976) used Ibsen's play to demonstrate the existence of the universal 'It', which is personified by Peer Gynt. Another psychologist, Wilhelm Reich, extolled Peer's free-roaming spirit which exemplified free-flowing 'orgone energy'. Reich used the tale to emphasise the unfortunate end which civil society metes out to such spirits.[2] Perhaps, it was his belief in the tragic hero, as well as harsh convention, which drove Reich to his paranoid and miserable end.

In many ways, Ibsen's drama more aptly illustrates *Freud*'s view of the oedipal stage of development than Sophocles' *Oedipus the King*. Peer is not adopted. He has an exclusive, narcissistic relationship with his mother. He spurns his lovers, including his mother. He grows up to become an adventurer but not a man of wisdom. Unlike Oedipus, his tendency is to run away from responsibility and from the complexity of any difficult situation. Peer enters a forbidden kingdom. He answers the riddle of the Trolls. He has illicit intercourse with the Troll King's daughter, out of which union a monster is conceived. Finally, he returns home a broken man to a maternal figure, Solveig. More than Oedipus' acts of self-mutilation, Peer's return to Solveig exemplifies Freud's belief in the renunciation of illicit oedipal wishes at the behest of castration. In both Freud's interpretation of *Oedipus the King* and Ibsen's rendition of *Peer Gynt*, we encounter a similar attitude towards the growth of knowledge: curiosity propels the enquirer into illicit sexuality, and thus into incest, for which pollution the adventurer must be punished either by society's edicts or through the promptings of inner conscience and guilt. This same parable of licentious, 'selfish' living and of final atonement and forgiveness is told in the story of the Prodigal Son.

Knowledge and the tragic vision

In this chapter, I have outlined a common psychoanalytic approach to the origins of human knowledge. I have called this the tragic vision – a vision which originates in Freud's work and continues to permeate the work of contemporary authors such as the Kleinian analyst, W. R. Bion. This vision is tied to a model of early infancy; the infant is a need-orientated, autistic creature who does not wish to know about his reality or to relate to the beings who inhabit it. He comes to relate to his reality through pain and suffering – primarily, through the frustration of his needs and the inevitable absences of those persons or objects (such as the breast) who might satisfy these needs. Like an affectional attachment, curiosity is not primary but secondary to the absence of the need-satisfying object.

13
'A holy curiosity'

> The important thing is not to stop questioning. Curiosity has its own reason for existence. One cannot help but be in awe when one contemplates the mysteries of eternity, of life, of the marvellous structure of a reality. It is enough if one tries to comprehend a little of this mystery each day. Never lose a holy curiosity.
>
> (Einstein, in Clark, 1973)

Contemporary views on exploration

In this chapter, I attempt to outline an alternative view of thinking and exploration in which the varieties of mental functioning develop in the context of presence and minimal frustration and are linked to the emergence of transitional objects and phenomena. Knowledge and pain, thought and absence, are not necessarily connected although knowledge, thinking and speech are related in some sense to negation. A sense of separateness and the experience of separation *may* influence the development of verbal thought and speech, but traditional Freudian/Kleinian theory represents the mental processes involved in differentiation and separation-individuation in polarised terms (e.g. splitting and hatching). These theories reflect the pathologies they explain in that, like the psychotic child, they posit a gap where there should be a bridge.

Nevertheless, the theories examined in this book, psychoanalytic and communicational, are united in their assumption and observation that words and thoughts depend, *in some way*, upon *negation*. The child who cannot tolerate the perception of not-there, not-me or 'don't' will be unable to make the leap out of the concrete world of presences into the abstract world of absence (i.e. no-things) of which thoughts and ideas consist. Verbal communication depends upon the axiom that the map is not the territory. In a similar vein, Freud remarked that we never discover a 'No' in the unconscious, implying that the 'No' is intrinsic to the secondary processes. Winnicott has studied the child's use of the transitional object as a way of dealing with the first *me/not-me* distinction. Bion and other contemporary Kleinian psychoanalysts have focused upon the experience of the no-breast, the negative realisation, as the precursor of thinking. Bateson suggests that the leap from analogical to digital communication depends upon the simple negative, which is often preceded by the negative command 'Don't'. All agree that psychotic processes proliferate when the negative is avoided.[1] In psychotherapy with autistic and psychotic children, Tustin claims that autistic objects must give way to transitional objects and symbol formation. Play, a transitional phenomenon, marks a crucial step in the discovery of map-territory relations and is important in the development from primary to secondary process thinking. Tustin describes how traumatic oral frustration, imbued with 'unspeakable terror', has been experienced 'as a blow on the mouth which brought an agony of consciousness which could not be borne' (1972, pp. 79–88). The autistic child has tried to cope with the ensuing 'black hole depression' by denying separateness and negation. He uses the therapist as an undifferentiated object which can be entered and controlled. The child oscillates between two extremes: fusion and annihilation. In therapy, 'in' and 'out' reactions become modified, it is hoped, into reciprocal 'to' and 'fro' responses. Communication begins when there is a *shared area* between mother and child. Tustin tells us that the psychotic child has a gap or hole at a place where there should be a *point of contact* or a bridge from me to you (p. 160). However, this therapeutic goal, reflective of a view of *normal* development, suggests a concept of difference and differentiation which is not often formulated or understood in traditional Freudian and Kleinian theory.

Thus, the experience of negation, or the 'negative realisation', and the formulation of the simple negative are linked to separation, absence, separateness, differentiation, to the perception of contrast and differences, to the making of distinctions, to the command 'Don't', etc. However, in my view, these communications are *tolerated* in a context of togetherness, reciprocity, play, secure attachment and, above all, predictable presence or reunion. When differentiation is linked to the use of transitional objects and transitional phenomena – i.e. to bridging phenomena – physical separation or a lack of holding become tolerable, even welcome, and black hole depression and defences against the many forms of negation do not set in. In play, map and territory are both equated and discriminated, thereby freeing the child from the black and white, all-or-nothing, quality of concrete thought. Play offers an intermediate area in which primary and secondary processes, action and reason, combine. Play ceases to exist if the person either *totally* forgets or can*not* forget the context marker 'This is play'.

To illustrate the important role of play in the individuation process and in the tolerance of negation, I reproduce a vignette presented by a member of a seminar group in which I participated. We had been discussing the all-or-nothing nature of a mother's interaction with her four-year-old daughter in which the mother oscillated between delivering rational explanations to her daughter and acting together with her as a peer. I remarked on how there seemed to be no intermediate or bridging types of communication. I did not use the word 'play', but the student went on to present the following material. The child had come to treatment because of excessive faecal and urinary retentiveness to the extent of contracting infections. Much of the treatment had focused upon the child's panicky reluctance to give up her nappy or diaper. The diaper was experienced both as a body-part or another skin and as the external container of terrifying inner objects and body products. It was held on to as an autistic-transitional object in the absence of a secure holding relationship with the mother, who was extremely anxious about separateness. The problem was not that the mother did not actually hold her child, since the child would often spend a whole session in her mother's lap, burrowed inside her just as the mother was burrowed into the armchair. But this burrowing inside, which was so close and warm, did not provide this child with the support that comes from being held by a person who has strength in her arms. The mother herself would collapse into the chair. On the session presented, the child was in her mother's lap and the therapist and the mother were trying to communicate to the little girl that it was really time *now* for her to give up the diaper. However, to the message 'No diaper', the child screamed in distress and clung to her mother.

Without thinking, the therapist picked up the child's doll and started to undress her, taking off her diaper. Interestingly, on arrival for her sessions, this little girl often undressed completely, as if wishing to rid herself of the second skin which held her together outside but, nevertheless, was also experienced as foreign and defensive. When the therapist asked the little girl what she should put on the naked doll, the little girl replied, quite definitely, 'nothing'. This exchange was repeated two or three times. Meanwhile, the child had left her mother's lap and, absorbed with the therapist in the exchange about the doll, made no further request for the diaper. The doll play, apart from its obvious representational content, liberated this little girl from continuous physical contact with her mother and provided the necessary transitional space between physical presence and the naked, raw exposure of being separate. Play made the negative tolerable and moreover, suggested to the mother that perhaps there was a middle way between the two extremes of physical fusion and traumatic separation.

Although learning and thinking may be inhibited by an intolerance of separation, negation, frustration and separateness, it does not follow that they *arise* under such conditions. Much of the research cited in this book emphasises that the newborn does not only wish to be *fused;* therefore, he does not need to be prised away. He may seek out near-continual proximity, togetherness, mutuality and synchrony, but these goals are very different to the wish for total womb-like fusion, as described in the primary narcissism thesis. Togetherness and the appreciation of contrast and difference are not incompatible in the same way as fusion and fission. When a child is secure about his or her mother's whereabouts, thus ensuring reunion, he is free to turn his attention away from her. Pleasure in problem-solving gives even the neonate a freedom from proximity-seeking actions.

Spitz's account of 'scanning' as the precedent of both incorporation and evacuation is relevant to this view of the growth of knowledge and exploration. Spitz points out that the activity of rooting in newborns is essentially a striving toward activity and is 'a behaviour which is neither splitting out nor taking in, but . . . a *scanning* behaviour . . .' (1957, p. 90). According to Spitz, communication originates from scanning behaviour. This point of view emphasises the questioning, and forward-looking, origins of communication. Spitz views rooting as 'a prestage of communication' (1957, p. 89). This view implies that the search for knowledge and for reality itself, as the consummation of scanning, does not originate solely from frustration. The scanning part of the total rooting pattern precedes both incorporation and evacuation. Spitz's thesis may be compared with Fairbairn's concept of 'object-seeking' as opposed to the concept of 'satisfaction-seeking' (1941).

When the baby 'scans', he picks up information. Bateson points out that in order to produce 'news of difference', that is information, there must be two entities. The scanning infant notices contrast and loses interest in repetition. A three-week-old infant I observed was riveted by the contrast between a dark jacket hanging on the door of a white cupboard. Over and over again, his attention was drawn not to one *object* but to the boundary line which created the outline of the object. When I placed three soft toys of varying colours and shapes across Stephen's cradle when he was about six weeks of age, his eyes first flitted over the objects from left to right and then back again; he then fingered each object in turn, systematically going back and forth along the string. It seemed to me that it was the perception of differences which intrigued and delighted him. The infant registers contrast, such as the contrasts between loud and soft, high-pitched and low, sounds and voices, or between light and dark, pattern and uniformity, hardness and softness. On the most general level, he notices the contrast between the familiar and the strange. He *prefers* the familiar but none the less is *attracted* to novelty. News of difference disturbs monotony; it can be sought out or avoided. The autistic child seems to find the plethora of differences so overwhelming that he tries to blot out all contrast and to replace it by the monotony of perseverative activity. For most securely attached children under the age of three years, the news of difference which is triggered by the mother's departure is registered as an unwelcome disturbance. However, the mothers of such children often remark that the child's equilibrium is quickly restored once the mother has actually left the room, thereby freeing the child to settle in to the relationship with another familiar, loved figure. The disturbing contrast dissolves with the mother's departure.

Tolpin's paradigm for the step-by-step development of the tolerance of frustrations aroused by unfamiliarity is Bowlby's model of eight months' anxiety: in his examination of stranger anxiety, Bowlby describes the situation of the infant on *the mother's knee* (1969, pp. 324–6). This model draws our attention to the enormous difference in the infant's anxiety level in a strange situation when he or she is seated on the mother's knee. The baby is then able to use the mother as a safe base for exploration. Bowlby's point is that, initially, exploration develops *in the presence of the mother*. For example, an infant who is in the presence of his mother but seated at a distance of four feet from her will show more fear of the stranger than when he is seated at closer proximity. However, extreme proximity such as burrowing in the mother's lap also precludes exploration. Using Bowlby's model, Tolpin points out that the small anxiety responses we observe when the infant is on the mother's knee are in sharp contrast to the overwhelming panic-like reactions that the infant experiences in the *absence* of the mother's alleviating behaviour. From the mother's knee, contrast is not traumatic, but stimulating.

Bowlby's account of the child's response to the stranger when on the mother's knee is similar to Winnicott's view of the development of the capacity to be alone whilst in the presence of the mother (Winnicott, 1958a). Both describe overlapping situations in which difference is agreeable. It might be argued that these situations occur towards the end of the first year of life and are not relevant to the first weeks when the infant is subjected to massive automatic traumatic and persecutory anxiety. However, in Tolpin's view, there has been insufficient emphasis on the fact that in the good-enough mother-infant unit, the infant experiences mothering interventions which mitigate the magnitude and duration of these states and prevent distress from reaching traumatic proportions. Even in the earliest days, when the baby is vulnerable to overwhelming and disrupting anxiety, the terrifying experience of 'nameless dread' (Bion, 1962a, p. 96) is closely modulated by the mother's state of 'primary maternal preoccupation' (Winnicott, 1956) and 'reverie' (Bion, 1962a, p. 36). Eventually, the infant perceives the beginning of distress not as the precursor of overwhelming persecution, but as the forerunner of activities which bring relief. Tolpin suggests that the attitude of optimistic expectation in an adult, that challenge may be overcome by appropriate means, is grounded in these infantile experiences of anxiety which can be tolerated because relief is expected. The infant has a picture of 'an average expectable environment' (Hartmann, 1939) out of which he begins to discriminate aspects of the mother's anxiety-relieving functions. Later, the infant builds up transitional structures, such as the blanket, in which some of these discretely perceived functions amalgamate.

Tolpin (1971, p. 333) proposes that

> the necessary foundations for what Freud called the ability 'to subject the affect of anxiety . . . to the normal workings of the mind' [Freud, 1926, p. 150] are laid when the mother 'subjects' the infant's anxiety experiences (or what may be more precisely considered their precursors (Benjamin, 1961)) to 'the normal workings' of the infant- mother relationship of the pre-oedipal years.

Both Bion and Tolpin emphasise the importance of the mother's soothing functions such as her capacity for reverie. However, the model of the 'infant-mother unit' and the model of 'container-contained' entail different views about early relationship. The first implies interdependence whereas the second is derived from the evacuation theory. In Bion's model, the experience of the unit or the couple is not primary. The infant internalises the idea of 'twoness' (Bion, 1962b,) *after* the mother has transformed the infant's projected pain through her capacity for reverie. The 'creative pair' (Bion, 1959, p. 311) introject, the forerunner of linking and knowing, is formed by a metabolising container who is open to the baby's projected need and, second, by the baby who, through projective identification, places his intolerable feelings in her (the contained). When envy of the creative couple is excessive, the infant and the mother form a 'frustrated couple' (Bion, 1958, p. 145). Central to the view proposed by Bowlby, Tolpin and Winnicott, by contrast, is the thesis that the search for knowledge is stultified when the child's familiar base, i.e. the mother's presence, disappears. Anxiety becomes quickly intolerable to the young infant in the absence of the *primary link* to the mother.

Bion and Winnicott have expanded the boundaries of psychoanalytic work to the very foundations of mental functioning. I have compared the approaches to knowledge of these two thinkers and contrasted their views of absence and *emptiness* out of which the varieties of mental functioning take their form. These two analysts have called attention to that area of human development which Piaget has named 'genetic epistemology'. Both attempt to describe the area of 'formlessness' or 'emptiness' out of which knowing, thinking, playing, dreaming, imagining, fantasying, etc. take shape. In the language of cybernetics, Bateson refers to this area as 'noise': 'All that is not information, not redundancy, not form and not restraints – is noise, the only possible source of *new* patterns' (Bateson, 1967, p. 410). Bion views emptiness under its negative aspect as a state of isolation, deprivation, psychic pain or unbearable chaos. Winnicott, like Bateson, contemplates the positive aspect of formlessness as a space of potentiality. In therapy, the therapist and patient enter the area of formlessness together in the same way that a mother may join in in the 'free play' or 'nonsense' of her child.

Not surprisingly, both men have found themselves working in borderline areas of mental functioning. Winnicott's experience has been drawn from paediatrics and child psychiatry whilst Bion's work has been with groups and with schizophrenics. Both have extended the psychoanalytic method to areas which, formerly, lay outside the domain of psychoanalysis. Where Bion has investigated the preconditions for, and attacks upon, 'linking', Winnicott has articulated the 'transitional areas' without which life is not worth 'living' (1971a, pp. 26–37). Where Bion emphasises the link between knowing and truth, Winnicott stresses the transition between playing and reality. The ' "K" link' evokes the image of man the discoverer or seeker of a truth outside him, whereas the transitional phenomenon of 'playing' pictures man as the creator of that which he finds. The contrast between these two conceptions of absence is reflected in the respective formulations of the 'psychoanalytic object' (Bion) or setting. For Bion, the psychoanalytic object is a transcendental, non-sensual object. For Winnicott, psychotherapy is a transitional object.[2] The transcendental object is ineffable and inaccessible; it is an absent object. The transitional object is neither mental nor physical; it is a present object, accessible and personal, though neither subjective nor objective.

Although both Freud and Klein acknowledged the child's search for knowledge in the concept of the 'epistemophilic instinct', the object of this desire is nevertheless a *forbidden* knowledge. Whereas the Kleinians have promoted a feeding, incorporative model of knowledge, Freud linked the arousal of scientific curiosity with the primal scene – a scene from which the child is *excluded*. Curiosity is thereby associated with *intrusiveness* and with the discovery of a *forbidden* secret. In my view, sexuality is one aspect of exploratory activity rather than its cause. If babies find that problem solving is motivating in itself, 'we don't have to search for ways to make babies learn to acquire knowledge' (Bower, 1977, p. 108). Tinbergen also points out that there are specific behaviour patterns, the exclusive function of which is to create the opportunity to learn certain things. In my clinical experience, a strong association between knowledge and sexuality is often the source of phobias about, or inhibitions in, learning. Finding out is associated with intruding into the forbidden intercourse. With this observation, many psychoanalysts would agree. Why, then, do they hold on to a theory of the origins of knowledge appropriate to pathology but long since challenged by psychologists and ethologists? *Ambivalence* about knowing may be interpreted as a conflict either between feelings of disgust and fascination or between omnipotent phantasies of replacing the father/teacher and fears of castration. However, we may also view ambivalence from the parameter familiar/strange, as well as from more usual parameters such as good/bad or inclusion/exclusion. From an ethological viewpoint, exploratory and withdrawal behaviours must appear together. Tinbergen (1972) interprets 'eight months anxiety' as an essential stage in adapted behaviour. Child-stranger encounters create in the child a state of motivational conflict. The child is both attracted and reluctant. In autistic children, this adaptive ambivalence has reached paralysing proportions. Thus, knowledge and ambivalence go hand in hand but, in normal circumstances, ambivalence is not necessarily a source of pain. This view of ambivalence as contributing to survival acknowledges both sides of the coin – attraction and fear – which are lost in the tragic vision.

Tinbergen suggests that the requirements for survival may be 'adjustability, open-mindedness, ability to judge and to plan far ahead' (1973, p. 225). The optimal conditions for the flourishing of exploratory behaviour are 'security, a minimum amount of interference by adults (as distinct from guarding), time and opportunity, and an environment which invites exploration' (p. 224).[3] These conditions are not always met by mothers who respond to modern, stressful living conditions by behaving in either over-intrusive or sub-motherly ways. They may over-expose their children to unfamiliar situations or solicit over-intrusive behaviour in visitors. An over-intrusive mother may interfere at moments when the child wants to play alone or with his peers, and thus force him to withdraw. Tinbergen considers that the increase in autism in our day is a real increase due to increased social stress (1972). Winnicott's view of the mature capacity to be alone rests upon the infant's experience of being alone in the presence of another (Winnicott, 1958a). This kind of togetherness is usually impossible under conditions of stress. The neurotic state of ambivalence over closeness may reflect a deprivation of this type of companionship. Solitude and togetherness seem incompatible. The person oscillates between active engagement and withdrawal with accompanying fears of engulfment and abandonment.

In my practice in the United States, I have been struck by a deprivation in the area of independence. Here I witness a paucity of privacy through over-possessiveness and an insistence on shared experience at the expense of a personal world. In England, working in a National Health Clinic, I met young people who suffered from emotional deprivation in the sense of loneliness, unreliability, comparative poverty and frequent separations from attachment figures. I think of four gifted people in therapy with me in the United States, all of whom experienced personal success as a kind of robbery because of a lack of privacy. In therapy, the couch became the forerunner of solitude which was treasured. To begin with, all four persons felt a frightening loss of contact and mindlessness but soon found that, in the wall or window opposite them, they could forget about their mother's face. It took a great deal of courage for them to turn their backs on me, particularly as I could still see them. All had suffered throughout childhood from a lack of friendships with anyone other than their mothers. None could remember consciously turning their backs on their mothers in order to play alone or with their friends or even siblings. All four stuck adhesively to face-to-face contact and to the infinite mirroring thereby imposed. All were part-time performers: two dancers, one lecturer and one singer. Each had many talents. The restoration of their creativity coincided with their liberation from the response of their audiences – which was without exception admiring. My point is that, in the therapy, it took tremendous effort and courage for these people to forget about me, and to make their own creative gesture to the world outside me. If I made an interpretation along these lines, they would feel suspicious: either I was pushing them out or I wished for their success for my own ends, my own self-aggrandisement. To turn away, they needed my permission but that very permission robbed them of their own creativeness and initiative. The wave of goodbye did not come naturally, since it signified rejection.

Further research into ambivalent behaviours has been undertaken by Anderson (1972) and Blurton Jones and Leach (1972); these writers employ an ethological approach in their research on mother-infant interaction. Blurton Jones and Leach observed that, although clinging behaviour signifying over-dependence may result from too little mothering, some nursery school children who cling and appear to lack exploratory curiosity nevertheless have responsive mothers. Previously, Bowlby had proposed an inverse relationship between clinging, crying and adequate mothering. Hinde and Spencer-Booth, on the other hand, suggest that the development of independence in rhesus monkeys results from an increase in *rejection* by the mother. Their research indicates that the mother's active support is required if independence and exploratory activity are to get off the ground. In rhesus monkeys, the mother will push her infant out whilst she remains where she is as a secure base to return to. Through the mother's rejecting support of the child's tentative departure, mother and child help each other out of the potentially vicious circle of rejection-clinging behaviour. It may be that some degree of sensitive rejection on the part of the mother in the context of motivational conflict supports the child and frees him, and probably herself, from an ambivalence which is irresoluble within itself. This type of releasing rejection, coinciding with encouragement, is exemplified by the mother who, with a warm and confident push, says to her child, 'Go on, I'll be here.'

Blurton Jones and Leach suggest that both Bowlby's view and the opposing view of Hinde and Spencer-Booth may be valid, but that the factors they stress are related to age. Too little mothering at a very early age makes the infant clinging and insecure so that he is unable to deal with rejecting behaviour at a later age, when he is capable of increased independence and enjoyment of other children. In their study of separation and greeting, Blurton Jones and Leach observed that the mothers of criers and non-criers under three years old were equally responsive to the child's behaviour. However, in their study of older children, the mothers of children who cried at separation were *less* responsive and smiling exchanges were also considerably reduced. In early infancy, smiling, clinging and crying have been thought by Bowlby, Ainsworth and others to increase proximity between mother and child and, therefore, to strengthen the attachment bonds between mother and child. However, Jones and Leach found that smiling at a later age no longer correlated with clinging and crying. Indeed, these two behaviours were found to be exclusive of each other. Children who smiled more at their mothers tended to be those who cried little on separating and who explored more. According to this study, it would appear that smiling at a *later* stage in development no longer increases proximity. At a later stage smiling, in contrast to clinging, may be an appropriate attachment behaviour over distance. Clinging precludes distance and therefore might tend to inhibit exploration. Crying demands approach. Smiling, however, like the wave of goodbye, may communicate both attachment and independence.

In a comparative study of normal and problem children, Leach (1972) discovered that bad separators seemed unable to *join in* in laughing and joking or mock-fighting. She suggests that smiling between a mother and child may have more to do with developing interactions with people in general rather than the formation of an exclusive attachment to the mother. Bad separators are unwilling to let their mothers leave and yet, when their mothers stay, they are often unresponsive to them. They neither smile at their mothers nor at others. This trait seems to be connected with their inability to join in. These children end up in a vicious circle of general unresponsiveness. Leach also observed that bad separators tend to initiate more *actions* than speech in their mothers. In this respect, they compare with younger, normal children. Unlike the child who both plays with his peers and smiles and waves to his mother, these children are locked in a negative ambivalence which is completely incapacitating. Speech is unusable since it implies spatial distance which these children cannot tolerate because of the loss of contact it signifies. Such children usually lack the quality of playfulness.

An adolescent who is reluctant to go out in the evenings with his or her own friends may fear that he is rejecting his parents and leaving them alone to age or die without him. He may feel enormously relieved when his parents go out or when the therapist goes on holiday. Jean dreaded all separations from me, particularly when I took a long summer holiday. She would beg to come for sessions right up to the last morning of departure. Once, she got herself marooned in a different part of town a week before my departure and called me in tears begging me to come and collect her. (In Los Angeles, there is barely any public transport and no local taxi service.) On the two occasions we made an appointment for the morning prior to my departure, she phoned me after I had arrived at my office to say that she was sick. She was genuinely sick, but she also could not bear to make a session the last. Her parents took frequent trips which often extended well over the weekend into the week. All the children were expected to accompany them. Jean, however, was six years older than the others and it became increasingly detrimental to her education to miss school. She was unable to reject her parents' generosity or to face staying behind at home while they flew off to a strange and exciting place. However, on two occasions, she left with them but returned two to four days ahead of them. To her astonishment, she found that she loved to be at home without them, enjoying both solitude and her own friends.

Sometimes, the parents of teenage children have become so unaccustomed to being alone together that they lack the motivation to assist their child in the resolution of separation conflicts. I think this was the case with Jean, to whom her father was enormously attached. The breakthrough in Doreen's 'school phobia' or refusal to leave home and the consequent paralysis in her social life paralleled her parents' first visit to a pub alone together since the birth of their two children. It was most strange for them to find themselves alone, even though the pub was their 'local' and was frequently visited by the father either alone or with his friends.

One of the most important factors in the growth of independent exploration is the child's knowledge of his parents' whereabouts. Bowlby observes a marked difference in the child's behaviour between those occasions when the mother leaves the child and those in which the child leaves the mother who remains in a known place. In the former situation, the separation leads to anxiety whereas, in the latter, it is conducive to adventurousness and relative contentment. In studies of separation, this difference may be obscured. Behaviour on *reunion* is of equal importance. In the psychoanalytic study of separation reactions during treatment, there is a marked absence of observations of separations in which the analys*and* leaves the analyst in a known place. Also, more emphasis is usually placed on the patient's behaviour *prior* to separation than upon reunion. I have noticed significant changes in the treatment of two adolescents on their return from school camps or family holidays which they took *during the analytic term*. A therapist might interpret to the patient that he or she is taking a break during the analytic term in order to avoid something unpleasant, such as the therapist's own vacations and freedom, or in order to reject and triumph over the therapist who is left behind to work. However, this interpretation might mask an important development in which the patient steps forth out of the familiar and safe routine, whilst leaving the familiar figure behind in his usual place.

Fleeting and distant contacts can also be effective during periods of separation. In therapy, the therapist decides whether to send his patient a post card. The post card might make the patient feel more left out, abandoned or envious or, on the other hand, he might feel remembered, cared for and included in the analyst's mind. Tinbergen (1972, p. 191) discusses the importance of 'by proxy' bonding, an example of which is given by a working mother who leaves a snack out for the child who returns home from school before his mother gets home. In their films of separation reactions in children, James and Joyce Robertson have demonstrated beautifully the value of this type of contact. In their 'foster' care of children whose mothers and fathers are absent, the Robertsons use photographs and doll families in order to keep alive the memory and thoughts of the absent parents. The child enacts what he imagines his parents are doing. The doll children express the child's tears, anger, disappointment and hope of reunion.

In the arrest of exploratory behaviour, it seems that over-protectiveness and sub-motherliness are of equal importance. An adhesive presence with minimal physical separation or verbal contact can interfere (as much as absence) with the child's approach to novelty. There is also the mother's attitude towards novelty and exploration, which includes her responses to strangers and unfamiliar situations. Tinbergen (1972) observes that mothers often respond with uncanny perceptiveness to even slight negative responses of their children. A mother may throw the stranger a slightly defensive glance or show a friendly and understanding reaction. The situation is complex; as well as the mother's attitude to novelty and strangeness and her reactions to her child's reactions, there is the responsiveness of the stranger. Over-effusive approaches, such as exclaiming and touching, are likely to effect withdrawal or rebuff. Again, the emphasis is on joining in when approached. Not until the bond is well-established, is face-to-face, eye-to-eye, hand-to-hand, contact likely to achieve bonding. The most effective principle for the stranger in this very complex series of interactions is to hold back until the child is positively longing for more intense contact (1972, pp. 190–91).

Contemporary research on attachment and exploration in infants and young children suggests a smoother transition between the two positions denoted in psychoanalysis by primary narcissism and the Oedipus complex. In relation to the state of absolute primary narcissism, the 'first grand problem of life' seemed a dramatic imposition on the child's early family life. Reality was harsh. The father, the herald of the external world, cast his shadow on a past idyllic unity, as rippleless as the pool into which Narcissus first gazed. The undoing of the beloved Narcissus was to hold the face that was most dear to him too near – 'my very plenty makes me poor . . . a new prayer this, for a lover, to wish the things he loves away'. In Stephen's case, it would be hard to *date* the onset of exploration, since curiosity marked his attitude to the outside world from the moment of birth when he first looked into his mother's face and eyes. From six months onward, he crawled outwards in expanding concentric circles around his mother at a steady rate of about a foot every few days.

Freud's anecdote of the eighteen-month-old boy, who played with the cotton reel when his mother had gone (Freud, 1920, pp. 14–16), has been adopted by psychoanalysts as the dominant model of the origins of children's play. Play develops as a secondary process, the function of which is to deal with separation and pain. Play is linked with the mastery of anxiety whereas, from an ethological viewpoint, creative play is more likely to develop in the conditions enumerated by Tinbergen. That *some* play is linked with the pain of separation or that scientific research may sometimes be motivated by sexual curiosity and exclusion from the primal scene is not in dispute.

In my view, the *Oedipus Rex* is about man's frailty *and* man's greatness in the face of knowledge: it is about what men do or do not do with knowledge. The 'chaste' man commits no less a 'sin' than the incestuous dare-devil. The biblical story of Genesis and Sophocles' *Oedipus Rex* are about the bounds of knowledge, about how to know about life without meddling in its seasonal rhythm. Adam and Eve *eat* the fruit of the tree of knowledge: Laius and Jocasta interfere with the process and proceeds of life. The two cardinal sins of humanity, identified by Freud, erupt when *individuals* disrupt blindly a vast pattern of movement which they do not comprehend. This is the message of ecology. In Sophocles' play, Oedipus realises that the efforts of a mere mortal such as himself could not rectify the pollution of Thebes. He does not bother about whether he is guilty or innocent:

> If I could have stifled my hearing at its source,
> I would have done it and made all this body
> A tight cell of misery, blank to light and sound:
> So I should have been safe in a dark agony
> Beyond all recollection.

This too is the prayer of an autistic child. A senseless world is 'the empty fortress' (Bettleheim, 1967) he seeks in vain. The knowledge which seeps through his senses is too painful. But

Oedipus is an old man who has spent his life in the pursuit of truth. The autistic child, who seems to have seen through it all,[4] has turned away too soon. When a monk has not even tasted sensual life, ascetic withdrawal is meaningless. The story of the Buddha – which is not a tragedy – is about a prince who experienced everything which power and fame could offer. Such riches he left for the discovery of his inner life.

14
The limits of knowledge and the castration complex

Freud linked the resolution of the Oedipus complex with the 'castration complex'. Thus, for Freud, the castration complex was associated with questions of knowledge as well as the very particular reference it held in relation to the penis. I suggest that the castration complex is linked with the realisation that individual knowledge is *limited*. The resolution of the Oedipus complex entails a renunciation; not only must the child give up the fantasy that he can have an exclusive relationship with the parent of the opposite sex, he must also accept that there is an objective order of things which he will never completely understand or control. In *some* cases, this realisation is experienced as a castration or narcissistic blow. The blow is to the child's budding feelings of power and curiosity and to the satisfactions gained by learning.

Psychoanalysis has interpreted Oedipus' acts of banishment and self-mutilation as evidence of the castration complex (Freud, 1940, p. 200). Oedipus, it is said, punishes himself for his incestuous relationship with Jocasta. In my view, Oedipus' self-mutilation does not only signify guilt, but his renunciation of power in the face of forces over which he has no control. Freud spoke of the *fate* of the Oedipus complex in different ways. In 'The dissolution of the Oedipus complex' (1924), Freud writes that the Oedipus complex is *dissolved,* it succumbs to repression and is followed by the latency period. Freud also discusses the *'demolition'* and *'destruction'* of the Oedipus complex. He asks, 'What is it that brings about its destruction?' It is the experience of *painful* disappointments which the boy suffers from his mother's transference of her love to a new arrival and which the girl suffers from harsh punishments from her father who she liked to think loved her above all else. Even when none of these special events occur, the absence of satisfaction 'must in the end lead the small lover to turn away from his hopeless longing. In this way, the Oedipus Complex would go to its destruction from its lack of success, and from the effects of its internal impossibility' (Freud, 1924, p. 173).

Thus, Freud spoke of the resolution of the Oedipus complex in both absolute and relative terms. On the one hand, the ego turns away from the Oedipus complex through repression, despite the fact that, in most cases, repression requires the participation of the super-ego, which is just being formed; on the other hand, the process is 'equivalent, if it is ideally carried out, to a destruction and an abolition of the complex' (1924, p. 177). In this distinction between the repression and the destruction of the Oedipus complex, Freud says we come upon a borderline, which is not sharply drawn, between the normal and the pathological. When the ego achieves no more than a repression, the Oedipus complex 'persists in an unconscious state in the id and will later manifest its pathogenic effect' (p. 177).

In a later work, *An Outline of Psycho-Analysis* (1940), Freud says that the Oedipus complex is never dissolved, it is merely 'modified' through repression. In the earlier paper, Freud regarded repression as no more than a partial and neurotic solution to the oedipal conflict; the normal outcome would be that the complex would dissolve absolutely.

In the case of the little girl, however, threats of castration do not occur; thus the castration complex is not the agent of dissolution or repression. The Oedipus complex is given up because of the little girl's upbringing and because of certain intimidations from the outside, which threaten her with loss of love. However, in renouncing the penis, she makes a symbolic equation between the penis and the baby. Her Oedipus complex culminates in the desire to receive from her father a baby as a gift. 'One has an impression that the Oedipus Complex is then gradually given up because this wish is never fulfilled' (1924, p. 179). Freud concludes that his insight into the development of girls is 'unsatisfactory, incomplete and vague'. He was to elaborate upon these views in a paper written in 1925, entitled 'Some psychical consequences of the anatomical distinction between the sexes'.

Freud also discussed a genetic solution to the Oedipus complex. According to the phylogenetic view, the Oedipus complex must collapse 'just as the milk teeth fall out' (Freud, 1924, p. 173). 'Although the majority of human beings go through the Oedipus complex as an individual experience, it is nevertheless a phenomenon which is determined and laid down by heredity and which is bound to pass away according to programme when the next pre-ordained phase of development sets in. This being so, it is of no great importance what the occasions are which allow this to happen, or, indeed, whether any such occasions can be discovered at all.' Thus, both these views are compatible and it 'remains of interest to follow out how this innate programme is carried out and in what way accidental noxae exploit this disposition' (Freud, 1924, p. 174).

Freud gave several accounts of the origin and function of the castration complex. The castration complex is, first, an agent of repression or destruction, second, a hereditary phenomenon and, third, an effect of environmental influences. Throughout his work, Freud was concerned with the roles played in development by heredity and experience. In one of his last works, *Moses and Monotheism* (1939), Freud says that the behaviour of neurotic children towards their parents in the oedipal and castration complexes can only be explained phylogenetically. The archaic heritage comprises not only dispositions but also memory-traces of the experience of early generations quite independently of direct communication and the influence of education (Freud, 1939, pp. 98–100). Although Freud remarked that the only evidence for these memory-traces was the residual phenomena of the work of analysis, he found it necessary to postulate the presence of memory-traces in order to connect both individual and group psychology. Freud sought a comprehensive theory which would account for both individual and social psychology and which would link biological and evolutionary phenomena with intra-psychic experience.

When Freud discusses the onset of the latency period, he considers the connection between the castration complex and environmental influences; the castration complex relates both to external threats and to early experiences of separateness. Freud quotes examples of the brutal threats which were made, usually by women, when the child masturbated or touched, and expressed interest in, his genitals. The threat of castration was also given as a common punishment for bed-wetting. However, the castration complex has its precursors in (1) the birth experience and the loss of the intra-uterine state, (2) the withdrawal of the mother's breast, and (3) the daily demand to give up the contents of the bowels. Thus, the castration complex is linked with the loss of individual control and with the loss of an early attachment. Freud says that, although these experiences of separation and of separateness underlie the castration complex, they do not effect it until a fresh experience comes the child's way. This experience, which finally dispels the child's state of unbelief, is the sight of the female genitals.

Freud said that the Oedipus complex offers the child only two possibilities of satisfaction: one, the identification with one parent and, two, the relinquishment of the other. The child who wishes to replace one parent and to set up an exclusive relationship with the other is compelled to repeat the painful experience which he seeks to avoid – the experience of exclusion. Renunciation frees the child from the pain of exclusion. A person might get married on an oedipal premise, the primary motive being to get in on an intimacy from which he or she has been excluded. But the marriage is a disappointment because the primary wish is not to be with one other person but to be part of a couple which is ready-made.

At about five years of age, the young child, who has been torn by the conflict between his oedipal wishes and his narcissistic attachment to his penis, eventually gives up the 'object-cathexes' which are then 'replaced by identifications'. These identifications lead to the formation of the super-ego which is the internalised parental authority.[1] In identification with his father, the boy attempts various sexual attacks on his mother but he gives these up under the threat of castration which has an 'extraordinarily powerful traumatic effect' on him (Freud, 1939, p. 79). In reaction to his mother's threats, the boy now adopts a passive attitude towards his father and, furthermore, provokes him to administer corporal punishment. Thus, the child passes into the latency period which is usually free from any marked disturbances and, as often happens, the child becomes an exemplary boy. But, with puberty and adolescence, the trauma returns and is often accompanied by 'the symptom of sexual impotence' and 'sado-masochistic phantasies' (Freud, 1939, p. 79).

Freud considered the fluidity of the ego to be a defect and a weakness. With maturation, the ego was to become entrenched in an increasingly defensive, rather than an exploratory, position.

> Thus the ego is fighting on two fronts: it has to defend its existence against an external world which threatens it with annihilation as well as against an internal world that makes excessive demands. It adopts the same methods of defence against both, but its defence against the internal enemy is particularly inadequate. (Freud, 1940, p. 200)

The child's attempts at a defence – repressions – are effective only for the moment. Freud concludes:

> If this is so, it would have to be said from a biological standpoint that the ego comes to grief over the task of mastering the excitations of the early sexual period, at a time when its immaturity makes it incompetent to do so. It is in this lagging of ego development behind libidinal development that we see the essential precondition of neurosis; and we cannot escape the conclusion that neuroses could be avoided if the childish ego were spared this task – if, that is to say, the child's sexual life were allowed free play, as happens among many primitive peoples. (Freud, 1940, p. 200)

Such 'an early attempt at damming up the sexual instinct, so decided a partisanship by the young ego in favour of the external as opposed to the internal world, brought about by the prohibition of infantile sexuality, cannot be without its effect on the individual's later readiness for culture' (Freud, 1940, p. 201).

Within the schema of development which I am presenting, the ego does not occupy such a defensive position. First, the child does not start off enclosed in an autistic world but within a relationship: second, since the child's exploratory motivation is not exclusively sexual, it is not required that excitement be forgone in favour of participation in the social world. The crucial conflict occurs between exploratory behaviour on the one hand and the inhibition, through anxiety, of approaches on the other. This dilemma may be overcome or decreased when the parent figure, and the stranger, avoid stimulating withdrawal and enhance approach and contact by waiting for the child to take the initiative. The Victorian attitude of disapproval and threat towards curiosity would tend to enhance withdrawal and frustrate social urges. If the child's curiosity is deemed incestuous and thus socially destructive, there is no way for an unreformed child to participate in culture. In Freud's day, development and learning involved elaborate detours.[2]

Freud's super-ego has its base in paranoia – in watching, ordering, judging, threatening and punishing. In my view, this type of watching agency interferes with the individual's approach to his culture. Freud pointed out that the severity of the super-ego is not always matched by the actual behaviour of the person's parents. However, a person may be pursued by a feeling of being watched, even when his parents are not punitive. A parent may be intrusive and over-protective and thereby refuse the child the space in which to play and think; he 'castrates' the child in a different way. Freud also said that it is not just the personal qualities of the parents that make themselves felt in the super-ego representation; it represents everything which had a determining effect on them themselves, 'the tastes and standards of the social class in which they lived and the innate dispositions and traditions of the race from which they sprang' (Freud, 1940, p. 206). John Bowlby observes that many adult phobias and illnesses have their roots in childhood because of the *threats* made, and stories told, by parents to their children. Bowlby emphasises the realistic fears which are aroused by parental threats of separation. Despite the clear connection which Freud made between the castration complex and threats of loss, Freud presents the case of Little Hans as if he did not take these threats seriously. In his interpretation of the *Oedipus Rex* in terms of unconscious wishes and guilt, Freud perhaps underestimated the importance of real events. However, Freud stated many times that the torments caused by the reproaches of conscience correspond precisely to a child's fear of loss of love. The severity and tenacity of self-reproaches and self-criticism usually reflect an insecurity in the primary attachment bond.

Thus, in my view, the castration complex is the culmination of the tragic view of the origins, growth and limitation of human knowledge. Curiosity, leading to illicit intercourse, must be prohibited. Tied to such overwhelmingly anti-social wishes as parricide and incest, exploration and the urge to know about the origins of life become a source of crippling guilt. With the traditional, psychoanalytic models of the narcissistic and oedipal stages, it is hard to envisage how a healthy and lively child ever gets out of them and progresses. It is also difficult to see how an infant would break out of the mirroring relationship, as described by Kohut. Freud's many accounts of both the resolution of the Oedipus complex and the origins of the castration complex would seem to demonstrate some of the inadequacies of a non-relational, egocentric, view of childhood. Freud's phylogenetic views are also unsatisfactory. A prohibitory and threatening agent, such as castration, then becomes the prototype for the termination, or resolution, of a previous condition.

Epilogue

How do we feel about the 'external world'? About the ever-shifting boundary between us and the larger environment? How does a patient leave an analysis? Or an adolescent leave home? How do we approach certain death? I suggest that our responses to limitation are consequent upon our images or concepts of beginning and development. For instance, the bird's egg model of the beginning of life creates the hatching image of growth. We *break out* of our shells. Change is dramatic. What are the forces which crack the shell? Are they internal or external? If internal, the agent might be guilt. If external, reward or punishment seem suitable candidates. Into what do we hatch? How do we conceive of this outside world? Is it a container in which we feel contained? Or does something *other* lie beyond? If so, is there some way, super-human or extraterrestrial, in which we can glimpse this beyond? Is our relationship to what lies outside us one of participation, immanence, transcendence, inclusion or expulsion?

In this book, I have tried to develop two themes which I recapitulate in the question 'Does the infant seek out, or avoid, reality?' On the one hand, some thinkers say Yes, of course; the baby wants to be attached, he looks outwards, he fingers the world around him. In this view, withdrawal is temporary and one aspect of a rhythmic cycle of attention and withdrawal. *At times*, the contrast is too great between the infant's powers of co-ordination and the differences he registers in the environment. He responds to the outside as a threat. This is the attachment or interactional view – positions 3 and 4 on my spectrum. On the other hand, others say No, the infant does not want to know reality; he prefers the world of phantasy and wish. He views reality and the harsh boundary he perceives between inside and outside as a source of pain. Therefore, he must be helped or forced to face the outside world. Luckily, at a certain point in development, internal forces collaborate. The child feels guilty about enacted wishes which, since they are usually unrealised, are deemed 'omnipotent' or egocentric. However, under the force of external and internal prohibitions, the infant now wishes to repair the damage he has done to the objects which he has mindlessly shrouded with wishful projections, both idealising and destructive. This is the primary narcissism or primary persecutory anxiety view – positions 1 and 2 on my spectrum. This second view of the forces of change leading to the acceptance of the reality principle is based upon the assumption that the dominant desire of the infant is to be *inside*. Both Freud's primary narcissism hypothesis and Klein's theory of projective identification (the most primitive mode of communication) are founded on this premise. These theories are united in that they use the container/contained metaphor to delineate the process of development. The child grows out of one container and into another.

In support of the view that the infant seeks out reality and relationship, I have emphasised a different image of neonatal safety to that of a bird's egg: I envisage the picture of the infant held in his mother's arms. The infant wants to be held in the familiar arms *and* to investigate the world around him. Even in the first hours of post-partum existence, he does not *only* want to be closed inside his mother's womb or breast; he solicits almost continuous holding. But the infant in his mother's arms is not contained within a container. His sensory apparatus is open to the outside world. And yet he may retreat into his mother's breast and arms, which serve from time to time as the post-partum extension of the womb.

In the holding image, the barrier between inside and outside is soft and permeable. As the infant develops beyond the intra-uterine form of relating, he expands his sensibilities and comes to know reality *provided that he has a secure base*. In analysis, we encounter defences which have been erected against an expansion of sensibilities which proved painful. It may seem, therefore, that the analysand does not want to know reality. The outside is threatening. Phantasy is familiar and safe. At such times, both analyst and analysand work towards understanding in a dominant context of pain. Illogically, some analysts conclude that, in analytic *and* ontological development, pain precedes knowledge and insight.

Freud accepted the 'rule that analysis must be carried out "in a state of frustration" ' (Freud, 1940, p. 231). In his paper 'Analysis terminable and interminable', he concludes 'Analytic experience has taught us that the better is always the enemy of the good and that in every phase of the patient's recovery we have to fight against his inertia, which is ready to be content with an incomplete solution' (1937, p. 231). This view of analytic work coincides with the patient's attitude towards knowing, which is neurotic. The patient approaches reality and the boundary between phantasy and reality fearfully, defiantly or aggressively. But these are defences against the *absence of a link*. In my view, a strong wish to be inside is often a manifestation of a failure in holding. The patient cannot conceive of a relationship of *mutuality* between self and other or of overlap between inside and outside. The search for containment is part of his pathology. Connected to these feelings about boundary are phantasies of punishment or prohibition, which may form part of normal oedipal development but may also represent fixated oral or sexualised phantasies about knowing. In the absence of mutuality because of a failure in holding, the search for knowledge is coloured by phantasies of intrusion, incorporation, or voyeurism. Within the phantasy construction, the way to find out is to break down a door into a forbidden space.

The cracked shell of primary narcissism or autism opens on to the door closing upon the primal scene. A forceful element in the Oedipus complex is the child's desire to gain entry. The child is the outsider. In the early days, the temporary wish to be inside and to extend the intra-uterine existence was reciprocated by the mother's response to her infant as an inside-being. But the parental intercourse is a closed, dyadic relationship in which the young child may not join. Nevertheless, the child will continue his efforts to break in until he meets a new force – the castration complex. The castration complex cuts off the thrust of actions promoted by anti-social, pleasure-seeking wishes. The child of three to five years is thereby forced to know reality.

In his paper 'The use of an object' (1969), Winnicott proposes a view of the child's approach to reality which is the converse of the Freudian view. Using the container/contained framework (rather than a more relational model), Winnicott emphasises the *child's* destruction of illusion. 'It is generally understood that the reality principle involves the individual in anger and reactive destruction, but my thesis is that the destruction plays its part in making the reality, placing the object outside the self. For this to happen, favourable conditions are necessary' (Winnicott, 1969, p. 91). The child or analysand himself punctures the containment and seeks to draw the outline between illusion and reality. Central to this view of destructiveness is the assumption that the child, left to his own devices, wishes to live reality rather than the wish-fulfilling dream. In analysis, the patient strives to know his analyst outside the area of projective phenomena.

The view of curiosity and knowing I have proposed in this book has implications for analytic theory and technique. In Part I, I suggest that some narcissistic pathologies ensue from a lack of differentiation and exploratoriness. In the Narcissus myth, the message of the soothsayer is that Narcissus will live to a ripe old age provided that he never knows himself. The relationship portrayed between Narcissus and Echo and which I envisage between Narcissus and Leiriope is bound by mirroring and echoing. In Part II, I interpret the *Oedipus Rex* as a drama about knowing – a tragedy wrought by deception and distortion. Taking off from Einstein's attitude to the *mystery* of life, I propose an alternative view of knowing which is not tragic but expansive. I link the tragic view with phantasies about inclusion and exclusion, incest and sterility, which coexist with the container/contained metaphor of growth and development.

In analytic practice, our conceptions of change and of limitation affect the way we interpret a patient's approach to termination and to individuation as it arises throughout the course of treatment. In the psychoanalytic theory of technique, more emphasis is usually placed on the *gathering* of the transference than upon its dissolution. For much of the analysis, the patient may try to avoid the transference, since it re-evokes painful relationships, particularly the close relationship between two people. Transference works two ways to create a self-enclosed system: the analyst interpreting within the context of the transference will see himself as the representative of outside figures who are also used by the patient to represent the analyst. However, if treatment has proved helpful, the patient may begin to wonder how he will leave the analysis. What happens when the patient tries to place the analyst 'outside the area of omnipotent control' – that is, outside the transference of outside or past figures? I suggest that we label the class of interactions engaged in at this stage as 'the differentiating transferences'.

The differentiating transferences raise issues connected to map-territory distinctions. Much has been written about the content of the transference in analytic work but little has been said about the patient's *perception* of transference, which requires the perception of a different order of abstraction. In the differentiating transferences, the patient continues to transfer onto the analyst the interactions and role-relationships involved in his earlier attempts at individuation and differentiation. However, as these transferences are sorted out and understood within the analysis the previously inhibited process of separation-individuation evolves *for the first time*. This means that the analyst must at times exist as a person outside the differentiating transference. The patient, now freed from the compulsion to repeat familiar patterns, approaches the strange, a domain which includes the analyst, who has remained largely unknown outside the transference. Here, there is ample room for map-territory confusions. The process of differentiation, which has been facilitated by the analysis, is not part of the differentiating transference. If the patient is to acknowledge his analyst as a person outside the area of projection, the analyst must accept extra-transferential communications. Not everything is *contained* in the transference relationship or frame.

When the differentiating transference is allowed to proceed, the transferential aspect of the relationship recedes, thus enabling the analysand to differentiate himself from the analytic process. Like the teddy bear, the maximally used analyst is not forgotten, but 'loses meaning' as a phantasy, and (later in the analysis) transitional, object.

Notes

Introduction

1 In his original formulation (Bowlby, 1958, pp. 365–6) Bowlby listed five behavioural systems which contribute to attachment – sucking, clinging, following, crying and smiling. In later accounts, Bowlby and others have elaborated upon this early formulation. (Bowlby, 1969; Ainsworth, 1969, pp. 969–1025; Ainsworth, 1972, pp. 97–137.)

The myth of Narcissus

1 This version of the myth is taken from both Ovid's and Robert Graves's accounts. Graves's sources include Ovid, Pausanias, Conon and Pliny. I use Mary Innes's translation of 'Echo and Narcissus' from The Metamorphoses by Ovid.

1 *Primary narcissism and primary fusion/union*

1 'The relationship to the mother is not the infant's first relationship to the environment. What precedes it is an earlier phase in which not the object world but the body needs and their satisfaction or frustration play the decisive part . . . In the struggle for satisfaction of the vital needs and drives the object merely serves the purpose of wish fulfillment, its status being no more than that of a means to an end, a "convenience". The libidinal cathexis at this time is shown to be attached, not to the image of the object, but to the blissful experience of satisfaction and relief.' (A. Freud, 1954).

2 '*Normal autistic phase*. The first weeks of extrauterine life, during which the neonate or young infant appears to be an almost purely biological organism, his instinctual responses to stimuli being on a reflex and thalamic level. During this phase we can speak only of primitive unintegrated ego apparatuses and purely somatic defense mechan-

isms, consisting of overflow and discharge reactions, the goal of which is the maintenance of homeostatic equilibrium. The libido position is a predominantly visceral one with no discrimination between inside and outside, animate and inanimate. Initially, because of his very high threshold for external stimuli, the infant seems to be in a state of primitive negative hallucinatory disorientation, in which need satisfaction belongs to his own omnipotent autistic orbit.'

3 '*Normal symbiotic phase*. Normal symbiosis is ushered in by the lifting of the innate strong stimulus barrier that protected the young infant from internal and external stimuli up to the third or fourth week of life. Since, in the human young the instinct for self-preservation has atrophied, the ego has to take over the role of managing the human being's adaptation to reality. However, the rudimentary ego of the young infant is not adequate to the task of organizing his inner and outer stimuli in such a way as to ensure his survival; it is the psychobiological rapport between the nursing mother and the baby that complements the infant's undifferentiated ego. Empathy on the part of a mother is, under normal circumstances, the substitute among human beings for those instincts on which the altricial animal relies for its survival. Normal symbiosis develops concomitantly with the lowering of the innate stimulus barrier, through the predictably repetitious experience of an outside mothering agency alleviating need, hunger, and tension coming from within, that is, functioning as an auxiliary ego (Spitz).
Symbiosis refers to a stage of sociobiological interdependence between the 1- to 5-month-old infant and his mother, a stage of preobject or need-satisfying relationship, in which self and maternal intrapsychic representations have not yet been differentiated. From the second month on, the infant behaves and functions as though he and his mother were an omnipotent dual unity within one common boundary (the "symbiotic membrane").
The mother's availability and the infant's innate capacity to engage in the symbiotic relationship are essential at this point. This relationship marks the inception of ego organization by the establishment of intrapsychic connections on the infant's part between memory traces of gratification and the gestalt of the human face; there is a shift of cathexis from inside the body, from the predominantly visceral position of the autistic phase to the periphery, the sensory perceptive organs (from coenesthetic to diacritic organization).'

4 '*Separation-individuation phase*. The phase of normal development commencing around 4 to 5 months of age, at the height of symbiosis and overlapping it. The infant shows increasing capacity to recognize mother as a special person, to cathect and inspect the nonmother world, and to move ever so slightly, and later quite deliberately, away from mother. It is a phase of development that lasts from about 5 months to 2½ years, and moves along two separate but intertwining tracks: the one of separation, leading to intrapsychic awareness of separateness, and the other of individuation, leading to the acquisi-

tion of a distinct and unique individuality. Four subphases of the separation-individuation process have been identified. Although they overlap, each subphase has its own characteristic clusters of behaviors that distinguish it from the preceding and following ones. The four subphases are: (1) Differentiation, (2) Practicing, (3) Rapprochement, and (4) Consolidation of individuality and beginning emotional object constancy.'

5 '*Primary Narcissism*. A state prevailing during the first weeks of life in which need-satisfaction is not perceived as coming from the outside and in which there is no awareness of a mothering agent. It is akin to Ferenczi's "absolute infantile omnipotence." This stage is followed by one of dim awareness that need-satisfaction cannot be provided by oneself.'

6 '*Hatching*. The process of emerging from the symbiotic state of oneness with mother, in the intrapsychic sense. It is the "second," the psychological, birth experience – the process by which the "other-than-mother" world begins to be cathected. The hatched infant has left the vague twilight state of symbiosis and has become more permanently alert and perceptive to the stimuli of his environment, rather than to his own bodily sensations, or to sensations emanating within the symbiotic orbit only.'

7 'From the beginning the child molds and unfolds in the matrix of the mother-infant dual unit. Whatever adaptations the mother may make to the child, and whether she is sensitive and empathic or not, it is our strong conviction that the child's fresh and pliable adaptive capacity, and his need for adaptation (in order to gain satisfaction), is far greater than that of the mother, whose personality, with all its patterns of character and defense, is firmly and often rigidly set' (1975, p. 5).

8 'Self-Object' is sometimes written as 'selfobject' in more recent formulations of self-psychology.

9 The concept of '*transmuting internalisations*' refers to the process of analytic cure. When problems are 'worked through' in analysis, certain 'structural transformations' are produced. These transformations are not the consequence of intellectual insights but of the gradual internalisations of old experiences as these are relived repeatedly 'by the more mature psyche'. The curative process in self-pathology is 'structure building'. Using an analogy from physics, Kohut discusses 'microstructural' changes as follows: 'Little by little, as a result of innumerable processes of microinternalization, the anxiety-assuaging, delay-tolerating, and other realistic aspects of the analyst's image become part of the analysand's psychological equipment, *pari passu* with the "micro" -frustration of the analysand's need for the analyst's permanent presence and perfect functioning in this respect. In brief: through the process of transmuting internalization, new psychological structure is built' (Kohut, 1977, p. 32).

Notes

2 *Primary internal object-relationships*

1 'In projective identification parts of the self and internal objects are split off and projected into the external object, which then becomes possessed by, controlled and identified with the projected parts.' (Segal, 1973, p. 27.)

4 *Interactional synchrony and mutuality*

1 'each new thrust of activity in the growing infant requires a new period of interactional adjustment with the caretaking environment to reach stable coordination on the bases of new changes' (Sander, 1970).

5 *Narcissus: an 'average' history*

1 'If, in the fantasy of early growth, there is contained *death*, then at adolescence there is contained *murder*. Even when growth at the period of puberty goes ahead without major crises, one may need to deal with acute problems of management because growing up means taking the parent's place. *It really does*.' (Winnicott, 1971a, p. 144.)

7 *The concept of transitional schemas*

1 Bower points out that the interactional synchrony displayed by newborns is characteristic of human communication. 'Whenever two people from the same culture group talk to each other, a detailed analysis of their movements will show that they engage in a kind of dance with each other' (Bower, 1977, p. 30)
2 Throughout this book, I quote from the *Oedipus Rex* by Sophocles, trans. Dudley Fitts and Robert Fitzgerald, London, Faber & Faber, 1951.
3 The recent publication of the book *Between Reality and Fantasy – Transitional Objects and Phenomena* pays tribute to Winnicott's innovation.
4 In the introduction to his book *Therapeutic Consultations in Child Psychiatry*, much of which is concerned with the use of transitional objects and phenomena as an aid to diagnosis, Winnicott says, 'I wish to emphasise, however, that my aim in presenting these consultations is not to give a series illustrating symptomatic cure. I am rather aiming to report examples of *communication with children*' (1971b, p. 8).
5 'in analysis we never discover a "no" in the unconscious' (Freud, 1925, p. 239).
6 In his consultations with children, Winnicott devised the 'squiggle game' as a free associative kind of playing through which frightening and forgotten experiences could be communicated. With some chil-

dren, there was a tremendous desire, when anxiety threatened, to turn the game into a 'points game' such as Os and Xs, where the focus is on winning and losing (Winnicott, 1971b).

7 'Perhaps it is to be accepted that there are patients who at times need the therapist to note the nonsense that belongs to the mental state of the individual at rest without the need even for the patient to communicate this nonsense, that is to say, without the need for the patient to organize nonsense. Organized nonsense is already a defence, just as organized chaos is a denial of chaos. The therapist who cannot take this communication becomes engaged in a futile attempt to find some organization in the nonsense, as a result of which the patient leaves the nonsense area because of hopelessness about communicating nonsense. An opportunity for rest has been missed because of the therapist's need to find sense where nonsense is.' (Winnicott, 1971a, p. 56.)

8 *The 'fate' of the transitional object*

1 'While especially evident during early childhood attachment behaviour is held to characterize the human being from the cradle to the grave. It includes crying and calling, which elicit care, following and clinging, and also strong protest should a child be left alone or with strangers. With age the frequency and the intensity with which such behaviour is exhibited diminish steadily. Nevertheless, all these forms of behaviour persist as an important part of man's behavioural equipment. In adults they are especially evident when a person is distressed, ill or afraid. The particular patterns of attachment behaviour shown by an individual turn partly on his present age, sex and circumstances and partly on the experiences he has had with attachment figures earlier in his life' (Bowlby, 1976, p. 203).

2 'In very many species, it is now known, whatever situation has become familiar to an individual is treated as though it provided safety, whereas any other situation is treated with reserve. Strangeness is responded to ambivalently: on the one hand it elicits fear and withdrawal, on the other it elicits curiosity and investigation' (Bowlby, 1973, p. 115).

3 'At the point of development that is under survey the subject is creating the object in the sense of finding externality itself, and it has to be added that this experience depends on the object's capacity to survive. (It is important that "survive", in this context, means "not retaliate".) If it is in an analysis that these matters are taking place, then the analyst, the analytic technique, and the analytic setting all come in as surviving or not surviving the patient's destructive attacks. This destructive activity is the patient's attempt to place the analyst outside the area of omnipotent control, that is, out in the world. Without the experience of maximum destructiveness (object not protected) the subject never places the analyst outside and therefore can

never do more than experience a kind of self-analysis, using the analyst as a projection of a part of the self. In terms of feeding, the patient, then, can feed only on the self and cannot use the breast for getting fat. The patient may even enjoy the analytic experience but will not fundamentally change' (Winnicott, 1969, p. 91).

9 *The watching agency and its products*

1 See 'Attacks on Linking' (Bion, 1959).
2 'It has been claimed that the repertoire of the babbling baby in the first half-year contains all the sounds of all the languages of man. This vast repertoire does not persist. By the second half-year of life the baby is producing pretty much only the sounds of the language community in which he finds himself' (Bower, 1977, p. 135).
3 'an infant's babbling and the way in which an older child goes over a repertory of songs and tunes while preparing for sleep come within this intermediate area as transitional phenomena' (1953, p. 2).
4 In an experiment with twenty-one infants aged three months, Rheingold, Gewirtz and Ross (1959) varied the frequency of babbling in a very short time by their social behaviour. The experimenter elicited babbling by leaning over the baby and looking at him with an expressionless face for a period of three minutes. On days one and two, the experimenter remained unresponsive to the ensuing babbles. On days three and four, she made an immediate response each time the infant vocalised; each of her responses was threefold – a broad smile, three 'tsk' sounds, and a light squeeze of the infant's abdomen. On days five and six, she was again unresponsive. Results were unambiguous. When the infant's vocalisations were responded to, the infants vocalised more: on the second of the two rewarded days, vocalisations had almost doubled. When the infants' vocalisations were no longer responded to, they diminished again (reported in Bowlby, 1969, vol. 1, pp. 288–9).
5 Bateson suggests that the evolution from analogical to digital communication depends upon the achievement of the simple negative. This step would endow signals with a degree of freedom from their referents. If an animal wishes to interact with another in playful combat, it cannot say 'I will not bite you.' It must propose combat, for instance by baring fangs, and then oppose the forbidden action, for instance by appeasement behaviour. The animal must find postures to communicate both aggression and friendliness (Bateson, 1968, and 1955).
6 'Their mental processes operate at great speed. Even when dominated by repetitiveness, the rapidity with which new combinations and permutations of the same basic configuration of phantasy are evolved, is quite dazzling. Their accessibility to sensory data both from the body and from the outside world gives the impression of an apparatus naked to the wind. Consequently their discrimination of the details of

the environment and of alterations in these details is quite intimidating. The complexity of their mental functioning taxes the therapist at every point. Added to this there is a subtlety of emotive response and sensitivity to the mental and physical state of the therapist which far exceeds that encountered in child analysis generally, and certainly is in quite a different category from the atmosphere of the adult consulting room.

Added to this intelligence and the factors of perceptual sensitivity connected with it, the children present an emotional sensibility which we would wish to describe as a kind of gentleness of disposition. Their awareness of the mental states of the person to whom they feel intimately related . . . is in the nature of a primitive permeability to the emotions of others – another aspect of the "nakedness" mentioned above' (Meltzer *et al.*, 1975, p. 9).

7 'it is only in recent years that I have become able to wait and wait for the natural evolution of the transference arising out of the patient's growing trust in the psychoanalytic technique and setting, and to avoid breaking up this natural process by making interpretations. It will be noticed that I am talking about the making of interpretations and not about interpretations as such. It appals me to think how much deep change I have prevented or delayed in patients *in a certain classification category* by my personal need to interpret. If only we can wait, the patient arrives at understanding creatively and with immense joy, and I now enjoy this joy more than I used to enjoy the sense of having been clever. I think I interpret mainly to let the patient know the limits of my understanding. The principle is that it is the patient and only the patient who has the answers' (Winnicott, 1969, also in 1971a, pp. 86–7).

8 'Now, what happens when the mother leaves the baby with someone else? The baby's only partner in communication is gone, and the baby is left with a stranger, someone who doesn't "speak the same language," who doesn't respond to the baby's social gestures, social invitations, social ploys, or other forms of interaction. The baby is, in effect, left alone. He is isolated from other adults by the very development of the communication routines he shares with his mother' (Bower, 1977, p. 56).

9 ' "Wouldn't it be awful if the child looked into the mirror and saw nothing?" ' (Winnicott, 1967, p. 116.)

11 *The riddle of life*

1 'If we speculate about the evolution of communication, it is evident that a very important stage in this evolution occurs when the organism gradually ceases to respond quite "automatically" to the mood-signs of another and becomes able to recognize the sign as a signal: that is, to recognize that the other individual's and its own signals are only

signals, which can be trusted, distrusted, falsified, denied, amplified, corrected, and so forth' (Bateson, 1955, p. 178).

2 'At the instigation of these feelings and worries, [arising out of confrontation with the arrival of a new baby], the child now comes to be occupied with the first, grand problem of life and asks himself the question: "*Where do babies come from?*" – a question which, there can be no doubt, first ran: "Where did this particular, intruding baby come from?" We seem to hear the echoes of this first riddle in innumerable riddles of myth and legend. The question itself is, like all research, the product of a vital exigency, as though thinking were entrusted with the task of preventing the recurrence of such dreaded events' (Freud, 1908, p. 212).

3 'There can be no doubt about Hans' sexual curiosity; but it also roused the spirit of enquiry in him and enabled him to arrive at genuine abstract knowledge. . . . Thirst for knowledge seems to be inseparable from sexual curiosity' (Freud, 1909, p. 9).

4 'If children could follow the hints given by the excitation of the penis they would get a little nearer to the solution of their problem. That the baby grows inside the mother's body is obviously not a sufficient explanation. How does it get inside? What starts its development? That the father has something to do with it seems likely; he says that the baby is *his* baby as well. Again, the penis certainly has a share, too, in these mysterious happenings; the excitation in it which accompanies all these activities of the child's thoughts bears witness to this. Attached to this excitation are impulsions which the child cannot account for – obscure urges to do something violent, to press in, to knock to pieces, to tear open a hole somewhere. But when the child thus seems to be well on the way to postulating the existence of the vagina and to concluding that an incursion of this kind by his father's penis into his mother is the act by means of which the baby is created in his mother's body – at this juncture his enquiry is broken off in helpless perplexity. For standing in its way is his theory that his mother possesses a penis just as a man does, and the existence of the cavity which receives the penis remains undiscovered by him' (Freud, 1908, p. 218).

12 *Knowledge and the tragic vision*

1 'The study of judgement affords us, perhaps for the first time, an insight into the origin of an intellectual function from the interplay of the primary instinctual impulses' (Freud, 1925, pp. 238–9).

2 'Through Peer Gynt, a great poet gave voice to his perceptions of world and life . . . Ibsen had simply dramatized the misery of unconventional people. At first Peer Gynt has a great many fantastic ideas and feels strong. He is out of tune with everyday life, a dreamer, an idler. The others diligently go to school or to work and laugh at the dreamer. . . . Peer Gynt feels the pulse of life, which dashes on

impetuously. Everyday life is narrow and demands a strict course. . . . Fearing the infinite, the practical man shuts himself off on a patch of earth and establishes security for his life. It is a modest problem to which he as a scientist devotes his whole life. It is a modest trade that he plies as a shoemaker. He does not think about life: he goes to the office, into the fields, to the factory, pays visits to patients, goes to school. He does his duty and holds his peace. He has long since disposed of the Peer Gynt in himself. Thinking is too troublesome and too dangerous. The Peer Gynts are a threat to his peace of mind. It would be too tempting to be like them' (Reich, 1978, pp. 37–8).

13 *'A holy curiosity'*

1 'In normal development, the mother seems to be able to allow her infant to have a "salting" of the terror associated with bodily separateness so that he can gradually develop a preparedness for that situation. Part of this preparedness is the capacity to hold an image of the absent mother in the mind so that both mother and infant are freed from the necessity for constant bodily contact. As we have seen, autistic children have never reached this stage, constant bodily contact is demanded, and the illusion that it is present is maintained by autistic activities which impede the use of the actual mother. The real mother is negated as a source of "not-me" dread and so she is prevented from giving the nurturing of which she is capable' (Tustin, 1972, p. 84).
2 'psychotherapy is done in the overlap of two play areas' (1971a, p. 54).
3 'I cannot resist relating one little incident which, although one would hardly expect this from the literature on child development, is in my experience representative. A 12-month-old boy, guarded by his aunt and his grandmother, was observed crawling about over a sandy slope which was bare but for isolated rosettes of ragwort and occasional thistle plants. After having moved over many ragwort rosettes without showing any reaction to them, he happened to crawl over a thistle, whose prickly leaves slightly scratched his foot. Giving a barely perceptible start, he crawled on at first, but stopped a second or so later, and looked back over his shoulder. Then, moving slightly back, he rubbed his foot once more over the thistle. Next he turned to the plant, looked at it with intense concentration and moved his hand back and forth over it. This was followed by a perfect control experiment: he looked round, selected a ragwort rosette and touched that in the same way. After this he touched the thistle once more, and only then did he continue his journey. To ethologists this is only one of many examples of true experimentation in a pre-verbal child: of highly sophisticated exploration' (Tinbergen, 1973, pp. 224–5).
4 The idiot savant (see Tustin, 1972, p. 132).

14 *The limits of knowledge and the castration complex*

1 'A portion of the external world has, at least partially, been abandoned as an object and has instead, by identification, been taken into the ego and thus become an integral part of the internal world. This new psychical agency continues to carry on the functions which have hitherto been performed by the people (the abandoned objects) in the external world: it observes the ego, gives it orders, judges it and threatens it with punishments, exactly like the parents whose place it has taken. We call this agency the *super-ego* and are aware of it in its judicial functions as our *conscience*. It is a remarkable thing that the super-ego often displays a severity for which no model has been provided by the real parents, and moreover that it calls the ego to account not only for its deeds but equally for its thoughts and unexecuted intentions, of which the super-ego seems to have knowledge. This reminds us that the hero of the Oedipus legend too felt guilty for his deeds and submitted himself to self-punishment, although the coercive power of the oracle should have acquitted him of guilt in our judgement and his own. The super-ego is in fact heir to the Oedipus complex and is only established after that complex has been disposed of. For that reason its excessive severity does not follow a real model but corresponds to the strength of the defence used against the temptation of the Oedipus complex' (Freud, 1940, p. 205).

2 'The instinctual demands forced away from direct satisfaction are compelled to enter on new paths leading to substitutive satisfaction, and in the course of these *détours* they may become desexualised and their connection with their original instinctual aims may become looser. At this point we may anticipate the thesis that many of the highly valued assets of our civilisation were acquired at the cost of sexuality and by the restriction of sexual motive forces' (Freud, 1940, p. 201).

Bibliography

Abraham, K. (1924), *Selected Papers on Psycho-Analysis*, London, The Hogarth Press; 8th impression 1973, London, The Institute of Psycho-Analysis.

Ainsworth, M. D. S. (1969), 'Object relations, dependency, and attachment: A theoretical review of the infant-mother relationship', *Child Development*, 1969, vol. 40, pp. 969–1025.

Ainsworth, M. D. S. (1972), 'Attachment and dependency: A comparison', in J. L. Gerwirtz (ed.), *Attachment and Dependence*, Washington D.C., Winston (distributed by Wiley, New York).

Ainsworth, M. D. S., and Bell, Silvia M. (1970a), 'Attachment, exploration and separation: illustrated by the behavior of one-year-olds in a strange situation', *Child Development*, vol. 41, pp. 49–67.

Ainsworth, M. D. S., and Bell, Silvia M. (1970b), 'Some contemporary patterns of mother-infant interaction in the feeding situation', in *The Functions of Stimulation in Early Post-natal development*, (ed.) Ambrose, J. A., London, Academic Press.

Anderson, J. W. (1972), 'Attachment behaviour out of doors', in N. Blurton Jones (ed.), *Ethological Studies of Child Behaviour*, Cambridge University Press, pp. 199–217.

Bach, Sheldon (1975), 'Narcissism, continuity and the uncanny', *International Journal of Psycho-Analysis*, vol. 56, pp. 77–86.

Bach, Sheldon (1977a), 'On the narcissistic state of consciousness', *International Journal of Pyscho-Analysis*, vol. 58, pp. 290–334.

Bach, Sheldon (1977b), 'On narcissistic fantasies', *International Review of Psycho-Analysis*, vol. 4, pp. 281–93.

Balint, M. (1937), 'Early developmental states of the ego. Primary object love', in *Primary Love and Psycho-Analytic Technique*, New York, Liveright Publishing Corp., 1965.

Balint, M. (1957), *The Doctor, his Patient, and the Illness*, New York, International Universities Press, Inc.

Balint, M. (1968), *The Basic Fault: Therapeutic Aspects of Regression*, London, Tavistock Publications.

Balint, M. (1969), 'Trauma and object relationship', *International Journal of Psycho-Analysis*, vol. 50, pp. 429–35.

Bibliography

Bateson, G. (1936), *Naven: A Survey of the Problems Suggested by a Composite Picture of the Culture of a New Guinea Tribe Drawn from Three Points of View*, Cambridge University Press, rep. New York, Macmillan, 1937.

Bateson, G. (1955), 'A theory of play and fantasy; a report on theoretical aspects of the project for study of the role of paradoxes of abstraction in communication', *American Psychiatric Association, Psychiatric Research Reports*, II, 1955 and in *Steps to an Ecology of Mind* (1972), New York, Ballantine Books, pp. 177–93.

Bateson, G. (1960), 'Minimal requirements for a theory of schizophrenia', *Archives of General Psychiatry*, vol. 2, pp. 477–91. Reprinted in *Steps to an Ecology of Mind* (1972), New York, Ballantine, pp. 244–70.

Bateson, G. (1967), 'Cybernetic explanation', *American Behavioral Scientist*, vol. 10, no. 6, pp. 29–32. Reprinted in *Steps to an Ecology of Mind* (1972), New York, Ballantine Books, pp. 399–410.

Bateson, G. (1968), 'Redundancy and coding', in Thomas A. Sebeok (ed.), *Animal Communication; Techniques of Study and Results of Research*, Bloomington, Indiana and London, Indiana University Press. Reprinted in *Steps to an Ecology of Mind* (1972), New York, Ballantine Books, pp. 411–25.

Bateson, G. (1969), 'Double bind, 1969', in *Steps to an Ecology of Mind* (1972), New York, Ballantine Books, pp. 271–8.

Bateson, G. (1970), 'Form, substance and difference', *General Semantics bulletin*, no. 37, 1970. Reprinted in *Steps to an Ecology of Mind* (1972), New York, Ballantine Books, pp. 448–66.

Bateson, G. (1979), *Mind and Nature*, New York, E. P. Dutton.

Bell, R. Q. (1974), 'Contributions of human infants to caregiving and social interaction', in M. Lewis and L. A. Rosenblum (1974).

Bell, Silvia M. (1970), 'The development of the concept of object as related to infant – mother attachment', *Child Development*, vol. 41, pp. 291–311.

Bettleheim, B. (1967), *The Empty Fortress: Infantile Autism and the Birth of the Self*, London, Collier/Macmillan.

Bion, W. R. (1958), 'On arrogance', *International Journal of Psycho-Analysis*, vol. 39, pp. 144–6.

Bion, W. R. (1959), 'Attacks on linking', *International Journal of Psycho-Analysis*, vol. 40, pp. 308–15.

Bion, W. R. (1962a), *Learning from Experience*, London, Heinemann.

Bion, W. R. (1962b), 'A theory of thinking', *International Journal of Psycho-Analysis*, vol. 43, pp. 306–10.

Bion, W. R. (1963), *Elements of Psycho-Analysis*, in *Seven Servants* – four works – New York, Jason Aronson, 1977.

Bion, W. R. (1965), *Transformations*, in *Seven Servants* – four works – New York, Jason Aronson, 1977.

Bion, W. R. (1970), *Attention and Interpretation*, London, Tavistock Publications.

Blurton Jones, N. and Leach, G. M. (1972), 'Behaviour of children and their mothers at separation and greeting', in *Ethological Studies of Child Behaviour* (1972), Cambridge University Press, pp. 217–49.

Bower, T. G. R. (1977), *A Primer of Infant Development*, California, W. H. Freeman.

Bowlby, J. (1951), *Child Care and the Growth of Love*, Harmondsworth, Penguin, 2nd edn 1965.

Bowlby, J. (1958), 'The nature of the child's tie to his mother', *International Journal of Psycho-Analysis*, vol. 39, pt 5, pp. 350–73.

Bowlby, J. (1969), *Attachment and Loss Vol. 1. Attachment*, The Hogarth Press, London.

Bowlby, J. (1973), 'Self-reliance and some conditions that promote it', in *The Making and Breaking of Affectioral Bonds*, London, Tavistock Publications, 1979.

Bowlby, J. (1976), 'The making and breaking of affectional bonds', *The British Journal of Psychiatry*, 1977, vol. 130, pp. 201–10.

Brazelton, T. B. (1969), *Infants and Mothers – differences in development*, New York, Dell Publishing Co.

Brazelton, T. B., Koslowski, B., and Main, M. (1974), 'The origins of reciprocity: the early mother-infant interaction', in Michael Lewis and Leonard A. Rosenblum (eds), *The Effect of the Infant on its Caregiver*, New York, John Wiley.

Breger, L. (1980), *Freud's Unfinished Journey*, London, Routledge & Kegan Paul.

Clark, R. W. (1973), *Einstein: The Life and Times*, London, Hodder & Stoughton.

Condon, W. S., and Sander, L. (1974), 'Neonate movement is synchronised with adult speech: interactional participation and language acquisition', *Science*, 183, pp. 99–101.

Descartes, R. (1961), *Philosophical Writings*, eds E. Anscombe and P. Geach, Edinburgh, Thomas Nelson & Sons.

Dodds, E. R. (1973), 'On misunderstanding the *Oedipus Rex*', in *The Ancient Concept of Progress*, Oxford University Press.

Eliot, T. S. (1971), *Four Quartets*, 'Little Gidding', New York, Harcourt, Brace & World, Inc.

Ellis, H. (1927), 'The conception of narcissism', *Psychoanalytic Review*, vol. 14, pp. 129–53.

Fairbairn, W. R. D. (1941), 'A revised psychopathology of the psychoses and psychoneuroses', *International Journal of Psycho-Analysis*, vol. 22, pp. 250–79.

Feder, L. (1974), 'Adoption trauma: Oedipus myth/clinical reality', *International Journal of Psycho-Analysis*, 1974, vol. 55, pp. 491–3.

Flew, A. (1978), 'Transitional objects and transitional phenomena: comments and interpretations', in Simon A. Grolnik, Leonard Barkin and Werner Muensterberger (eds), *Between Reality and Fantasy*, New York, Jason Aronson, Inc.

Fordham, M. (1966), 'Notes on the psychotherapy of infantile autism', *British Journal of Medical Psychology*, vol. 39, pp. 299–312.

Freud, A. (1954), 'Psycho-analysis and education', *Psychoanalytic Study of the Child*, vol. 9, pp. 9–15.

Freud, A., and Burlingham, D. (1974), *Infants Without Families and*

Reports on the Hampstead Nurseries 1939–1945, London, The Hogarth Press.
Freud, A., and Dann, S. (1951), 'An experiment in group upbringing', *Psychoanalytic Study of the Child*, vol. 6, pp. 127–68.
Freud, S. (1908), 'On the sexual theories of children', *The Standard Edition of the Complete Psychological Works of Sigmund Freud* (1906–1908), *SE* 9, pp. 207–26, London, The Hogarth Press and The Institute of Psycho-Analysis.
Freud, S. (1909), *Two Case Histories* ('Little Hans' and the 'Rat Man'), *SE* 10, pp. 3–149.
Freud, S. (1911), 'Formulations on the two principles of mental functioning', *SE* 12, pp. 215–26.
Freud, S. (1914), 'On narcissism', *SE* 14, pp. 69–102.
Freud, S. (1916–17), *Introductory Lectures on Psycho-Analysis*, Part III, Lecture 26, *SE* 16, pp. 412–30.
Freud, S. (1916–17), *Introductory Lectures on Psychoanalysis*, Part III, General theory of the neuroses, Lectures XXVI and XXVII, *SE* 16, pp. 412–47.
Freud, S. (1917), 'A difficulty in the path of psycho-analysis', *SE* 17, pp. 136–44.
Freud, S. (1920), *Beyond the Pleasure Principle*, *SE* 18, pp. 7–64.
Freud, S. (1924), 'The dissolution of the Oedipus complex', *SE* 19, pp. 173–83.
Freud, S. (1925a), 'Negation', *SE* 19, pp. 235–9.
Freud, S. (1925b), 'Some psychical consequences of the anatomical distinction between the sexes', *SE* 19, pp. 243–58.
Freud, S. (1926), *Inhibitions, Symptoms and Anxiety*, *SE* 20, pp. 77–175.
Freud, S. (1930), *Civilisation and its Discontents* (1929), *SE* 21, pp. 59–145.
Freud, S. (1937), 'Analysis terminable and interminable', *SE* 23, pp. 211–53.
Freud, S. (1939), *Moses and Monotheism* (1934–38), *SE* 23, pp. 7–137.
Freud, S. (1940), *An Outline of Psycho-Analysis* (1938), *SE* 23, pp. 144–207.
Von Glaserfeld, E. (1977), 'A radical constructivist view of knowledge', paper for symposium on Constructivism and Cognitive Development, American Educational Research Association, New York, April.
Goldberg, A. (1972), 'On the incapacity to love', *Archives of General Psychiatry*, vol. 26, pp. 3–7.
Goldberg, A. (1975), 'Narcissism and the readiness for psychotherapy termination', *Archives of General Psychiatry*, vol. 32, June, pp. 695–9.
Goldmann, L. (1964), *The Hidden God*, London, Routledge & Kegan Paul.
Graves, R. (1955), *The Greek Myths* 2 vols: Oedipus; vol. 1, no. 85, Narcissus, vol. 2, no. 1. Harmondsworth, Penguin.
Green, A. (1978), 'Potential space in psychoanalysis: the object in the setting', in *Between Reality and Fantasy*, eds S. A. Grolnick, L. Barkin and W. Muensterberger, New York, Jason Aronson.
Greenacre, P. (1957), 'The childhood of the artist' in *Emotional Growth*, pp. 479–504, New York, International Universities Press.

Greenacre, P. (1964), 'A study of the nature of inspiration', in *Emotional Growth*, pp. 225–48, New York, International Universities Press.
Groddeck, G. (1976), *The Book of the It*, New York, International Universities Press.
Hartmann, H. (1939), Ego Psychology and the Problem of Adaptation, New York, International Universities Press (1958).
Heinicke, C. (1956), 'Some effects of separating two-year-old children from their parents: a comparative study', *Human Relations*, 9, pp. 105–76.
Heinicke, C. and Westheimer, I. (1966), *Brief Separations*, New York, International Universities Press, London, Longmans Green.
Heraclitus, Fragment 235, in Kirk, G. S. and Raven, J. E. (1966), *The Pre Socratic Philosophers*, Cambridge University Press.
Hoxter, S. (1975), 'The residual autistic condition and its effect upon learning – Piffie', in *Explorations in Autism*, Scotland, The Clunie Press.
Jones, E. (1961), *The Life and Work of Sigmund Freud*, New York, Basic Books.
Kant, I., *Critique of Pure Reason*, Transl. Norman Kemp Smith (1963), London, Macmillan.
Kernberg, O. F. (1969), 'A contribution to the ego-psychological critique of the Kleinian School', *The International Journal of Psycho-Analysis*, vol. 50, pp. 317–33.
Kernberg, O. F. (1974), 'Further contributions to the treatment of narcissistic personalities', *The International Journal of Psycho-Analysis*, vol. 55, pp. 215–40.
Kernberg, O. F. (1975), 'Further contributions to the treatment of narcissistic personalities: a reply to the discussion by Paul H. Ornstein', *The International Journal of Psychoanalysis*, vol. 56, pp. 247–7.
Klein, M. (1952), 'On observing the behaviour of young infants', in Klein, M., Heimann, P., Isaacs, S., Riviere, J. (1952), *Developments in Psycho-Analysis*, pp. 237–271, London, The Hogarth Press.
Kohut, H. (1971), *The Analysis of the Self*, New York, International Universities Press.
Kohut, H. (1977), *The Restoration of the Self*, New York, International Universities Press.
Kohut, H. (1978), *The Search for the Self*, New York, International Universities Press.
Kohut, H. (1979), 'The two analyses of Mr. Z', *The International Journal of Psycho-Analysis*, vol. 60, pt 3, pp. 3–27.
Kohut, H. and Wolff, E. S. (1978), 'The disorders of the self and their treatment: an outline', *The International Journal of Psycho-Analysis* vol. 59, pp. 413–25.
Kuhn, T. (1962), *The Structure of Scientific Revolutions*, University of Chicago Press.
Laing, R. D. (1960), *The Divided Self*, London, Tavistock Publications.
Laudan, L. (1977), *Progress and Its Problem: Towards a Theory of Scientific Growth*, London, Routledge & Kegan Paul.
Leach, G. M. (1972), 'A comparison of the social behaviour of some

normal and problem children', in N. Blurton Jones (ed.), *Ethological Studies of Child Behaviour* (1972), Cambridge University Press, pp. 249–85.

Lewis, M. and Rosenblum, L. A. (1974), *The Effect of the Infant on its Caregiver*, New York, John Wiley.

Lichtenstein, H. (1964), 'The role of narcissism in the emergence and maintenance of a primary identity', *International Journal of Psycho-Analysis*, vol. 45, pp. 49–56.

Mahler, M. S., Pine, F. and Bergman, A. (1975), *The Psychological Birth of the Human Infant*, New York, Basic Books.

Mandelstam, O. (1937), 'I look into the frost's face, alone', in *Osip Mandelstam*, poems chosen and translated by James Greene (1977), p. 72, London, Elek Books.

Meltzer, D., Bremner, J., Hoxter, S., Weddell, D., and Wittenberg, I. (1975), *Explorations in Autism*, Scotland, The Clunie Press.

Metcalf, D. R., and Spitz, R. A. (1978), 'The transitional object: critical developmental period and organizer of the psyche', in S. A. Grolnik, L. Barkin and W. Muensterberger (eds), *Between Reality and Fantasy*, New York, Jason Aronson.

Milner, M. (1952), 'Aspects of symbolism in comprehension of the not-self', *The International Journal of Psycho-Analysis*, vol. 33, pp. 181–95.

Ornstein, P. H. (1974), 'A discussion of the paper by O. F. Kernberg on "Further contributions to the treatment of narcissistic personalities" ', *International Journal of Psycho-Analysis*, vol. 55, pp. 241–7.

O'Shaugnessy, E. (1964), 'The absent object', *Journal of Child Psychotherapy*, vol. 1, no. 2, pp. 34–43.

Ovid (1955), *The Metamorphoses*, Book III, Echo and Narcissus, trans. M. M. Innes, Harmondsworth, Penguin, pp. 83–7.

Padel, J. H. (1977a), 'The use of identification', The fourth of six talks in the series, 'The state of depth psychology' (Radio 3), printed in the *Listener*, 17 November 1977.

Padel, J. H. (1977b), 'The creative narcissist', *The Times Literary Supplement*, 9 December 1977.

Pruyser, P. W. (1975), 'What splits in "splitting"? A scrutiny of the concept of splitting in psychoanalysis and psychiatry', *Bulletin of the Menninger Clinic*, vol. 39, no. 1, January 1975, pp. 1–47.

Reich, W. (1978), *The Function of the Orgasm*, New York, Pocket Books.

Rheingold, H. L., Gewirtz, J. L. and Ross, A. W. (1959), 'Social conditioning of vocalisations in the infant', *The Journal of Comparative and Physiological Psychology*, vol. 52, pp. 68–73.

Robertson, J. and J. (1967), Film: *KATE, 2 Years 5 Months, in Foster Care for 27 Days*, 16mm, b/w, sound, 33 mins (English, Danish, French, Swedish), guide, Concord Films Council and New York University Film Library, and film libraries throughout the world.

Robertson, J. and J. (1968), Film: *JANE, 17 Months, in Foster Care for 10 Days*, 16mm, b/w, sound, 37 mins (English, Danish, French, German, Swedish), guide, available as above.

Robertson, J. and J. (1969), Film: *JOHN, 17 Months, for 9 Days in a*

Residential Nursery, 16mm, b/w, sound, 43 mins (English, Danish, French, German, Swedish), guide, available as above.
Robertson, J. and J. (1971), Film: *THOMAS, 2 Years 4 Months, in Foster Care for 10 Days*, 16mm, b/w, sound, 38 mins (English only because of live conversations), guide, available as above.
Robertson, J. and J. (1976a), Film: *LUCY, 21 Months, in Foster Care for 19 Days*, 16mm, b/w, sound, 38 mins (other language versions pending), guide, available as above.
Robertson, J. and J. (1976b), Film: *The Importance of Substitute Mothering*, 16mm, b/w, sound, 20 mins (Scenes from *JOHN* and *JANE*; sale only to owners of film *JOHN*, Concord Films Council.
Rosenfeld, H. (1964), 'On the psychopathology of narcissism: a clinical approach', *International Journal of Psycho-Analysis*, vol. 45, pp. 332–7.
Sacks, O. (1973), *Awakenings*, London, Gerald Duckworth.
Sander, L. W. (1970), 'Regulation and organization in the early infant-caretaker system', in R. Robinson (ed.), *Brains and Early Behavior*, London, Academic Press, pp. 313–31.
Schafer, R. (1976), *A New Language for Psychoanalysis*, New Haven and London, Yale University Press.
Schaffer, H. R. (1971), *The Growth of Sociability*, Harmondsworth, Penguin.
Schaffer, H. R. and Emerson, P. E. (1964), 'The development of social attachments in infancy', *Monographs of the Society for Research in Child Development*, vol. 29, p.3.
Segal, H. (1973), *Introduction to the Work of Melanie Klein*, London, The Hogarth Press.
Sophocles (1951), *Oedipus Rex*, trans. Dudley Fitts and Robert Fitzgerald, London, Faber & Faber.
Spitz, R. A. (1957), *No and Yes. On the Genesis of Human Communication*, New York, International Universities Press.
Tinbergen, N. (1964), 'The search for animal roots of human behaviour', in *The Animal in its World – explorations of an ethologist, 1932–1972*, vol. 2, London, Allen & Unwin, 1973, pp. 161–74.
Tinbergen, N. (1972), 'Early childhood autism – an ethological approach', in *The Animal in its World – explorations of an ethologist, 1932–1972*, vol. 2, Laboratory experiments and general papers, London, Allen & Unwin, 1973.
Tinbergen, N. (1973), *The Animal in its World – explorations of an ethologist, 1932–1972*, vol. 2, Laboratory experiments and general papers, London, Allen & Unwin.
Tolpin, M. (1971), 'On the beginnings of a cohesive self', *The Psychoanalytic Study of the Child*, vol. 26, pp. 316–52.
Tolstoy, L. (1964), *Childhood, Boyhood and Youth*, trans. R. Edmonds, Harmondsworth, Penguin.
Tustin, F. (1972), *Autism and Childhood Psychosis*, London, The Hogarth Press.
Wahler, R. G. (1967), 'Infant social attachments: a reinforcement theory

interpretation and investigation', *Child Development*, vol. 38, pp. 1079–88.

Weich, M. J. (1978), 'Transitional language', in Simon A. Grolnik, L. Barkin and W. Muensterberger (eds), *Between Fantasy and Reality*, New York, Jason Aronson, pp. 413–23.

Wieder, H. (1977), 'The family romance fantasies of adopted children', *Psychoanalytic Quarterly*, vol. 46, pp. 185–99.

Winnicott, D. W. (1953), 'Transitional objects and transitional phenomena', *The International Journal of Psycho-Analysis*, vol. 34, pt 2. Reprinted in *Playing and Reality*, London, Tavistock Publication, 1971a, pp. 1–25.

Winnicott, D. W. (1956), 'Primary maternal preoccupation', in *Collected Papers: Through Paediatrics to Psycho-Analysis*, London, Tavistock Publications, 1958.

Winnicott, D. W. (1957a), *The Child and the Family: First Relationships*, London, Tavistock Publications.

Winnicott, D. W. (1957b), *The Child and the Outside World: Studies in Developing Relationships*, London, Tavistock Publications.

Winnicott, D. W. (1958a), 'The capacity to be alone', *International Journal of Psycho-Analysis*, vol. 39, pp. 416–20. Reprinted in *The Maturational Process and the Facilitating Environment*, New York, International Universities Press, 1965.

Winnicott, D. W. (1958b), *Collected Papers: Through Paediatrics to Psycho-Analysis*, London, Tavistock Publications: New York, International Universities Press.

Winnicott, D. W. (1960), 'The theory of the parent-infant relationship', in *The Maturational Processes and the Facilitating Environment – Studies in the Theory of Emotional Development, 1965*, New York, International Universities Press, Inc.

Winnicott, D. W. (1965a), *The Family and Individual Development*, London, Tavistock Publications.

Winnicott, D. W. (1965b), *The Maturational Processes and the Facilitating Environment*, London, The Hogarth Press and The Institute of Psycho-Analysis; New York, International Universities Press.

Winnicott, D. W. (1967), 'Mirror-role of mother and family in child development', in *Playing and Reality* (1971a), London, Tavistock Publications, pp. 111–18.

Winnicott, D. W. (1969), 'The use of an object and relating through identifications', *International Journal of Psycho-Analysis*, vol. 50, and in *Playing and Reality* (1971a), London, Tavistock Publications, pp. 86–94.

Winnicott, D. W. (1970), 'The mother-infant experience of mutuality', in E. J. Anthony and T. Benedek (eds), *Parenthood*, Boston, Little, Brown & Co.

Winnicott, D. W. (1971a), *Playing and Reality*, London, Tavistock Publications.

Winnicott, D. W. (1971b), *Therapeutic Consultations in Child Psychiatry*, London, The Hogarth Press and The Institute of Psycho-Analysis.

Wollheim, Richard (1969), 'The mind and the mind's image of itself', *International Journal of Psycho-Analysis*, vol. 50, pp. 209–20.
Wordsworth, W. (1971), *The Prelude*, ed. J. C. Maxwell, Harmondsworth, Penguin, Bk. II.
Yates, F. A. (1966), *The Art of Memory*, London, Peregrine Books, 1969.

Index

Index

Index

Index

Index